AF238751

Jürgen Beyerer, Marco Huber (Eds.)

Proceedings of the 2010 Joint Workshop of Fraunhofer IOSB and Institute for Anthropomatics, Vision and Fusion Laboratory

Karlsruher Schriften zur Anthropomatik
Band 7
Herausgeber: Prof. Dr.-Ing. Jürgen Beyerer

Lehrstuhl für Interaktive Echtzeitsysteme
Karlsruher Institut für Technologie

Fraunhofer-Institut für Optronik, Systemtechnik und
Bildauswertung IOSB Karlsruhe

Eine Übersicht über alle bisher in dieser Schriftenreihe erschienene
Bände finden Sie am Ende des Buchs.

Proceedings of the 2010 Joint Workshop of Fraunhofer IOSB and Institute for Anthropomatics, Vision and Fusion Laboratory

Edited by
Jürgen Beyerer
Marco Huber

Impressum

Karlsruher Institut für Technologie (KIT)
KIT Scientific Publishing
Straße am Forum 2
D-76131 Karlsruhe
www.ksp.kit.edu

KIT – Universität des Landes Baden-Württemberg und nationales
Forschungszentrum in der Helmholtz-Gemeinschaft

KIT Scientific Publishing 2011
Print on Demand

ISSN: 1863-6489
ISBN: 978-3-86644-609-0

Preface

For the second time, the annual joint workshop of the Fraunhofer Institute of Optronics, System Technologies and Image Exploitation IOSB and the Vision and Fusion Laboratory (Institute for Anthropomatics, Karlsruhe Institute of Technology (KIT)) was held in La Bresse, France. From July 19 to July 23 the 2010 joint workshop provided a forum for the doctoral students of both institutions to present their latest research and development findings. It further allows discussing potential research avenues and alternative scientific approaches. The research results presented on the 2010 joint workshop are put down in this book in form of a collection of technical reports. Thus, it provides are a valuable insight into the scientific and developmental progress in the research fields of the Vision and Fusion Laboratory and the Fraunhofer IOSB. These research fields mainly are image processing, pattern recognition, system technologies, and information fusion.

The editors thank all the organizers of the workshop for their efforts that led in a pleasant and rewarding stay in France. The editors further thank the doctoral students for writing and reviewing the technical reports as well as for responding to comments and suggestions of their colleagues.

Prof. Dr.-Ing. Jürgen Beyerer
Dr.-Ing. Marco Huber

Contents

Probabilistic Active Vision: An Overview

Marco F. Huber

Variable Image Acquisition and Processing Research Group (VBV)
Fraunhofer Institute of
Optronics, System Technologies and Image Exploitation (IOSB)
marco.huber@ieee.org

Technical Report IES-2010-01

Abstract: In active vision, the configuration of a camera system is adapted automatically in order to acquire the most informative observations for a given task. This paper gives an overview of a probabilistic approach for active vision. Planning the camera parameters is described as a partially observable Markov decision process. Here, the relevant components of the image acquisition task, i.e., object and camera, are represented by means of probabilistic models for incorporating uncertainties into planning. Additionally including reinforcement learning allows a priori unknown probabilistic models.

1 Introduction

Research on computer vision mostly focuses on the object or scene observed by the camera system. It is assumed that the parameters of the camera (e.g., position, illumination, or focus) are given or determined off-line in a time-consuming trial-and-error process involving human interaction. Particular operations are then applied on the acquired images in order to solve the given vision task, e.g., object localization or surface reconstruction. Thus, in so-called *passive* vision systems, the camera configuration is not adapted on-line. This is in contrast to an *active* vision system, where the configuration for the next camera observation is carefully planned based on the so far acquired information and the employed models of the scene dynamics and camera system (see Figure 1.1).

Ideally, by utilizing active vision, no irrelevant or non-informative data is processed. This in turn reduces the consumption of costly or rare resources like computation power, memory, or energy. Furthermore, adapting the configuration of the camera to the current conditions improves the performance of subsequent

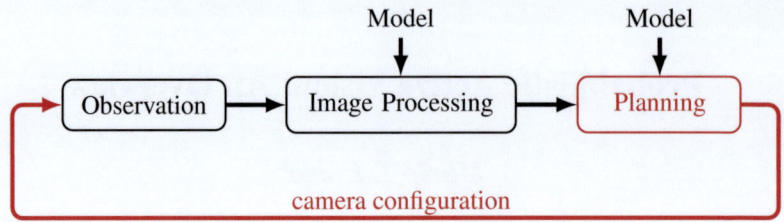

Figure 1.1: Processing chain in an active vision system. The red components are not part of a passive vision system.

computer vision algorithms like feature detection or image segmentation. Consider for example an object recognition task. Here, a single camera configuration may not be sufficient due to occlusions or near-symmetrical or similar objects. By moving the camera, ambiguities can be resolved, which improves the recognition performance [RCB04].

To attain these benefits, an active vision algorithm 1. has to incorporate uncertainties into the planning of the configurations and 2. has to deal with several camera specific constraints. As in any sensor system, data/information acquisition is always to some degree uncertain. In case of a camera sensor, uncertainties arise from noise and the finite resolution in terms of for example space, intensity, or contrast. A common practice in computer vision is to process features instead of the raw camera images. The calculation of features can be considered a dimensionality reduction [CV08]. This leads to a loss of information or in other words, increases the uncertainty about the observed object or scene depending on the expressiveness and dimensionality of the used features [PP00].[1] Typical constraints an active vision algorithm has to deal with are for example the limited field-of-view of a camera or (partial) occlusion of the object. In case of a movable camera, kinematic or geometric restrictions have to be considered as well.

Most of the existing active vision algorithms are designed for a specific application. Furthermore, heuristics or rule-of-thumbs are applied. For a survey see for example [TA95]. In this report, planning camera configurations under uncertainties is formalized via the general mathematical framework of *partially observable Markov decision processes* (POMDPs). A brief introduced into POMDPs is given in the next section. POMDPs rely on the assumption that probabilistic models of the sensor and the scene/object dynamics are given. If this assumptions is not

---

[1]It is worth mentioning that carefully selected features are typically more expressive than the intensities of the image pixels.

valid, reinforcement learning (RL) introduced in Section 3 allows the simultaneous learning of the models and planning of the camera configuration. In Section 4, it is shown how typical active vision tasks can be mapped to the introduced probabilistic active vision framework. The technical report closes with a summary.

2 Theoretical Framework: POMDPs

For characterizing the object's state and dynamics as well as the observations and their relation to the object, probabilistic models are employed. The object state vector $\underline{x}_k \in \mathcal{X} \subseteq \mathbb{R}^{n_x}$ is the quantity of interest, which has to be estimated from the observations and which may vary over the time[2] $k \in \mathbb{N}^+$. Depending on the vision task, the state vector may comprise the position and orientation of the object, its shape or color information. Initially, at time step $k = 0$, the state $\underline{x}_0$ is described by means of the probability density function $f_0^x(\underline{x}_0)$, which usually is quite uninformative.

The observation vector $\underline{z}_k \in \mathcal{Z} \subseteq \mathbb{R}^{n_z}$ with density function $f_k^z(\underline{z}_k)$ may consist of the whole image. But due to the high dimension of the raw image date, it is common practice that features are extracted from the image during the image processing step and thus, $\underline{z}_k$ comprises the extracted features.

Finally, with the camera configuration vector $\underline{a}_k \in \mathcal{A} \subseteq \mathbb{R}^{n_a}$ it is possible to modify the image acquisition by changing the parameters of the camera system, which may be the position, orientation, focus, or illumination, just to name a few. It is assumed that $\underline{a}_k$ is a deterministic variable.

Besides these variables, there are also probabilistic models describing the relations between the variables. The relationship between observations and the state depending on the camera configuration is characterized via the observation model $f(\underline{z}_k | \underline{x}_k, \underline{a}_k)$. The probabilistic nature of this models allows capturing uncertainties in the observation process resulting for example from camera noise or feature extraction.

Example 1 A 3-D point in the world with coordinates $\underline{x} = [x, y, z]^{\mathrm{T}}$ is observed via a camera. The projection of the point to the 2-D screen coordinates of the camera is typically modeled as a matrix multiplication in

---

[2] Discrete time steps are assumed.

homogeneous coordinates

$$\begin{bmatrix} u \\ v \\ w \end{bmatrix} = \begin{bmatrix} \xi_u(a) & 0 & \pi_u \\ 0 & \xi_v(a) & \pi_v \\ 0 & 0 & 1 \end{bmatrix} \cdot [\phi \ \underline{t}] \cdot \begin{bmatrix} \underline{x} \\ 1 \end{bmatrix} \ ,$$

where the affine transformation between camera coodinates and world co-ordinates is given by the rotation matrix $\phi \in \mathbb{R}^{3\times3}$ and the translation vector $\underline{t} = [t_x, t_y, t_z]^{\mathrm{T}}$. The internal camera parameters are the focal lengths $\xi_u(a), \xi_v(a)$ and the principal point $[\pi_u, \pi_v]^{\mathrm{T}}$. Here, the focal lengths depend on the parameter a. Thus, by modifying a it is possible to adapt the zoom of the camera.

The actual observation is given by

$$\underline{z} = \begin{bmatrix} z_x \\ z_y \end{bmatrix} = \begin{bmatrix} \frac{u}{w} \\ \frac{v}{w} \end{bmatrix} =: \underline{h}(\underline{x}, a) \ ,$$

where z_x and z_y are the horizontal and vertical coordinates reported by the camera and typically measured in pixels. This transformation $\underline{h}$ is nonlinear due to the division. Assuming additive zero-mean Gaussian noise on $\underline{z}$, the corresponding probabilistic observation model is

$$f(\underline{z}|\underline{x}, a) = \mathcal{N}(\underline{z}; \underline{h}(\underline{x}, a), \mathbf{R}) \ ,$$

where $\mathcal{N}(\underline{v}; \hat{\underline{v}}, \mathbf{R})$ is a Gaussian density with mean $\hat{\underline{v}}$ and covariance matrix $\mathbf{R}$.

If the state of the object varies over time, which is for example the case in object tracking applications, the transition or dynamics model $f(\underline{x}_{k+1}|\underline{x}_k)$ describes how the object state changes for the next time step based on the current state.

Example 2 The dynamic behavior of a mobile object in tracking scenarios (see Section 4.3) is often described by the so-called constant velocity model [May79], which is given by the linear transformation

$$\underline{x}_{k+1} = \mathbf{A} \cdot \underline{x}_k + \underline{w}_k \ .$$

The object state $\underline{x}_k = [x_k, \dot{x}_k, y_k, \dot{y}_k, z_k, \dot{z}_k]^{\mathrm{T}}$ comprises the 3-D position $[x_k, y_k, z_k]^{\mathrm{T}}$ and the velocities $[\dot{x}_k, \dot{y}_k, \dot{z}_k]^{\mathrm{T}}$ in x, y and z direction. The noise $\underline{w}_k$ is zero-mean Gaussian with covariance matrix $\mathbf{Q}$. The so-called system matrix $\mathbf{A}$ is

$$\mathbf{A} = \mathbf{I}_3 \otimes \begin{bmatrix} 1 & \Delta t \\ 0 & 1 \end{bmatrix} \ ,$$

where $\mathbf{I}_3$ is the 3×3 identity matrix, $\otimes$ is the Kronecker product, and Δt is the sampling time interval. Putting all together,

$$f(\underline{x}_{k+1}|\underline{x}_k) = \mathcal{N}(\underline{x}_{k+1}; \mathbf{A} \cdot \underline{x}_k, \mathbf{Q})$$

is the corresponding probabilistic transition model.

2.1 Bayesian Inference

Based on the previously introduced probabilistic models, the so-called Bayesian inference allows predicting future object states or updating the estimate of the object state based on new observations. Therefore, Bayesian inference performs two alternating steps, i.e., prediction and filtering. In the prediction step, the result $f_k^x(\underline{x}_k|\underline{z}_{0:k}, \underline{a}_{0:k})$ of the previous filter step is propagated from time step k to $k+1$ by means of the Chapman-Kolmogorov equation

$$f_{k+1}^x(\underline{x}_{k+1}|\underline{z}_{0:k}, \underline{a}_{0:k}) = \int f(\underline{x}_{k+1}|\underline{x}_k) \cdot f_k^x(\underline{x}_k|\underline{z}_{0:k}, \underline{a}_{0:k}) \, \mathrm{d}\underline{x}_k \ . \qquad (2.1)$$

Here, $\underline{z}_{0:k} = (\underline{z}_1, \ldots, \underline{z}_k)$ and $\underline{a}_{0:k} = (\underline{a}_0, \ldots, \underline{a}_k)$ summarize all observations and camera configurations up to and including time step k.

In the filtering step, the current observation $\underline{z}_k$ given the camera configuration $\underline{a}_k$ is used for updating the result of the prediction step $f_k^x(\underline{x}_k|\underline{z}_{0:k-1}, \underline{a}_{0:k-1})$ according to Bayes's rule

$$f_k^x(\underline{x}_k|\underline{z}_{0:k}, \underline{a}_{0:k}) = \frac{f(\underline{z}_k|\underline{x}_k, \underline{a}_k) \cdot f_k^x(\underline{x}_k|\underline{z}_{0:k-1}, \underline{a}_{0:k-1})}{f_k^z(\underline{z}_k|\underline{z}_{0:k-1}, \underline{a}_{0:k})} \ , \qquad (2.2)$$

where $f_k^z(\underline{z}_k|\underline{z}_{0:k-1}, \underline{a}_{0:k}) = \int f(\underline{z}_k|\underline{x}_k, \underline{a}_k) \cdot f_k^x(\underline{x}_k|\underline{z}_{0:k-1}, \underline{a}_{0:k-1}) \, \mathrm{d}\underline{x}_k$ is a normalization constant.

An analytic solution of Bayesian inference is only possible in some special cases. For instance, if the probabilistic models are linear Gaussian, the famous Kalman filter [Kal60] provides the optimal state estimate in closed form. A further special case is given in case of discrete states and observations, which leads to the Grid or HMM filter [AMGC02]. But in general, appropriate approximations have to be applied. Examples of approximate methods are Gaussian filters (see e.g. [HH08] and [JU04]), where the nonlinear non-Gaussian probabilistic models are approximated with Gaussians via moment matching, or particle filters [AMGC02], which employ a discretized representation of the state density $f_k^x(\underline{x}_k|\underline{z}_{0:k}, \underline{a}_{0:k})$.

2.2 Planning

The main task in active vision is the sequential selection of camera parameters, where planning over a (potentially infinite) time horizon with length N, i.e., planning N time steps ahead, is involved. Such sequential decision problems under probabilistic models are covered by the theory of *Markov decision processes* (MDPs). The primary assumption of MDPs is that the observations provide enough information for exactly determining the system state, i.e., perfect state information is assumed. This assumption does not hold for the considered active vision scenario. Due to the probabilistic observation model $f(\underline{z}_k | \underline{x}_k, \underline{a}_k)$, inferring the object state by means of observations leaves residual uncertainty concerning the object state. Problems of this type are covered by *partially observable Markov decision processes* (POMDPs), which are a generalization of MDPs [Dra62, Ast65].

2.2.1 Optimal Solution

Besides the observation and transition model, a partially observable Markov decision process consists of:

Cost function The primary goal of active vision is the determination of a sequence of camera configurations in order to gain maximum information about the observed object. To achieve this goal, a cost function (reward function) to be minimized (maximized) is specified. This function consists of two components: 1. the real-valued step costs $g_k(\underline{x}_k, \underline{a}_k)$, which are the costs if parameter $\underline{a}_k$ is applied at time k when the object state is $\underline{x}_k$, and 2. the terminal costs $g_N(\underline{x}_N)$, which is are costs when arriving in state $\underline{x}_N$ on completion of the planning. Typical cost functions in active vision consider informativeness of observations, which can be quantifies for example via the mutual information [CT91], classification accuracy, or the effort of acquiring and processing observations.

Decision state Since the object state $\underline{x}_k$ is not directly accessible, a so-called decision state X_k needs to be introduced. This state is a sufficient statistic for all past and present information upon which decisions about camera parameters can be made. It is assumed that the sufficient statistic forms a Markov process, i.e., subsequent states are independent of the past if the present state is given.

A POMDP can be reformulated as a fully observed MDP by introducing the so-called information set $\mathcal{I}_k = \{\underline{a}_0, \underline{z}_0, \ldots, \underline{a}_k, \underline{z}_k\}$ [CC07]. This set comprises the history of all applied configurations and the resulting observations. Thus, the information set is one possible choice of a decision state. Unfortunately, with increasing time k, the dimension of the information set increases as well. Instead of the information set, the probability density function $\underline{x}_k \sim f_k^x(\underline{x}_k | \underline{z}_{0:k-1}, \underline{a}_{0:k-1}) = f_k^x(\underline{x}_k | \mathcal{I}_{k-1})$ is an alternative choice of the decision state X_k and forms a sufficient statistic for the entire information set [BMWDW06]. Thus, merely the density function at time step k needs to be stored.

In order to minimize the costs over the considered planning horizon with length N, the expected costs

$$\mathrm{E}\left\{g_N(\underline{x}_N) + \sum_{k=0}^{N-1} g_k(\underline{x}_k, \underline{a}_k)\right\} \tag{2.3}$$

need to be considered, where the expectation $\mathrm{E}\{\cdot\}$ is with respect to the object states $\underline{x}_{0:N}$ and the observations $\underline{z}_{0:N-1}$. The optimization of (2.3) is over *policies*

$$\underline{a}_k = \underline{\mu}_k(f_k^x(\underline{x}_k | \mathcal{I}_{k-1})) \,,$$

i.e., rules for choosing $\underline{a}_k$ for each k and each possible decision state. How to determine the optimal policy will be shown below.

The optimization can be simplified by exploiting Bellman's principle of optimality. This results in the backward recursion

$$J_k(f_k^x(\underline{x}_k | \mathcal{I}_{k-1})) =$$
$$\min_{\underline{a}_k}\left\{\mathrm{E}_{\underline{x}_k, \underline{z}_k}\left\{g_k(\underline{x}_k, \underline{a}_k) + J_{k+1}(f_{k+1}^x(\underline{x}_{k+1} | \mathcal{I}_k)) | \mathcal{I}_{k-1}, \underline{a}_k\right\}\right\} \tag{2.4}$$

for $k = 0, \ldots, N-1$, commencing from the terminal costs. $J_N(f_N^x(\underline{x}_N | \mathcal{I}_{N-1})) = \mathrm{E}\{g_N(\underline{x}_N)\}$. This recursion is also known as Bellman's equations [Bel57] and the functions J_k are often referred to as *value functions* or *cost-to-go functions*. The density function $f_{k+1}^x(\underline{x}_{k+1} | \mathcal{I}_k)$ on the right hand side of (2.4) is calculated according to the prediction (2.1) and filtering (2.2) described above. According to the Bellman recursion, the optimal policy satisfies

$$\underline{a}_k^* = \underline{\mu}_k^*(f_k^x(\underline{x}_k | \mathcal{I}_{k-1}))$$
$$= \arg \min_{\underline{a}_k}\left\{\mathrm{E}_{\underline{x}_k, \underline{z}_k}\left\{g_k(\underline{x}_k, \underline{a}_k) + J_{k+1}(f_{k+1}^x(\underline{x}_{k+1} | \mathcal{I}_k)) | \mathcal{I}_{k-1}, \underline{a}_k\right\}\right\} \,.$$

Under certain assumptions, it is possible to prove that POMDPs for active vision converge, i.e., the uncertainty of the object state decreases over time [DB00]. However, solving POMDPs even for discrete states and discrete observations is

PSPACE-complete[3], as the size of $\mathcal{I}_k$ grows rapidly with the number of observations and camera parameters [PT87]. In case of continuous-valued states, solving POMDPs is intractable in general. A famous exception is LQG[4], where the separation principle leads to a decomposition into an estimation part and a control part [Ben92, Ber00]. For an survey of POMDP solution methods see [Hau00].

2.2.2 Closed-loop vs. Open-loop

The primary assumption of POMDPs is that state feedback is employed, i.e., the information about the object state is revealed to the planning component and the optimal policy utilizes that new information as it becomes available. This procedure corresponds to a *closed-loop* scheme. In many practical applications, however, the length N of the planning horizon may be too long and thus, the (approximate) calculation of the policy is too time consuming. Employing *open-loop planning* instead, where the primary assumption of POMDPs is not made, leads to an approximate procedure, where the optimal plan (that is a sequence of camera parameters rather than the sequence of policies as in the closed-loop case) can often be found with a significantly lower computational demand. Admittedly, no state feedback is employed.

As an compromise between open-loop and closed-loop, *open-loop feedback planning* (OLF) can be used alternatively. Like in open-loop planning, no future information is anticipated. But when a new observation becomes available, it is used for calculating an updated plan, i.e., the open-loop feedback planning component first determines the parameter sequence for the observation period in an open-loop fashion, executes one or more steps of the sequence, and then calculates a new sequence that incorporates the newly received observation. It can be shown, that OLF is no worse than open-loop planning, but the deviation from closed-loop planning can be arbitrarily large [Ber00]. The plans, however, are still constructed considering the total length N of the planning horizon.

To avoid the computational burden of optimizing over long time horizons, a model-predictive control scheme is often employed. Here, the planning component repeatedly determines the optimal configuration sequence over a moving or rolling horizon of length K. The length K of this moving horizon is considered to be much smaller than the planning horizon N, which may be infinite. Depending on the optimization type, two possible model-predictive schemes arise: at each time

---

[3]PSPACE is a superset of NP and is the set of decision problems that can be solved by a Turing machine using a polynomial amount of memory and unlimited computation time.

[4]LQG: *l*inear *q*uadratic *G*aussian control, i.e., Gaussian transition and observation models with quadratic cost function

step, the *closed-loop feedback* planner solves a POMDP for the moving horizon, while the *open-loop feedback* planner determines a plan for the moving horizon that does not anticipate the availability of future information[5]. Whenever a new observation is received, both schemes utilize this new information about the object state by calculating an updated policy and plan, respectively. Obviously, the open-loop feedback scheme provides an approximate solution to the closed-loop feedback problem. The computations, however, are typically less complicated since no expectations with respect to uncertain observations are necessary.

3   Reinforcement Learning

So far, it was assumed that the probabilistic observation and transition models are known to the planning component. This assumption may be valid in simple scenarios like tracking a point object as considered in Example 1 and 2. But in general, it is too involved or even not possible to identify these models or only oversimplified models can be derived. This problem arises when the observation vector $\underline{z}_k$ comprises complex features like intensity histograms or when the object state $\underline{x}_k$ comprises rather abstract elements like the class/type of the object. It becomes worse when dimensionality reduction techniques like principle component analysis are applied additionally in order to reduce the computation time and memory consumption.

A paradigm designed for this problem setup is reinforcement learning. Here, it is *learned*, which action[6] needs to be applied in which state in order to gain the maximum reduction of costs without knowledge about the models. There are no hints, which action is beneficial in which state. Instead, actions are applied based on a currently learned policy. The effects caused by the action are evaluated and the gained experience in terms of costs is used to modify the policy. This is different from many other learning methods in machine learning, where learning is performed on the basis of labeled examples.

Reinforcement learning methods can be divided into two classes. The *model-free* or direct approaches learn the policy without any probabilistic observation and transition models. In *model-based* approaches instead, the policy and the models are learned simultaneously. In Figure 3.1 on the next page, the more general second class is depicted. Removing the modeling component yields model-free

---

[5]The combination of model predictive control with closed-loop/open-loop planning is often also referred to as limited lookahead closed-loop/open-loop planning. Open-loop model-predictive planning can be considered as the combination of OLF with a limited and moving time horizon.

[6]In the context of active vision, the word action has to be replaced by camera parameter.

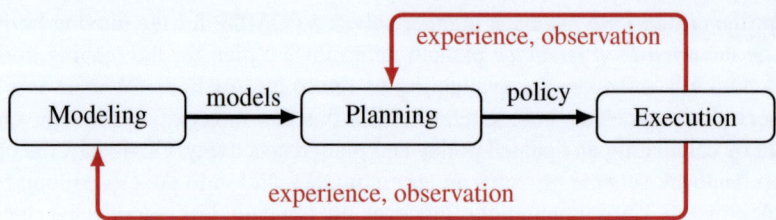

Figure 3.1: Extension of a POMDP by learning. The black blocks and arrows indicate planning as described in the previous section. Reinforcement learning utilizes experience from applying actions to learn and improve the policy as well as the probabilistic models.

reinforcement learning. In the following a brief introduction into both classes is provided. More details can found in [SB98].

From now on, the typical reinforcement learning assumption of an *infinite planning horizon* is made. An infinite horizon is appropriate in most of the active vision tasks, where observations are acquired over many time steps and the end of observing an object is not predefined. This assumption requires bounded, discounted, and stationary cost functions $\gamma^k \cdot g(\underline{x}_k, \underline{a}_k)$, where $\gamma \in (0, 1)$ is the discount factor that determines the importance of future costs. Furthermore, the policy and value function are stationary, i.e., it holds $\underline{\mu}_k(X_k) = \underline{\mu}(X_k)$ and $J_k(X_k) = J(X_k)$ for all k. Thus, the point in time for selecting a camera parameter is no longer relevant.

3.1 Model-free Planning

A common approach in model-free reinforcement learning is to learn the policy indirectly. For this purpose, the so-called *Q-function*

$$J(X_k) = \min_{\underline{a}_k}\{Q(X_k, \underline{a}_k)\}$$

is introduced, which is the argument of the minimization in (2.4). Hence, the Q-function can be written as

$$Q(X_k, \underline{a}_k) = \mathrm{E}\left\{g(\underline{x}_k, \underline{a}_k) + \gamma \cdot \min_{\underline{a} \in \mathcal{A}}\{Q(X_{k+1}, \underline{a})\}\right\} \qquad (3.1)$$

In case of a finite decision state X and a finite set of actions $\mathcal{A}$, the Q-function can be considered a table that stores for each combination of states and actions the expected costs. In case of continuous decision states and actions, universal function approximators like neural networks or radial basis functions are employed for representing the Q-function. The policy then can be derived from the Q-function by means of $\mu(X_k) = \arg\min_{\underline{a}_k}\{Q(X_k,\underline{a}_k)\}$. Thus, by learning the optimal Q-function Q^*, the optimal policy is learned by the way.

One of the mostly used algorithms for learning the Q-function is *Q-learning*, which is given by

$$Q(X_k,\underline{a}_k) \leftarrow Q(X_k,\underline{a}_k) +$$

$$\alpha \cdot \left(g(X_k,\underline{a}_k) + \gamma \cdot \min_{\underline{a}\in\mathcal{A}}\{Q(X_{k+1},\underline{a})\} - Q(X_k,\underline{a}_k) \right) , \quad (3.2)$$

where X_{k+1} results from selection $\underline{a}_k$ according to the currently learned policy. $\alpha \in (0,1]$ is the learning rate and determines to what extent newly acquired information will override old information. Equation (3.2) is obtained from (3.1) by first considering a general version of (3.1) by including $(1-\alpha) \cdot Q(\cdot)$, which leads to

$$Q(X_k,\underline{a}_k) \leftarrow (1-\alpha) \cdot Q(X_k,\underline{a}_k) +$$

$$\alpha \cdot \mathrm{E}\left\{ g(\underline{x}_k,\underline{a}_k) + \gamma \cdot \min_{\underline{a}\in\mathcal{A}}\{Q(X_{k+1},\underline{a})\} \right\} .$$

Evaluating the expectation requires the knowledge about the probabilistic transition model and observation model. An approximate version can be derived when replacing the expectation by a single sample. That is, when applying action $\underline{a}_k$ in state X_k, it is assumed that the cost $g(\cdot)$ and the subsequent decision state X_{k+1} can be acquired directly[7] by interaction with the environment. This and some minor arrangements of terms lead to the Q-learning equation (3.2).

In case of finite states and actions, it can be shown that Q-learning converges towards the optimal Q-function if each combination of states and actions if visited infinitely often [BT96]. In the continuous case, no convergence towards the optimal Q-function can be proven in general.

An alternative to learning the Q-function is to learn the policy directly. For this purpose, the policy is now represented via a function approximator. The parameters of the function approximator are then adapted by applying the currently learned policy and by utilizing the acquired observations and costs. A typical approach are policy gradients for modifying the parameters of the policy [PS08]. The main problem with policy gradients is obtaining a good estimator for the gradient since no model is available and thus, the gradients have to be estimated from the acquired

---

[7]This assumption holds for example, if the decision state is equal to the observation vector, i.e., the decision state is the image itself or comprises features generated from the image.

observations and costs. On the other hand, policy gradient algorithms are well suited to continuous problems and are guaranteed to converge to locally optimal policies.

3.2 Simultaneous Planning and Model Learning

Convergence of reinforcement learning towards the optimal policy can be significantly improved, if the probabilistic models are learned simultaneously with the policy [AS97, RN09]. Due to utilizing the observations for additionally building up the observation and transition models, observations are used more effectively in a model-based approach since information about the object and the vision system is exploited explicitly. For instance, consider Q-learning for a fully observed scenario, i.e., the underlying planning problem is an MDP, where $X_k = \underline{x}_k$. The policy is (indirectly) adjusted to agree with the observed successor state X_{k+1} (see equation (3.2)). A model-based approach instead exploits the learned transition model for updating the policy in order to agree with *all* successor states weighted by their probabilities. Examples for model-based reinforcement learners are for example adaptive dynamic programing [RN09] or Gaussian process dynamic programming [DRP09].

The benefits of model-based reinforcement learning, however, come at the expense of additional computations for learning the models. In case of fully observed scenarios, it is just necessary to learn the transition model. This is a supervised learning task, where the input is a state-action pair and the output is the subsequent state. Things become more complicated in the partially observed case. Now, the states are not directly accessible. Both the transition and observation model have to be learned merely on the basis the observations instead. A general framework to solve this unsupervised learning problem is expectation maximization (EM) [DLR77]. Representing the probabilistic models by means of parametric function approximators, EM could be employed for learning the parameters of the approximators.

4   Active Vision Tasks

So far, probabilistic active vision was only discussed on a rather abstract mathematical level. In the following, some specific vision tasks are introduced and connected with the introduced theoretical framework. For this purpose typical assumptions are clarified, i.e., what typical camera parameters and states are and whether the task is a dynamic problem or not.

4.1 Object Recognition

In object recognition or classification the goal is to identify an object as one of a given database of known objects. The camera is varied in position and orientation in order to improve classification performance. The object state is discrete and indicates the class of the object. Correspondingly, the decision state is the discrete probability distribution of the class. Since the object class is not changing with the time, there is no need for a transition model. Sometimes, however, not only the class of an object is of interest but also its 3-D position in the world. In this case, the state becomes a mixed discrete-continuous one. But still, a static (non moving) object is assumed.

4.2 Reconstruction

To gain an accurate surface model of an object, especially if it is large and/or if its shape is complex, multiple views from different positions are necessary. As in the object recognition problem, typical camera parameters in the reconstruction problem are the position and orientation of the camera. Furthermore, a static object is typically assumed. The state and observations instead comprise the points on the object's surface and thus, are continuous. For reconstructing the surface from observations, interpolation methods like splines or Gaussian processes [RW06] can be used.

Based on the reconstructed surface, further planning tasks are often conducted, e.g., grasp planning for humanoid robots. If a very accurate object model in form of a CAD model is given, *inspection planning* aims at setting up a visual inspection machine for identifying anomalies on industrial goods. This includes the number and positions of the cameras or the illumination of the object. Here, it is typically sufficient to construct a plan rather than a policy, since the inspection machine will not alter the inspection procedure in order to allow a high throughput of goods.

4.3 Tracking

In surveillance tasks, it is common to track the location of an object. Therefore, stationary cameras are used and thus, camera parameters that can be varied are mainly the focal length and the orientation. In some applications, selecting an subset of active cameras for tracking in a camera network is subject to parameterization as well. This selection or scheduling task is discussed in more detail in Section 4.5. Contrary to the previously considered vision tasks, the object is now assumed to be moving. This requires the incorporation of a transition model into planning, where the state is the position and often the velocity of the object.

4.4 SLAM

Simultaneous localization and mapping (SLAM) is a common problem in robotics, where a robot creates a map of its environment while using this map to locate itself [TBF05]. The SLAM problem can be turned into an active vision problem, if 1. the robot uses cameras for observing the environment and 2. the path of the robot is planned. Planning here means dealing with the tradeoff between visiting unknown areas of the environment (exploration) and revisiting known regions in order to reduce uncertainty (exploitation). This so-called *active SLAM* problem has some special properties. The state comprises not only the location of the robot, it also comprises the map and thus, the dimension of the state may grow with increasing time. Furthermore, adapting camera parameters affects the robot and thus the state of the entire system and not only the observations.

4.5 Scheduling

In the scheduling or selection problem, the focus is on selecting only a subset of the cameras at each time step for observation. This task is of special interest in camera networks with limited communication bandwidth, computational power, or energy capacity. As only those observations are informative that are provided by camera in close vicinity of the observed object, considering not all cameras at each time step allows trading of estimation accuracy against operational lifetime. The camera parameter vector is binary in this task and indicates which cameras should be switch on and which off.

5 Summary

In this report, a probabilistic framework for active vision was introduced. Selecting the optimal parameters for adapting the perception of visual information can be modeled as a partially observable Markov decision process (POMDP). Solving a POMDP requires probabilistic models of the used camera system and the dynamics of the observed object. Both models however, might be unknown in many applications. To still allow planning the optimal camera parameters, model-free reinforcement learning can be exploited. Although well established, model-free approaches typically converge very slowly towards the optimal policy. This draw-back can be avoided by simultaneously learning the policy and the probabilistic models. Finally, some common active vision task were mapped on the introduced probabilistic framework. Future work is concerned with developing well-designed instantiations of this framework for the different tasks.

Bibliography

[AMGC02]   M. Sanjeev Arulampalam, Simon Maskell, Neil Gordon, and Tim Clapp. A Tuto-rial on Particle Filters for Online Nonlinear/Non-Gaussian Bayesian Tracking. *IEEE Transactions on Signal Processing*, 50(2):174–188, February 2002.

[AS97]   Christopher G. Atkeson and Juan Carlos Santamaría. A Comparison of Direct and Model-Based Reinforcement Learning. In *Proceedings of the 1997 IEEE Interna-tional Conference on Robotics and Automation*, pages 3557–3564, Albuquerque, New Mexico, April 1997.

[Ast65]   Karl J. Aström. Optimal control of Markov decision processes with incomplete state estimation. *Journal of Mathematical Analysis and Applications*, 10:174–205, 1965.

[Bel57]   Richard E. Bellman. *Dynamic Programming*. Princeton University Press, 1957.

[Ben92]   Alain Bensoussan. *Stochastic Control of Partially Observable Systems*. Cambridge University Press, 1992.

[Ber00]   Dimitri P. Bertsekas. *Dynamic Programming and Optimal Control*, volume 1. Athena Scientific, Belmont, Massachusetts, U.S.A., 2nd edition, 2000.

[BMWDW06] Alex Brooks, Alexei Makarenko, Stefan Williams, and Hugh Durrant-Whyte. Para-metric POMDPs for planning in continuous state spaces. *Robotics and Autonomous Systems*, 54(11):887–897, November 2006.

[BT96]   Dimitri P. Bertsekas and John Tsitsiklis. *Neuro-Dynamic Programming*. Athena Scientific, Belmont, Massachusetts, U.S.A., 1996.

[CC07]   David A. Castañón and Lawrence Carin. *Foundations and Applications of Sensor Management*, chapter 2. Springer, Berlin, 2007.

[CT91]   Thomas M. Cover and Joy A. Thomas. *Elements of Information Theory*. John Wiley & Sons, Inc., 1991.

[CV08]   Francesco Camastra and Alessandro Vinciarelli. *Machine Learning for Audio, Image and Video Analysis: Theory and Applications*. Springer-Verlag London, 2008.

[DB00]   Joachim Denzler and Christopher Brown. Optimal Selection of Camera Parameters for State Estimation of Static Systems: An Information Theoretic Approach. Technical Report TR-732, Computer Science Department, University of Rochester, 2000.

[DLR77]   Arthur P. Dempster, Nan M. Laird, and Donald B. Rubin. Maximum Likelihood from Incomplete Data via the EM Algorithm. *Journal of the Royal Statistical Society*, Series B (Methodological) 39(1):1–38, 1977.

[Dra62]   Alvin W. Drake. *Observation of a Markov process through a noisy channel*. PhD thesis, Massachusetts Institute of Technology, 1962.

[DRP09]   Marc P. Deisenroth, Carl E. Rasmussen, and Jan Peters. Gaussian Process Dynamic Programming. *Neurocomputing*, 72(7–9):1508–1524, March 2009.

[Hau00]   Milos Hauskrecht. Value-function Approximations for Partially Observable Markov Decision Processes. *Journal of Artificial Intelligence Research*, 13:33–94, August 2000.

[HH08]   Marco F. Huber and Uwe D. Hanebeck. Gaussian Filter based on Deterministic Sampling for High Quality Nonlinear Estimation. In *Proceedings of the 17th IFAC World Congress*, Seoul, Republic of Korea, July 2008.

[JU04]   Simon J. Julier and Jeffrey K. Uhlmann. Unscented Filtering and Nonlinear Estimation. *Proceedings of the IEEE*, 92(3):401–422, 2004.

[Kal60]   Rudolf E. Kalman. A new Approach to Linear Filtering and Prediction Problems. *Transactions of the ASME, Journal of Basic Engineering*, 82 (Series D)(1):35–45, 1960.

[May79]   Peter Maybeck. *Stochastic Models, Estimation, and Control*. Academic Press, 1979.

[PP00]   Lucas Paletta and Axel Pinz. Active object recognition by view integration and reinforcement learning. *Robotics and Autonomous Systems*, 31(1):71–86, April 2000.

[PS08]   Jan Peters and Stefan Schaal. Reinforcement learning of motor skills with policy gradients. *Neural Networks*, 21:682–697, 2008.

[PT87]   Christos H. Papadimitriou and John N. Tsitsiklis. The Complexity of Markov Decision Processes. *Mathematics of Operations Research*, 12(3):441–450, 1987.

[RCB04]   Sumantra Dutta Roy, Santanu Chaudhury, and Subhashis Banerjee. Active recognition through next view planning: a survey. *Pattern Recognition*, 37(3):429–446, March 2004.

[RN09]   Stuart Russell and Peter Norvig. *Artificial Intelligence: A Modern Approach*. Prentice Hall, 3. auflage edition, 2009.

[RW06]   Carl Edward Rasmussen and Christopher K. I. Williams. *Gaussian Processes for Machine Learning*. The MIT Press, 2006.

[SB98]   Richard S. Sutton and Andrew G. Barto. *Reinforcement Learning: An Introduction*. MIT Press, 1998.

[TA95]   Konstantinos A. Tarabanis and Peter K. Allen. A Survey of Sensor Planning in Computer Vision. *IEEE Transactions on Robotics and Automation*, 11(1):86–104, February 1995.

[TBF05]   Sebastian Thrun, Wolfram Burgard, and Dieter Fox. *Probabilistic Robotics*. MIT Press, 2005.

World Modeling for Advanced Surveillance Systems

Yvonne Fischer

Vision and Fusion Laboratory
Institute for Anthropomatics
Karlsruhe Institute of Technology (KIT), Germany
yvonne.fischer@kit.edu

Technical Report IES-2010-02

Abstract: The objective of advanced surveillance systems is not only to collect as much sensor data as possible, but also to process and represent it in a meaningful way for supporting situation awareness of a decision maker. However, in today's surveillance systems, there is still a need for information processing methods that meet these higher-level objectives. In this article, the information flow inside of an advanced surveillance system is highlighted and the term situation is discussed with respect to different abstraction levels. Furthermore, several challenges are identified that an advanced system has to address. Therefore, methods selected for information processing should meet these challenges in order to provide a high-level functionality for situation awareness support.

1 Introduction

During the operation of complex systems that include human decision making, acquiring and interpreting information from the environment forms the basis for the state of knowledge of a decision maker. This state is often referred to as situation awareness. The most commonly used definition of situation awareness was provided by Endsley in [End95]:

"Situation awareness is the perception of the elements in the environment within a volume of time and space, the comprehension of their meaning, and the projection of their status in the near future."

Due to this definition, situation awareness consists of three levels, namely perception, comprehension, and projection, as depicted in Figure 1.1. The first level of situation awareness includes the detection of relevant elements and its characteristics in the environment. These elements are of course domain specific and

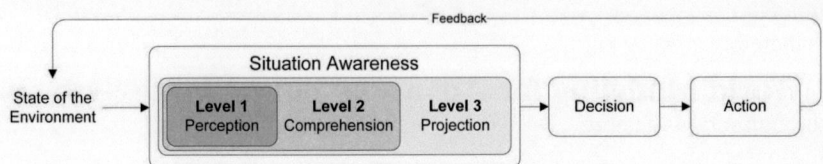

Figure 1.1: The process of dynamic decision making (adopted from [End95]).

their status, their attributes and their dynamics have to be observable by sensorial means. The second level of situation awareness is based on the relevant elements that have been detected on the first level and includes the understanding of the significance of these elements in relation to the operator's goals. The third and highest level of situation awareness is again based on the lower levels and deals with the ability to project future actions of elements in the environment.

Thus, a high level of situation awareness consists of much more than simply collecting information about elements in the environment. It is furthermore a result from the comprehension of its meaning and the projection of future states in order to make decisions on the most favorable actions. Situation awareness is therefore referred to as a mental state or a state of knowledge, whereas the processes to achieve and maintain that state are referred to as situation assessment. As a high level of situation awareness provides the complete knowledge which is necessary for effective decision making, the decision process itself and the performance of actions are separate stages of the dynamic decision making process as illustrated in Figure 1.1.

Endsley described several factors that have a major influence on the decision making process. First, individual factors influence the situation assessment process, for example the operator's abilities, experience, and training. But individuals do not only vary in their information processing mechanisms but also in their expectations and objectives. Other influencing factors can be summarized as system factors which include the system capabilities or the interface design, and also some features of the task environment like workload, stress or complexity.

The concept of situation awareness established by Endsley is applicable in many different domains and it can also be used for advanced surveillance systems. Especially in security-related tasks, like the surveillance of specific areas, decision makers should always have a high level of situation awareness. Situations of interest that take place in surveyed areas are often of a high complexity and dynamic, because they consist of multiple different objects that interact with each other and their activities evolve over time. In such a complex and dynamic environment, the limited capacity of a person's attention is quickly exhausted. The focus of attention is therefore a major limit on situation awareness.

In today's surveillance systems, level 1 situation awareness is highly supported through various heterogeneous sensors and appropriate signal-processing methods for extracting as much information as possible about the surveyed environment and its elements. The challenge of advanced surveillance systems is therefore not only to collect as much sensor data as possible, but also to process and represent them in an intelligent and meaningful way to give a sufficient information support to a decision maker. Or, in other words, to detect and assess complex situations that evolve over time as an automatic support to an operator's situation assessment process. The information overload is then reduced by providing only relevant or task-oriented information, which can be used to guide the focus of attention of a decision maker and allows him to decide and react in a timely and effective manner.

Working with heterogeneous sensors, the theories of multi-sensor data fusion [HM04], [Mit07] offer a powerful technique for supporting situation awareness. A lot of data fusion models have been developed and compared to Endsley's situation awareness model [IBRW07], whereas the most dominant model is the JDL model [SBW99]. However, there is still a need for concepts and methods supporting higher level situation awareness (level 2 and 3) that are able to infer real situations from observed elements in the environment and to project their status in the near future.

The paper is structured as follows. The next section gives an overview of the information flow inside an advanced surveillance system. Section 3.1 deals with a discussion on situational abstraction levels and tries to give a definition of the term situation. Section 3.2 is a first attempt of formalizing situations. In Section 4, several problems concerning automatic situation assessment in surveillance systems are identified. The paper finishes with a conclusion and outlook in Section 6.

2 Information Flow

Regarding data fusion in surveillance systems, the object-oriented world model (OOWM) is an approach to represent the relevant information extracted from sensor signals, fused into a single comprehensive, dynamic model of the monitored area. It was developed in [Bau09], whereas the basic ideas have been published in [EGB08]. A detailed description of the architecture can be found in [MRV10] and an application of the OOWM for wide area maritime surveillance is proposed in [FB10].

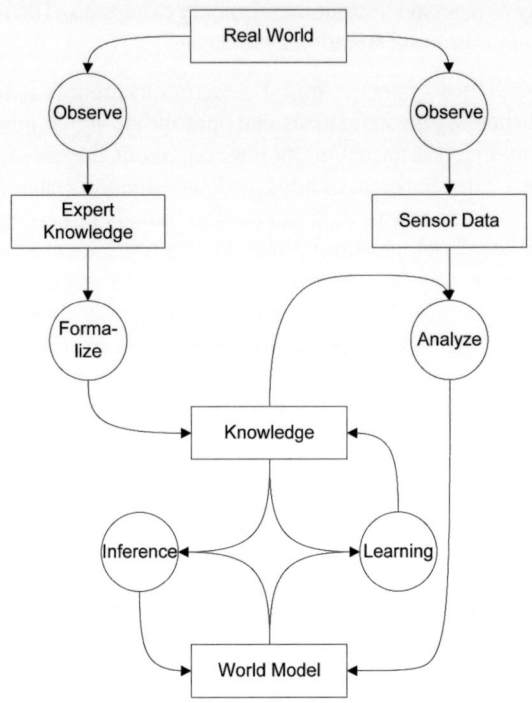

Figure 2.1: Information flow in surveillance systems.

In Figure 2.1, the information flow inside an advanced surveillance system is illustrated, whereas the real world is depicted on the top and the world model, i.e. the OOWM, is depicted on the bottom. Rectangular boxes represent aggregates of information and round boxes represent processes. The real world is defined as a spatio-temporal section of the physical world. Relevant parts of it can be observed by humans (or experts) and the result of this process is called expert knowledge. By formalizing the expert knowledge, knowledge-or more precisely-machine readable knowledge is generated.

The physical conditions of the real world can also be observed by appropriate sensors. The sensor data itself represents a spatio-temporal section of the real world and can be analyzed by using knowledge. The analyzed sensor data is transferred as information to the world model. The world model can be interpreted as a representation of the real world and its history, which is generated by using knowledge for analyzing sensor data, or by inference methods. Analyzing sensor data with knowledge includes for example data association and tracking methods, or consistency checks of the world model. Updating the world model with new sensor information is conducted by the inference process.

The knowledge includes all information that is needed for updating the world model by inference or for analyzing sensor data. It builds the basis for the description of relevant aspects of the real world in the world model. The knowledge is of course strongly dependent of the application domain, the context and the task. Furthermore, the knowledge is not static because it can be changed by new information coming from the world model or from expert knowledge. This dynamic aspect of the knowledge is also visualized by the learning process.

3 Higher-Level World Modeling

Regarding situational modeling, several concepts exist in literature. Roy proposed in [Roy01] the concept of situation analysis as a process to provide and maintain a state of situation awareness. He also proposed definitions of situational elements like entities, events and activities. Another refinement of the situational terminology with respect to the JDL data fusion model is given in [Sal07]. The concept of situation management in dynamic systems proposed by Jakobson [JBL07] includes not only the processes of perceiving and recognizing situations, but also the analysis of past situations and the prediction of future situations. In [Ste08], a rough taxonomy of functions related to situation assessment is proposed and a general overview of current approaches to automating this process is given.

3.1 Situational Abstraction Levels

In the revised version of the JDL data fusion model [SBW99], situation assessment (JDL-level 2) is defined as the estimation and prediction of relations among entities. The resulting network of relations among its elements is then referred to as the state of aggregation or the estimated situation. However, there is no formal representation of a situation, as the JDL definition admits any variety of relations to be considered. Types of relations exist at many different levels of abstraction, ranging from quantitative to highly abstract qualitative statements. Therefore, a formal representation of a situation, which fulfills the essential requirements in various application areas, is not easy to define. Situations are characterized mainly by their respective qualitative statements and their representation is therefore strongly dependent on the application domain.

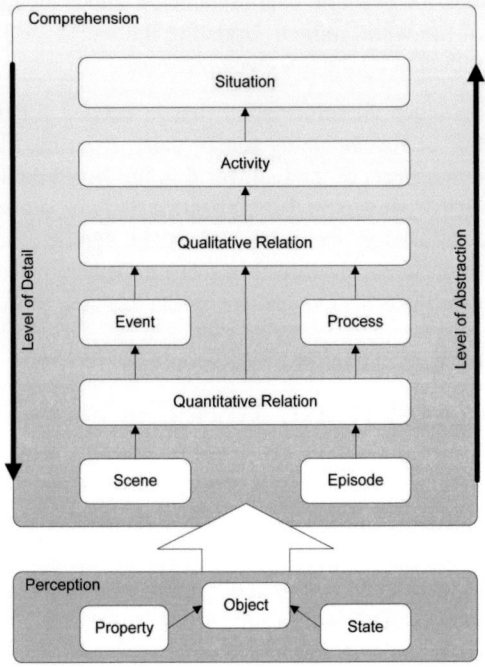

Figure 3.1: Situational Abstraction Levels.

Figure 3.1 shows a general decomposition of a situational description with respect to different abstraction levels. The level of abstraction is determined by the quantity of context information added to the observed element, whereas only relevant context information is used. The context information consists of knowledge that is not directly observable by sensors, for example expert knowledge. Its content and relevance is determined by the application domain and the task that an operator has to solve. The higher the level of abstraction, the lower is the level of detailed knowledge of a single, observed element. In the following, we will explain the decomposition in detail and give examples for each level of abstraction.

With the focus on surveillance systems, the perception stage includes the acquisition of object information by means of various sensors. Time invariant attributes about an object are summarized as properties and time variant attributes are summarized as the object's state. When observing for example human beings, the results from the perception stage are therefore the person's position and velocity as states and the height as property. This information is the input for the next stage, the comprehension of a situation.

At the lowest level of abstraction, a scene includes all observed objects at a certain point in time. A scene can therefore be interpreted as a snapshot or as a spatial subset of the world's observable objects at a point in time, whereas an episode includes also the time-dimension. An episode is the recording of all observed objects in a period of time (either discrete or continuous) and can therefore be defined as a spatio-temporal subset of the world's observable objects. Note, that at this level of abstraction, no relational aspects between objects are regarded.

The next level of abstraction deals with the description of quantitative relations that can be extracted directly from the information content of a scene or of an episode. Quantitative relations are quantitative statements about the connection between two or more relevant information values, mostly about the attribute values of some objects. The spatial distance measured in meter between two objects is for example a quantitative relation. Note that quantitative relations do not assume that the information values are derived from different objects. Another example of a quantitative relation is therefore the distance that an object has passed between two time points.

In Figure 3.1, special placements between quantitative and qualitative relations are given to events and processes. They can be interpreted as special cases of quantitative relations. An event is defined as the change of relevant object information at a point of time and a process describes the behavior of relevant object information during a time period. For example, the disappearance of an observed person could be tagged as an event or that a person's attribute value, indicating its speed, has changed to zero. A process would be the person's speed value or the direction of its movement over a time period. Events and processes are not limited to a single object. A process between two objects could be the decreasing distance between them and an event between them could be that the distance value of the respective quantitative relation changed to zero.

On the next higher level of abstraction, events, processes and quantitative relations can be summarized to qualitative relations. Detailed knowledge of attribute values of the observed objects goes lost at this level. A qualitative relation is an interpretation of the underlying events, processes and quantitative relations. Examples for qualitative relations are a person that is walking, a person that stops its movement, a person that is moving towards another object, or a person that meets another person.

Qualitative relations are strongly connected to activities. However, we state that activities take place in a longer period of time and are more complex in their construction. As qualitative relations can be interpreted as single and non-decomposable structures, an activity includes also the temporal relationships between them. An activity is a sequence of qualitative events, processes and relations. Temporal relationships of overlapping processes can for example be expressed by Allen's temporal interval logic [All83]. An example for this level of abstraction is a fighting activity between two human beings. The term behavior is often used if the focus is on activities conducted by humans or only by a single object. However, we will use the term activity for this level because it has a broader meaning.

At the highest level of abstraction, there is the situation itself. The human comprehension of a situation can be interpreted as the knowledge of everything of relevance that is going on. Therefore, based on our discussion so far, we give the following definition of the term situation:

A situation at time t is defined as a world state, which is characterized by the collection of relevant activities up to the time t and their interpretation with respect to the context knowledge.

As the world evolves over time, it changes from one state to another. Therefore, the change from one situation to another is due to the change of any activity that is going on or due to a change of the context. As an example, we assume a fighting activity between two humans that is going on so far. Regarding the context, the situation is completely different if the fighting takes place on the street or inside a boxing ring, although the underlying activity is the same.

The situation assessment process can therefore be described as the estimation and interpretation of the relevant state of the real world, which however does not only consist of the recognition of all activities that are going on. Moreover, it also includes contextual conditions like the environment in which an activity is taking place and its aim is to reduce the quantity of information with respect to its relevance.

3.2 Situational Configuration Spaces

In this subsection it is assumed that there are objects in the real world that have been observed. As described above, the objects have properties and states, which we will summarize as attributes. Attributes are for example the existence, the type, the position, the size or the color of an object. Objects can be divided into several classes, based on their type, whereas the number and style of attributes are determined by the object's type. Relations can be temporal or attributive and they can consider several objects. Most of the time only relations between two objects,

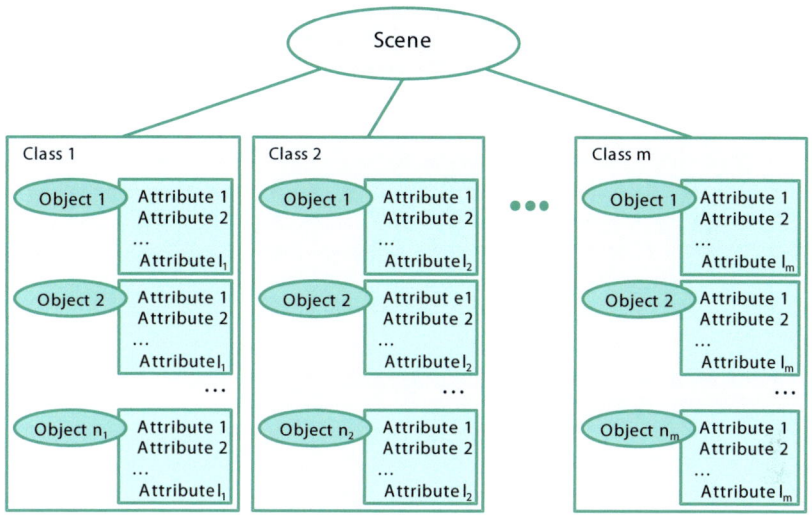

Figure 3.2: Formalization of a Scene.

binary relations are considered. As objects, also relations have attributes like the existence, the type or for example the relative distance between two objects. They can also be divided into classes based on their type.

If we interpret a scene as a snapshot of all observed objects at a certain point in time including their attributes, a scene can be formalized as depicted in Figure 3.2. Therefore, a configuration space K_{Scene} of a scene consists of

- the possible object classes $C_1, \ldots, C_m$,

- the number n_i of observed objects of class C_i, $i = 1, \ldots, m$, and

- the attributes $A_1^i, \ldots, A_{l_i}^i$ of Class C_i, $i = 1, \ldots, m$.

The configuration space of a scene can then be defined as

$$K_{Scene} = \prod_{i=1}^{m} \left(\prod_{j=1}^{n_i} \left(\prod_{k=1}^{l_i} A_k^i \right) \right) = \prod_{i=1}^{m} \left(\prod_{j=1}^{n_i} C_i \right)$$
$$= \underbrace{(C_1 \times \ldots C_1)}_{n_1} \times \underbrace{(C_2 \times \ldots C_2)}_{n_2} \times \ldots \times \underbrace{(C_m \times \ldots C_m)}_{n_m} .$$

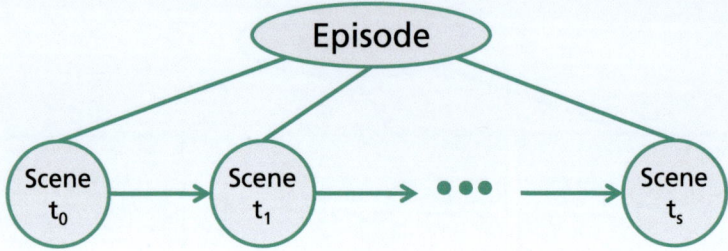

Figure 3.3: Scenes and Episodes.

The dimension of the configuration space K_{Scene} is therefore dependent on the number of observed objects per class:

$$\dim K_{Scene} = \sum_{i=1}^{m} n_i \cdot l_i \ .$$

Based on the definition of the configuration space of a scene, we can add the time-dimension for defining the configuration space of an episode, see Figure 3.3. The configuration space $K_{Episode}$ of an episode consists therefore of

- the configuration space of a scene K_{Scene}, and
- the time-sequence $\{t_0, t_1, \ldots, t_s\} := T$.

The configuration space of an episode can then be defined as

$$K_{Episode} = K_{Scene} \times T \ .$$

The dimension of the configuration space $K_{Episode}$ is therefore

$$\dim K_{Episode} = 1 + \dim K_{Scene} \ .$$

Situations can be interpreted as episodes enriched with relations and they include therefore higher-level information which is not included in a scene or an episode, see Figure 3.4. The configuration space $K_{Situation}$ of a situation consists therefore of

- the possible relational classes $R_1, \ldots, R_p$,
- the number q_i of relations of the relational class R_i, $i = 1, \ldots, p$,

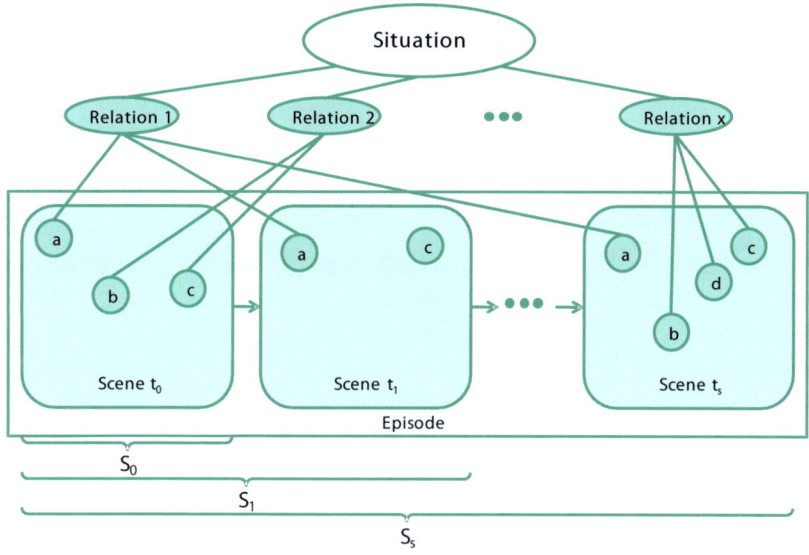

Figure 3.4: Formalization of a Situation.

- the attributes $B_1^i, \ldots, B_{r_i}^i$ of the relational class, and
- the configuration space of an episode $K_{Episode}$.

The configuration space of a situation can then be defined as

$$
\begin{aligned}
K_{Situation} &= K_{Episode} \times \prod_{i=1}^{p} \left(\prod_{j=1}^{q_i} \left(\prod_{k=1}^{r_i} B_k^i \right) \right) \\
&= K_{Episode} \times \prod_{i=1}^{p} \left(\prod_{j=1}^{q_i} R_i \right) \\
&= K_{Episode} \times \underbrace{\left(R_1 \times \ldots R_1 \right)}_{q_1} \times \ldots \times \underbrace{\left(R_p \times \ldots R_p \right)}_{q_p} .
\end{aligned}
$$

The dimension of the configuration space $K_{Situation}$ is therefore

$$
\dim K_{Situation} = \dim K_{Episode} + \sum_{i=1}^{p} q_i \cdot r_i = 1 + \sum_{i=1}^{m} n_i \cdot l_i + \sum_{i=1}^{p} q_i \cdot r_i .
$$

The definitions in this chapter are a first attempt of formalizing the term situation by the introduction of a configuration space. The formalizations are straightforward, based on the objects that have been observed in the environment. Obviously, the dimension of the configuration space is quite high, even if only few observed objects are present. The formalizations also show the complexity of defining situations.

4   Challenges of Advanced Surveillance Systems

In this Section we will identify the main problems and challenges of situation assessment in advanced surveillance systems. More advanced systems also support such high-level functions as described in general in [Das08]. Probabilistic methods like hidden Markov models can be used for situation recognition [MDPB09], but are strongly dependent on training data. Also several other approaches have been proposed, for example grammar-parsing detection of abnormal behavior of a person's movement in indoor surveillance [BF10] or logic based approaches for the recognition of human activities [IS10]. In [SNSS10], a heuristic graph matching approach for the identification of meaningful patterns in large volumes of data have been proposed as an enhancement to existing situation assessment methods. In [GGS06], Markov random fields are used to model contextual relationships and maximum a posteriori labeling is used to infer intentions of observed elements.

Mostly, there is a lack of training data, especially for critical situations that an operator wants to detect. For interventional reasons, critical situations have to be detected timely, which means during their development and not only when they are finished. Moreover, the system should be able to deal with uncertain observations, as signal processing methods usually provide estimated feature values and also false detections. The system should be able to deal with incomplete observations, whereas the incompleteness can be of spatial and of temporal type. Spatial incompleteness follows from incomplete sensor coverage, as for example in wide areas it is not possible to continuously observe every part of the environment. Temporal incompleteness follows from spatial incompleteness in the past. As situations evolve over time, it is possible that the beginning of a situation was not observed. Furthermore, the system should be able to predict the situation state in the near future and give a clue to the question: What might happen next?

The main challenges of situation assessment functions are therefore:

- dealing with no training data,

- detection of situations during their development,

- dealing with uncertainties,

- dealing with incomplete observations, as a result of

  – spatial incompleteness due to incomplete sensor coverage,

  – temporal incompleteness due to missing observations in the past, and

- predicttion of developments in the near future.

Due to these challenges, the result of the situation recognition should not be a binary decision if a certain situation is recognized or not. The result should be a Degree of Belief for each template situation, indicating the existence of the underlying and ongoing situation in the real world.

5 Conclusion and Outlook

In this article, the information flow inside of an advanced surveillance system has been highlighted and the term situation has been discussed with respect to different abstraction levels. A first attempt of formalizing the term situation via the introduction of a configuration space has been provided. Furthermore, several challenges has been identified that an advanced surveillance system has to address. Methods selected for situational assessment should meet these challenges in order to provide a high-level functionality for situation awareness support. Further research directions involve the generation of example situations in surveillance applications and the practical realization of various situation assessment methods. The objective is to support the situation awareness of a decision maker as best as possible because in today's surveillance systems, there is still a need for information processing methods that meet the higher-level objectives.

Bibliography

[All83]   James F. Allen. Maintaining Knowledge about Temporal Intervals. In *Communications of the ACM*, volume 26, 1983.

[BEVB09] Alexander Bauer, Thomas Emter, Hauke Vagts, and Jürgen Beyerer. Object oriented world model for surveillance systems. In *Future Security: 4th Security Research Conference, Fraunhofer Press*, pages 339–345, 2009.

[BF10]   Alexander Bauer and Yvonne Fischer. Task-oriented situation recognition. In *Proceedings of SPIE*, volume 7709, 2010.

[Das08]   Subrata Das. *High-Level Data Fusion*. Artech House, Inc, 2008.

[EGB08]   Thomas Emter, Ioana Gheta, and Jürgen Beyerer. Object oriented world model for video surveillance systems. In *Future Security: 3rd Security Research Conference, Fraunhofer Press*, pages 315–320, 2008.

[End95]   Mica R. Endsley. Toward a Theory of Situation Awareness in Dynamic Systems. *Human Factors: The Journal of the Human Factors and Ergonomics Society*, 37(1):32–64, 1995.

[FB10]   Yvonne Fischer and Alexander Bauer. Object-oriented sensor data fusion for wide maritime surveillance. In *2nd International Conference on Waterside Security, WSS*, 2010.

[GGS06]   Robin Glinton, Joseph Giampapa, and Katia Sycara. A Markov Random Field Model of Context for High-Level Information Fusion. In *9th International Conference on Information Fusion*, 2006.

[HM04]   David L. Hall and Sonya A. H. McMullen. *Mathematical Techniques in Multisensor Data Fusion*. Artech House, Inc., 2004.

[IS10]   Joris Ijsselmuiden and Rainer Stiefelhagen. Towards high-level human activity recognition through computer vision and temporal logic. In *KI 2010: Advances in Artificial Intelligence, Lecture Notes in Computer Science*, volume 6359, pages 426–435, 2010.

[JBL07]   Gabriel Jakobson, John Buford, and Lundy Lewis. Situation Management: Basic Concepts and Approaches. In *Information Fusion and Geographic Information Systems*, pages 18–33, 2007.

[lBRW07]   Éloi Bossé, Jean Roy, and Steve Wark. *Concepts, Models, and Tools for Information Fusion*. Artech House, Inc, 2007.

[MDPB09]   Daniel Meyer-Delius, Christian Plagemann, and Wolfram Burgard. Probabilistic Situation Recognition for Vehicular Traffic Scenarios. In *Proceedings of the 2009 IEEE international conference on Robotics and Automation*, pages 4161–4166, 2009.

[Mit07]   Harvey B. Mitchell. *Multi-Sensor Data Fusion: An Introduction*. Springer, 2007.

[MRV10]   Jürgen Moßgraber, Frank Reinert, and Hauke Vagts. An architecture for a task-oriented surveillance system: a service and event based approach. In *Proc. Fifth International Conference on Systems, ICONS*, pages 146–151, 2010.

[Roy01]   Jean Roy. From Data Fusion to Situation Analysis. In *Proceedings of the Fourth International Conference on Information Fusion*, 2001.

[Sal07]   John J. Salerno. Where's level 2/3 fusion - a look back over the past 10 years. In *10th International Conference on Information Fusion, IEEE*, 2007.

[SBW99]   Alan N. Steinberg, Christopher L. Bowman, and Franklin E. White. Revisions to the JDL Data Fusion Model. In *Sensor Fusion: Architectures, Algorithms, and Applications, Proceedings of the SPIE*, volume 3719, pages 430–441, 1999.

[SNSS10]   Kedar Sambhoos, Rakesh Nagi, Moises Sudit, and Adam Stotz. Enhancements to high level data fusion using graph matching and state space search. *Information Fusion*, 11(4, October):351–364, October 2010.

[Ste08]   Alan N. Steinberg. Foundations of Situation and Threat Assessment. In Martin E. Liggins, David L. Hall, and James Llinas, editors, *Handbook of Multisensor Data Fusion: Theory and Practice*, pages 437–501. CRC Press, 2nd edition, 2008.

Use of a Probability Interval Scheme for Focussed Bayesian Fusion

Jennifer Sander

Vision and Fusion Laboratory
Institute for Anthropomatics
Karlsruhe Institute of Technology (KIT), Germany
jennifer.sander@kit.edu

Technical Report IES-2010-03

Abstract: Focussed Bayesian fusion is a local Bayesian fusion technique by that high costs caused by Bayesian fusion can get circumvented. This publication constitutes an analysis with regard to the use of a probability interval scheme for focussed Bayesian fusion, which has been developed in previous publications. Its reduction to a unique posterior distribution by the Maximum Entropy method and its direct use for decision making are analyzed.

1   Introduction

Local Bayesian fusion approaches reduce costs caused by Bayesian fusion by a concentration of the actual Bayesian fusion task on a local context U. By a local context, we mean an appropriately chosen subset of the space Z that is spanned by the range of the Properties of Interest (PoI). Ignoring $\overline{U} := Z \setminus U$ completely, a straightforward fusion scheme, which we termed focussed Bayesian fusion, results. In [San09, SHGB10], a probability interval scheme for focussed Bayesian fusion has been developed. By this scheme, the uncertainty that results additionally from the focussing on U is represented explicitly in a non-probabilistic manner.

Provided that such a distinction of uncertainties is not used effectively, facts and corresponding uncertainties are represented in an adequate manner by probability in the sense of the Degree of Belief (DoB) interpretation. Hence, if the aim of the fusion task is to obtain a comprehensive representation of the posterior state of knowledge, a reduction of the probability interval scheme to a unique posterior distribution[1] should be done. For this, the use of the Maximum Entropy (ME) method

---

[1]According to the nature of the respective quantities, which may be discrete or continuous in a concrete fusion task, the term distribution has a mixed meaning as discrete probability function and probability density in this publication.

[Kap93, Ros77]–an established method to obtain objective DoB distributions–is self-evident. In Sec. 3, a closed solution for the ME problem given a probability interval scheme is derived and the result is analyzed critically.

Choosing a unique posterior distribution is a decision [BS04]. It appears not sensible to make such a decision if subsequently another decision problem is to be solved on basis of the posterior knowledge: doing so, two hard decisions are subsequent one another. It is shown in Sec. 4 how the probability interval scheme is usable directly for decision making. Under the assumption that the respective decision problem is one under linear partial information (LPI) [KM76, Pre02], common decision criteria under partial information are considered. Possibilities of improving the criteria by an enlargement of the local context and the inclusion of additional constraints are shown. Finally, the generalization of the derived concepts for the solution of arbitrary decision problems is sketched exemplarily.

2 Theoretical Foundations

2.1 Focussed Bayesian Fusion

At Bayesian fusion, we are interested in some PoI $z \in Z$ which adopt a certain "true" value. Instead of z, only the information d from several information sources is directly observable.

In the Bayesian theory, all quantities are assumed to be random and all available information is represented probabilistically in the sense of the DoB interpretation. The prior distribution $p(z)$ and the Likelihood function[2] $p(d|z)$ are combined via the Bayesian theorem to the posterior distribution $p(z|d) \propto p(d|z)\, p(z)$. Using concepts from decision theory, subsequent decisions can be derived from $p(z|d)$.

At focussed Bayesian fusion, the actual Bayesian fusion is performed only with respect to the local context. As explained in [SHGB09], the corresponding fusion scheme is given by

$$p(z|d, U) \propto p(d|z)\, p(z|U) \ .$$

In the focussed Bayesian model, events[3] $E \subseteq \overline{U}$ are assumed to be impossible. The probability of events $E \subseteq U$ gets distorted according to the posterior

---

[2]It holds $d := (d_1, \ldots, d_S)$ whereby d_s is the contribution of source number $s \in \{1, \ldots, S\}$, $S \in \mathbb{N}$. Especially in the case that $d_1, \ldots, d_S$ are conditionally independent given z, a sequential fusion scheme is easily realizable: by the use of source specific Likelihood functions, each information contribution can get incorporated individually into the posterior distribution [BHSG08]. We skip the respective exposition because it is not essential with regard to the aims of this publication.

[3]Events are sets to that a probability is assigned.

probability[4] $P(U|\boldsymbol{d}) = \int_U p(\boldsymbol{z}|\boldsymbol{d}) \; \mathrm{d}\boldsymbol{z}$ of the local context. More precisely, we have

$$p(\boldsymbol{z}|\boldsymbol{d}, U) = \begin{cases} \frac{p(\boldsymbol{z}|\boldsymbol{d})}{P(U|\boldsymbol{d})} \; , & \boldsymbol{z} \in U \; , \\ 0 \; , & \boldsymbol{z} \in \overline{U} \; . \end{cases} \tag{2.1}$$

A local context can be specified by a pre-evaluation of the available information. In the following, it is concretely assumed that U contains at least these values of the PoI whose Likelihood is larger than a suitable threshold. The rationale behind this specification, its extensions, and the threshold determination have been pointed up in several previous publications, see [SB08, SHGB09, SKB10].

2.2 Probability Interval Scheme

Assume we know that $p(\boldsymbol{d}|\boldsymbol{z}) \leq \delta$ holds for all $\boldsymbol{z} \in \overline{U}$ with a threshold $\delta \in (0, 1)$. As shown in [San09, SHGB10], this inequality delivers the following lower bound for the posterior probability of U in the non-focussed Bayesian model:

$$P(U|\boldsymbol{d}) \geq \frac{\int_U p(\boldsymbol{d}|\boldsymbol{z}) \, p(\boldsymbol{z}) \; \mathrm{d}\boldsymbol{z}}{\int_U p(\boldsymbol{d}|\boldsymbol{z}) \, p(\boldsymbol{z}) \; \mathrm{d}\boldsymbol{z} + (1 - P(U)) \delta} =: \beta \; . \tag{2.2}$$

β is computable in the focussed model if $P(U)$ is ratable.

Combining (2.1) and (2.2), general bounds for posterior probabilities are derived:

$$P(E|\boldsymbol{d}) \in [\mathrm{a}(E), \mathrm{b}(E)] := \begin{cases} [\beta \, P(E|\boldsymbol{d}, U), P(E|\boldsymbol{d}, U)] \; , & E \subseteq U \; , \\ [0, 1 - \beta] \; , & \emptyset \neq E \subseteq \overline{U} \; . \end{cases} \tag{2.3}$$

Additionally, from (2.1), one obtains for $\boldsymbol{z}^*, \boldsymbol{z}^{**} \in U$:

$$o(\boldsymbol{z}^*, \boldsymbol{z}^{**}) := \frac{p(\boldsymbol{z}^*|\boldsymbol{d}, U)}{p(\boldsymbol{z}^{**}|\boldsymbol{d}, U)} = \frac{p(\boldsymbol{z}^*|\boldsymbol{d})}{p(\boldsymbol{z}^{**}|\boldsymbol{d})} \; . \tag{2.4}$$

Hence, it is not possible that the posterior probabilities of events that are included in U vary arbitrarily within the corresponding intervals [SHGB10]: if $\boldsymbol{z}^* \in U$ is arbitrary but fixed, for each $E \subseteq U$, we have $P(E|\boldsymbol{d}) = p(\boldsymbol{z}^*|\boldsymbol{d}) \int_E o(\boldsymbol{z}, \boldsymbol{z}^*) \; \mathrm{d}\boldsymbol{z}$. This means that the posterior probability of E varies according to one parameter given by $p(\boldsymbol{z}^*|\boldsymbol{d})$. Obviously, it holds $p(\boldsymbol{z}^*|\boldsymbol{d}) \in [\beta \, p(\boldsymbol{z}^*|\boldsymbol{d}, U), p(\boldsymbol{z}^*|\boldsymbol{d}, U)]$.

---

[4]Integration with respect to the counting measure is summation. Because of this, generally, an integral notation is used for both, the summation of discrete and the integration of continuous quantities. A summation sign is used only if the respective formula is to refer exclusively to the discrete case.

3   Reduction to a Unique Probability Distribution

Let Π denote the set of all probability distributions on Z that are consistent with (2.3) and (2.4). The reduction of the probability interval scheme to a single ME distribution $p_{\text{ME}}(z|d)$ can be stated as[5]:

$$p_{\text{ME}}(z|d) = \arg \max_{p(z|d)\in\Pi} \text{H}[p(z|d)] \,, \tag{3.1}$$

$$\text{H}[p(z|d)] = -\int_Z p(z|d) \log_2 p(z|d) \ dz \,. \tag{3.2}$$

3.1   Formulation as One-Dimensional Optimization Problem

Lemma 1 *Let* $\text{H}[(P(U|d), P(\overline{U}|d))]$ *denote the entropy of the probability distribution on the set* $\{U, \overline{U}\}$ *that assigns* U *probability* $P(U|d)$*. It holds*

$$\begin{aligned} \text{H}[p(z|d)] =&\, \text{H}[(P(U|d), P(\overline{U}|d))] \\ &+ P(U|d)\,\text{H}[p(z|d, U)] + P(\overline{U}|d)\,\text{H}[p(z|d, \overline{U})] \,. \end{aligned} \tag{3.3}$$

PROOF. We have $p(z|d) = P(E|d)\,p(z|d, E)$, $E \in \{U, \overline{U}\}$, $z \in E$, compare (2.1). Together with (3.2), this delivers

$$\begin{aligned} \text{H}[p(z|d)] = &-P(U|d)\int_U p(z|d, U) \log_2 \left(p(z|d, U)\,P(U|d)\right) \ dz \\ &- P(\overline{U}|d)\int_{\overline{U}} p(z|d, \overline{U}) \log_2 \left(p(z|d, \overline{U})\,P(\overline{U}|d)\right) \ dz \,. \end{aligned}$$

Using the identity $\log_2\left(p(z|d, E)\,P(E|d)\right) = \log_2 p(z|d, E) + \log_2 P(E|d)$, $E \in \{U, \overline{U}\}$, and rearranging the resulting terms directly leads to (3.3).   □

Lemma 1 is also traceable back to the grouping axiom [DL75] for entropy. We will use the lemma to formulate the reduction of the probability interval scheme as optimization problem with respect to the value of $P(U|d)$ at the proof of the following theorem.

Theorem 1 *The reduction of the probability interval scheme by the ME method delivers*

$$p_{\text{ME}}(z|d) = \begin{cases} \pi\,p(z|d, U) \,, & \beta \leq \pi \,, \\ \beta\,p(z|d, U) \,, & \pi < \beta \,, \end{cases} \tag{3.4}$$

---

[5]For the shake of simplicity, it is assumed that all considered ME distributions exist.

with

$$\pi := \frac{2^{\mathrm{H}[p(\boldsymbol{z}|\boldsymbol{d},U)]}}{2^{\mathrm{H}[p(\boldsymbol{z}|\boldsymbol{d},U)]} + 2^{\mathrm{H}[p_{\mathrm{ME}}(\boldsymbol{z}|\boldsymbol{d},\overline{U})]}} .$$

Thereby, the quantity $\mathrm{H}[p_{\mathrm{ME}}(\boldsymbol{z}|\boldsymbol{d},\overline{U})]$ *denotes the entropy of the ME distribution on* $\overline{U}$*, which results if no knowledge–except that* $p_{\mathrm{ME}}(\boldsymbol{z}|\boldsymbol{d},\overline{U})$ *is a probability distribution–is imposed as constraint at the application of the ME method.*

PROOF. The maximization of $\mathrm{H}[p(\boldsymbol{z}|\boldsymbol{d})]$ is equivalent to the minimization of $-\mathrm{H}[p(\boldsymbol{z}|\boldsymbol{d})]$. Using the notation $x := P(U|\boldsymbol{d})$, lemma 1 delivers:

$$\begin{aligned}-\mathrm{H}[p(\boldsymbol{z}|\boldsymbol{d})] =& x \log_2 x + (1-x) \log_2(1-x) \\ & - x\,\mathrm{H}[p(\boldsymbol{z}|\boldsymbol{d},U)] - (1-x)\mathrm{H}[p(\boldsymbol{z}|\boldsymbol{d},\overline{U})] .\end{aligned} \tag{3.5}$$

At the focussing on U, $\overline{U}$ is ignored completely. Because no knowledge concerning $\overline{U}$ is available in the focussed Bayesian model, it gets clear from (3.5) that $-\mathrm{H}[p(\boldsymbol{z}|\boldsymbol{d})]$ becomes minimal if $\mathrm{H}[p(\boldsymbol{z}|\boldsymbol{d},\overline{U})]$ is chosen to be maximal, i.e., if $p(\boldsymbol{z}|\boldsymbol{d},\overline{U}) = p_{\mathrm{ME}}(\boldsymbol{z}|\boldsymbol{d},\overline{U})$. Hence, the reduction of the probability interval scheme by the ME method is equivalent to the minimization of the function

$$\mathrm{f}(x) := x \log_2 x + (1-x) \log_2(1-x) - x\,\mathrm{H}[p(\boldsymbol{z}|\boldsymbol{d},U)] - (1-x)\mathrm{H}[p_{\mathrm{ME}}(\boldsymbol{z}|\boldsymbol{d},\overline{U})]$$

under the constraint $\beta \leq x$, which corresponds to (2.2). Calculating the second derivative of $\mathrm{f}(x)$, one sees that this function is convex for $x \in (0,1)$. The corresponding Lagrangian function [BV05] is given by

$$\begin{aligned}\mathrm{L}(x,\lambda) =& x \log_2 x + (1-x) \log_2(1-x) - x\,\mathrm{H}[p(\boldsymbol{z}|\boldsymbol{d},U)] \\ & - (1-x)\mathrm{H}[p_{\mathrm{ME}}(\boldsymbol{z}|\boldsymbol{d},\overline{U})] + \lambda\,(\beta - x) .\end{aligned}$$

The Karush-Kuhn-Tucker (KKT) conditions [BV05] are:

(a) $\beta \leq x$,   (b) $\lambda \geq 0$,   (c) $\lambda = 0 \vee \beta = x$,

(d) $\log_2\left(\dfrac{x}{1-x}\right) - \mathrm{H}[p(\boldsymbol{z}|\boldsymbol{d},U)] + \mathrm{H}[p_{\mathrm{ME}}(\boldsymbol{z}|\boldsymbol{d},\overline{U})] - \lambda = 0$.

Now, we make a case distinction according to condition (c):

If $\lambda = 0$, condition (d) delivers

$$\frac{x}{1-x} = 2^{\mathrm{H}[p(\boldsymbol{z}|\boldsymbol{d},U)] - \mathrm{H}[p_{\mathrm{ME}}(\boldsymbol{z}|\boldsymbol{d},\overline{U})]} \Leftrightarrow x = \frac{2^{\mathrm{H}[p(\boldsymbol{z}|\boldsymbol{d},U)]}}{2^{\mathrm{H}[p(\boldsymbol{z}|\boldsymbol{d},U)]} + 2^{\mathrm{H}[p_{\mathrm{ME}}(\boldsymbol{z}|\boldsymbol{d},\overline{U})]}}$$

which holds according to condition (a) if $\beta \leq x$.

In the case that $\beta = x$, condition (d) delivers

$$\lambda = \log_2\left(\frac{\beta}{1-\beta}\right) - H[p(\boldsymbol{z}|\boldsymbol{d}, U)] + H[p_{\mathrm{ME}}(\boldsymbol{z}|\boldsymbol{d}, \overline{U})] \,.$$

Hence, according to condition (b), it must hold

$$\beta \geq \frac{2^{H[p(\boldsymbol{z}|\boldsymbol{d}, U)]}}{2^{H[p(\boldsymbol{z}|\boldsymbol{d}, U)]} + 2^{H[p_{\mathrm{ME}}(\boldsymbol{z}|\boldsymbol{d}, \overline{U})]}} \,.$$

$\square$

3.2 Direct Formulation

Let $z^* \in U$ be arbitrary but fixed. Because of (2.4), the ME distribution $p_{\mathrm{ME}}(\boldsymbol{z}|\boldsymbol{d})$ in (3.1) is exactly the probability distribution that minimizes

$$\int_{\overline{U}} p(\boldsymbol{z}|\boldsymbol{d}) \log_2 p(\boldsymbol{z}|\boldsymbol{d}) \ \mathrm{d}\boldsymbol{z} + \int_{U} p(\boldsymbol{z}^*|\boldsymbol{d}) o(\boldsymbol{z}, \boldsymbol{z}^*) \ \log_2\left(p(\boldsymbol{z}^*|\boldsymbol{d}) o(\boldsymbol{z}, \boldsymbol{z}^*)\right) \ \mathrm{d}\boldsymbol{z}$$

(3.6)

under the condition (2.2), i.e., $\beta - \int_U p(\boldsymbol{z}^*|\boldsymbol{d}) o(\boldsymbol{z}, \boldsymbol{z}^*) \ \mathrm{d}\boldsymbol{z} \leq 0$.

If $\overline{U}$ is a discrete set of cardinality $M \in \mathbb{N}$, this is a convex optimization problem on $\mathbb{R}^{M+1}$, which is also easily solvable by the consideration of the KKT conditions. The verification that the solution is identical to (3.4), which has been derived in Sec. 3.1 by an optimization on $\mathbb{R}$, is straightforward.

In the literature, finite ME problems under constraints on upper and lower bounds on probabilities have been discussed elaborately, see for example [Abb05]. By the formulation (3.6), constraints on probability ratios can get included additionally.

3.3 Discussion

Entropy is an inverse measure of DoB concentration. If $\beta \leq \pi$, it follows from (3.4) that[6] $P(U|d) \propto 2^{H[p(\boldsymbol{z}|\boldsymbol{d}, U)]} \leq |U|$ and $P(\overline{U}|d) \propto 2^{H[p_{\mathrm{ME}}(\boldsymbol{z}|\boldsymbol{d}, \overline{U})]} = |\overline{U}|$. Hence, the more concentrated $p(\boldsymbol{z}|\boldsymbol{d}, U)$ is, the more probability mass gets shifted on $\overline{U}$ at the transition from $p(\boldsymbol{z}|\boldsymbol{d}, U)$ to $p_{\mathrm{ME}}(\boldsymbol{z}|\boldsymbol{d})$. For the case of a finite Z with $|U| = |\overline{U}| = 2$, this phenomenon has been noted by Van Fraassen already in 1981 [Fra81]. In connection to his Judy Benjamin problem, it is analyzed and discussed to date [Bov10, DR09].

---

[6]The notation $|E|$ stands for the number of elements of a discrete event $E \subseteq Z$ and for the Lebesgue measure, respectively, if E is continuous.

Within the context of focussed Bayesian fusion, the described property of the ME method substantiates the interpretation that it corresponds to a worst case principle [Wal91]: the fact that $p(z|d, U)$ is highly concentrated may be misleading. Thereby, we mean that it may result from a high distortion at the transition from $p(z|d)$ to $p(z|d, U)$, which is done at the focussing.[7] The ME method assumes that such a situation is on hand and tries to correct the distortion.

To our mind, the application of the ME method for the reduction of the probability interval scheme may be conductive. We come to this conclusion also due to the fact that–if $P(U|d)$ is high and if β is a good bound for it–the condition $\beta \leq \pi$ in (3.4) may prevent the shifting of absurd much probability mass on $\overline{U}$.

4   Direct Use for Decision Making

4.1   Decisions under Risk, Partial Information, and LPI

It is assumed that a set A of actions is given and that $\tilde{u}(a, z)$ is the utility of action $a \in A$ provided that $z \in Z$ is the "true" value of the PoI.

If the posterior state of knowledge is represented by an unique posterior distribution $p(z|d)$, the decision making is done under risk [Rüg99]. According to the principle of expected utility [BS04], a rational decision maker should chose an action $a^* \in A$ such that it holds[8]

$$a^* = \arg \max_{a \in A} \mathrm{E}_{p(z|d)}[\tilde{u}(a, z)] , \tag{4.1}$$

$$\mathrm{E}_{p(z|d)}[\tilde{u}(a, z)] = \int_Z \tilde{u}(a, z)\, p(z|d)\ \mathrm{d}z . \tag{4.2}$$

In contrast, making decisions directly on the basis of the probability interval scheme is decision making under partial information [Pre02]. Here, it is only assumed that $p(z|d)$ is contained in the set of all probability distributions on Z that are consistent with (2.3) and (2.4). In this situation, a set of possible values for the expected utility of an action has to be considered explicitly–instead of one unique value as at decision making under risk. The next theorem shows that it may be possible to identify also here an action that is optimal in the sense of (4.1).

Theorem 2 *For events $E^* \subseteq U$, $E^{**} \subseteq Z$, we have $P(E^*|d) \geq P(E^{**}|d)$ if the corresponding interval bounds satisfy* $\mathrm{b}(E^{**} \cap \overline{U}) \leq \mathrm{a}(E^*) - \mathrm{a}(E^{**} \cap U)$.

---

[7]A high distortion is due to a low value of $P(U|d)$. See [San09, SB08] for a more comprehensive analysis of the critical effects of the distortion.

[8]We assume all used utility functions to be bounded and an act which maximizes (4.1) to exist.

Remark 1 Without loss of generality, it can be assumed that we have $E^* \cap E^{**} = \emptyset$ in theorem 2: if this does not hold, theorem 2 follows from a comparison of the posterior probabilities of $E^* \setminus (E^* \cap E^{**})$ and $E^{**} \setminus (E^* \cap E^{**})$.

Remark 2 Theorem 2 can be formulated as decision problem by defining[9] $A = \{E^*, E^{**}\}$, $\tilde{u}(E, \boldsymbol{z}) = \mathbf{1}_E(\boldsymbol{z})$ such that $\mathrm{E}_{p(\boldsymbol{z}|\boldsymbol{d})}[\tilde{u}(E, \boldsymbol{z})] = P(E|\boldsymbol{d})$, $E \in A$.

PROOF. $P(E^*|\boldsymbol{d}) \geq P(E^{**}|\boldsymbol{d})$ is equivalent to

$$P(E^{**} \cap \overline{U}|\boldsymbol{d}) \leq P(E^*|\boldsymbol{d}) - P(E^{**} \cap U|\boldsymbol{d}) . \tag{4.3}$$

Remembering (2.1) and (2.4), we obtain

$$P(E^{**} \cap U|\boldsymbol{d}) = P(E^*|\boldsymbol{d}) \frac{P(E^{**} \cap U|\boldsymbol{d}, U)}{P(E^*|\boldsymbol{d}, U)} = P(E^*|\boldsymbol{d}) \frac{\mathrm{a}(E^{**} \cap U)}{\mathrm{a}(E^*)} .$$

Hence, (4.3) is equivalent to

$$P(E^{**} \cap \overline{U}|\boldsymbol{d}) \leq P(E^*|\boldsymbol{d}) \left(1 - \frac{\mathrm{a}(E^{**} \cap U)}{\mathrm{a}(E^*)}\right) . \tag{4.4}$$

From (2.3), we know that $P(E^{**} \cap \overline{U}|\boldsymbol{d}) \leq \mathrm{b}(E^{**} \cap \overline{U})$ and $P(E^*|\boldsymbol{d}) \geq \mathrm{a}(E^*)$ hold[10]. Hence, (4.4) is surely satisfied if it holds

$$\mathrm{b}(E^{**} \cap \overline{U}) \leq \mathrm{a}(E^*) \left(1 - \frac{\mathrm{a}(E^{**} \cap U)}{\mathrm{a}(E^*)}\right) = \mathrm{a}(E^*) - \mathrm{a}(E^{**} \cap U) .$$

$\square$

Theorem 2 directly applies to Maximum-a-Posteriori (MAP) estimation:

Lemma 2 *Let Z be discrete. Then, $\hat{\boldsymbol{z}} \in U$ is a MAP estimate if* $\mathrm{a}(\boldsymbol{z}) \leq \mathrm{a}(\hat{\boldsymbol{z}})$ *holds for all $\boldsymbol{z} \in U$ and* $\mathrm{b}(\boldsymbol{z}) \leq \mathrm{a}(\hat{\boldsymbol{z}})$ *holds for all $\boldsymbol{z} \in \overline{U}$.*

Remark 3 The condition $\mathrm{a}(\boldsymbol{z}) \leq \mathrm{a}(\hat{\boldsymbol{z}})$ for all $\boldsymbol{z} \in U$ in lemma 2 is equivalent to the condition that $\hat{\boldsymbol{z}}$ must be a MAP estimate in the focussed Bayesian model.

The literature provides different criteria for decision making under partial information if it is not or only hardly possible to identify directly an action that is optimal in the sense of (4.1). See for example [KM76, Pre02, UA05, Wal91]. A lot of them are–partially with slight modifications–meaningful also at dealing with continuous

---

[9]$\mathbf{1}_E(\boldsymbol{z})$ is the indicator function of E: it has the value one if $\boldsymbol{z} \in E$ and the value zero if $\boldsymbol{z} \notin E$.
[10]Using additionally (2.4), one can derive that these bounds are reachable together.

distributions [Aug98, Wal91, Wei01]. However, at the present, the most feasible algorithms, which make their efficient application possible, deal only with quantities on finite sets. Their application to arbitrary decision problems is an actual research theme, see for example [OA07, UD09].

Assuming $\overline{U}$ to be a finite set, the given decision problem will be traced back to a decision problem under LPI. The following definition is based on [KM76]:

Definition 1 Partial information about a probability distribution over a finite set of cardinality k is LPI if the respective subarea W of the k-dimensional probability simplex can be specified by a system of inequalities such that it holds

$$W = \left\{ \boldsymbol{p}^{\mathrm{T}} = (p^1, \ldots, p^k)^{\mathrm{T}} \in \mathbb{R}^k \left| \sum_{i=1}^{k} p^i = 1, 0 \le p^i \text{ for } i \le k, \boldsymbol{A}\boldsymbol{p}^{\mathrm{T}} \ge \boldsymbol{b} \right. \right\}.$$

with $\boldsymbol{A} \in \mathbb{R}^{l \times k}$ and $\boldsymbol{b} \in \mathbb{R}^l$, $k, l \in \mathbb{N}$.

Because of (2.1), (4.2) can be rewritten to

$$\mathrm{E}_{p(\boldsymbol{z}|\boldsymbol{d})}[\tilde{u}(a, \boldsymbol{z})] = \int_{\overline{U}} \tilde{u}(a, \boldsymbol{z}) \, p(\boldsymbol{z}|\boldsymbol{d}) \ \mathrm{d}\boldsymbol{z} \ + P(U|\boldsymbol{d}) \, \mathrm{E}_{p(\boldsymbol{z}|\boldsymbol{d},U)}[\tilde{u}(a, \boldsymbol{z})] \,. \quad (4.5)$$

We assume that we have $\overline{U} = \{\boldsymbol{z}^1, \ldots, \boldsymbol{z}^M\}$, $M \in \mathbb{N}$. In the following, the notations $p^i := p(\boldsymbol{z}^i|\boldsymbol{d})$, $i \in \{1, \ldots, M\}$, $\boldsymbol{z}^{M+1} := U$, $p^{M+1} := P(U|\boldsymbol{d})$ are used. The quantity $\boldsymbol{p} := (p^1, \ldots, p^{M+1})$ specifies a discrete probability distribution on $Z_D := \{\boldsymbol{z}^1, \ldots, \boldsymbol{z}^{M+1}\}$.

If a probability distribution $p(\boldsymbol{z}|\boldsymbol{d})$ on Z satisfies (2.3) and (2.4), the respective discrete probability distribution $\boldsymbol{p}$ can be identified with an element of the set

$$W = \left\{ \boldsymbol{p}^{\mathrm{T}} = (p^1, \ldots, p^{M+1})^{\mathrm{T}} \left| \sum_{i=1}^{M+1} p^i = 1, 0 \le p^i \text{ for } i \le M, \beta \le p^{M+1} \right. \right\}.$$
$$(4.6)$$

Formula (4.6) makes clear that the given partial information is LPI.

For a given utility function $\tilde{u}(a, \boldsymbol{z})$ on $A \times Z$, we define

$$u(a, \boldsymbol{z}^i) := \begin{cases} \tilde{u}(a, \boldsymbol{z}^i) \,, & i \in \{1, \ldots, M\} \,, \\ \mathrm{E}_{p(\boldsymbol{z}|\boldsymbol{d},U)}[\tilde{u}(a, \boldsymbol{z})] \,, & i = M+1 \,, \end{cases}$$

and treat $u(a, \boldsymbol{z}^i)$ as appendant utility function on $A \times Z_D$: (4.5) becomes

$$\mathrm{E}_{\boldsymbol{p}}[u(a, \boldsymbol{z}^i)] = \sum_{i=1}^{M} \tilde{u}(a, \boldsymbol{z}^i) \, p^i + p^{M+1} \, \mathrm{E}_{p(\boldsymbol{z}|\boldsymbol{d},U)}[\tilde{u}(a, \boldsymbol{z})] \,. \quad (4.7)$$

4.2 Geometry of LPI and Linear Optimization

A set of probability functions that is specified by LPI constitutes a convex polyhedron [Fis01, KM76]. It is not hard to identify the edges of W in (4.6)
analytically:

Lemma 3 $p^{\mathrm{T}} = (p^1, \ldots, p^{M+1})^{\mathrm{T}} \in \mathbb{R}^{M+1}$ *is an edge of* W *in (4.6) if it holds*

$$p^i = \begin{cases} 0 , & i \leq M , \\ 1 , & i = M + 1 , \end{cases} \quad or \quad p^i = \begin{cases} 1 - \beta , & \text{for one } i_0 \in \{1, \ldots, M\} , \\ 0 , & i \leq M \wedge i \neq i_0 , \\ \beta , & i = M + 1 . \end{cases}$$

PROOF. It is known [KM76, Pre02] that a point of W is an edge if $M + 1$ of
the $M + 2$ conditions in (4.6) are satisfied as equations. Here, this means that the
values of M components of p must be equal to the respective lower bounds. □

Lemma 4 (see [NM04] or [Fis01]) *Let* $f : \mathbb{R}^k \to \mathbb{R}$ *be a linear function and* $W \subseteq$
$\mathbb{R}^k$ *a convex polyhedron,* $k \in \mathbb{N}$. *Then, there exists edges* $w_{\min}$ *and* $w_{\max}$ *of* W
such that $f(w_{\min}) = \min_{w \in W} f(w)$ *and* $f(w_{\max}) = \max_{w \in W} f(w)$.

4.3 Decision Criteria under LPI

Expected Utility Intervals Let LPI according to $W \subseteq \mathbb{R}^k$ be available.
$\mathrm{E}_p[u(a, z^i)]$ is a linear function with respect to p. Because W is convex and
lemma 4 holds, for each action $a \in A$, the set of possible expected utility values
with respect to the LPI according to W is given by an interval. Denoting the set of
edges of W by $V(W)$, this interval is given by

$$\left[\underline{\mathrm{E}}_p[u(a, z^i)], \overline{\mathrm{E}}_p[u(a, z^i)] \right]_W := \left[\min_{p \in V(W)} \mathrm{E}_p[u(a, z^i)], \max_{p \in V(W)} \mathrm{E}_p[u(a, z^i)] \right] .$$

Theorem 3 *If LPI according to* W *in (4.6) is on hand, we have*

$$\underline{\mathrm{E}}_p[u(a, z^i)] = \min \left\{ (1 - \beta) \min_{1 \leq i \leq M} \tilde{u}(a, z^i) + \beta \, \mathrm{E}_{p(z|d,U)}[\tilde{u}(a, z)], \right.$$
$$\left. \mathrm{E}_{p(z|d,U)}[\tilde{u}(a, z)] \right\} , \tag{4.8}$$

$$\overline{\mathrm{E}}_p[u(a, z^i)] = \max \left\{ (1 - \beta) \max_{1 \leq i \leq M} \tilde{u}(a, z^i) + \beta \, \mathrm{E}_{p(z|d,U)}[\tilde{u}(a, z)], \right.$$
$$\left. \mathrm{E}_{p(z|d,U)}[\tilde{u}(a, z)] \right\} . \tag{4.9}$$

PROOF. $V(W)$ has been identified in lemma 3. From (4.7), we obtain

$$\left\{\mathrm{E}_{\boldsymbol{p}}[u(a, \boldsymbol{z}^i)] \middle| \boldsymbol{p} \in V(W)\right\} = \left\{\mathrm{E}_{p(\boldsymbol{z}|\boldsymbol{d},U)}[\tilde{u}(a, \boldsymbol{z})]\right\}$$
$$\bigcup\left\{(1 - \beta)\,\tilde{u}(a, \boldsymbol{z}^i) + \beta\,\mathrm{E}_{p(\boldsymbol{z}|\boldsymbol{d},U)}[\tilde{u}(a, \boldsymbol{z})] \middle| i = 1, \dots, M\right\}.$$

$\boldsymbol{z}^{i_0} \in \{\boldsymbol{z}^1, \dots, \boldsymbol{z}^M\}$ minimizes the term contained in the second set on the right side if it holds that $\tilde{u}(a, \boldsymbol{z}^{i_0}) = \min_{1 \le i \le M} \tilde{u}(a, \boldsymbol{z}^i)$. This proves (4.8). An analog consideration with respect to maximization delivers (4.9).   □

Dominance of Actions   With respect to LPI given by $W \subseteq \mathbb{R}^k$, an action $a^* \in A$ dominates another action $a^{**} \in A \setminus \{a^*\}$ if, for all $\boldsymbol{p} \in W$, it holds that $\mathrm{E}_{\boldsymbol{p}}[u(a^{**}, \boldsymbol{z}^i)] \le \mathrm{E}_{\boldsymbol{p}}[u(a^*, \boldsymbol{z}^i)]$. In this case, a^{**} can be eliminated from A because a^* is definitively at least as good (in terms of expected utility) as a^{**} is.

Theorem 4 *If LPI according to W in (4.6) is on hand, an action $a^{**} \in A$ is dominated by another action $a^* \in A \setminus \{a^{**}\}$ if it holds that*

$$\max\left\{(1 - \beta) \max_{1 \le i \le M} \left\{\tilde{u}(a^{**}, \boldsymbol{z}^i) - \tilde{u}(a^*, \boldsymbol{z}^i)\right\} \right. \tag{4.10}$$
$$\left. + \beta\,\mathrm{E}_{p(\boldsymbol{z}|\boldsymbol{d},U)}[\tilde{u}(a^{**}, \boldsymbol{z}) - \tilde{u}(a^*, \boldsymbol{z})], \mathrm{E}_{p(\boldsymbol{z}|\boldsymbol{d},U)}[\tilde{u}(a^{**}, \boldsymbol{z}) - \tilde{u}(a^*, \boldsymbol{z})]\right\} \le 0.$$

A necessary prerequisite therefore that condition (4.10) is fulfilled is that a^* dominates a^{**} in the respective focussed model.

PROOF. a^{**} is dominated by a^* if, for all $\boldsymbol{p} \in W$, it holds that

$$\mathrm{E}_{\boldsymbol{p}}[u(a^{**}, \boldsymbol{z}^i)] - \mathrm{E}_{\boldsymbol{p}}[u(a^*, \boldsymbol{z}^i)] = \mathrm{E}_{\boldsymbol{p}}[u(a^{**}, \boldsymbol{z}^i) - u(a^*, \boldsymbol{z}^i)] \le 0.$$

This condition is satisfied if we have

$$\max_{\boldsymbol{p} \in W} \mathrm{E}_{\boldsymbol{p}}[u(a^{**}, \boldsymbol{z}^i) - u(a^*, \boldsymbol{z}^i)] \le 0. \tag{4.11}$$

Because $\mathrm{E}_{\boldsymbol{p}}[u(a^{**}, \boldsymbol{z}^i) - u(a^*, \boldsymbol{z}^i)]$ is also a linear function with respect to $\boldsymbol{p}$, it adopts its maximum at least in one edge of W. Compare lemma 4. Using the notation $\tilde{v}(a^*, a^{**}, \boldsymbol{z}) := \tilde{u}(a^{**}, \boldsymbol{z}^i) - \tilde{u}(a^*, \boldsymbol{z}^i)$, we obtain

$$\left\{\mathrm{E}_{\boldsymbol{p}}[u(a^{**}, \boldsymbol{z}^i) - u(a^*, \boldsymbol{z}^i)] \middle| \boldsymbol{p} \in V(W)\right\} = \left\{\mathrm{E}_{p(\boldsymbol{z}|\boldsymbol{d},U)}[\tilde{v}(a^*, a^{**}, \boldsymbol{z})]\right\} \tag{4.12}$$
$$\bigcup\left\{(1 - \beta)\,\tilde{v}(a^*, a^{**}, \boldsymbol{z}) + \beta\,\mathrm{E}_{p(\boldsymbol{z}|\boldsymbol{d},U)}[\tilde{v}(a^*, a^{**}, \boldsymbol{z})] \middle| i = 1, \dots, M\right\}.$$

From this, one sees that condition (4.10) is a sufficient dominance criterion: taking the maximum over (4.12), we just have to eliminate from the second set of the right side these elements for that $E_p[\tilde{v}(a^*, a^{**}, z)]$ is surely not maximal.

Condition (4.10) can be fulfilled only if it holds that $E_{p(z|d,U)}[\tilde{u}(a^{**}, z)] \leq E_{p(z|d,U)}[\tilde{u}(a^*, z)]$, i.e., if a^* dominates a^{**} with respect to $p(z|d, U)$. $\qquad\square$

Example By the use of theorem 4, another proof for theorem 2 will be given: we will show that E^* dominates E^{**} if the conditions in theorem 2 hold. To make the decision theoretic framework from remark 2 applicable, it has to be assumed, here, that there exist $I^*, I^{**} \subseteq \{1, \ldots, M\}$ such that $E^* = \bigcup_{i \in I^*} z^i$ and $E^{**} = \bigcup_{i \in I^{**}} z^i$ hold. Additionally, it is again assumed that E^* and E^{**} are disjoint, compare remark 1. Criterion (4.10) delivers the condition

$$\max \left\{ b(E^{**} \cap U) - b(E^*), b(E^{**} \cap \overline{U}) + a(E^{**} \cap U) - a(E^*) \right\} \leq 0 .$$
(4.13)

The second element of the set in (4.13) is not larger than zero if it holds

$$b(E^{**} \cap \overline{U}) \leq a(E^*) - a(E^{**} \cap U) .$$
(4.14)

The condition $b(E^{**} \cap U) - b(E^*) \leq 0$ holds if $a(E^{**} \cap U) - a(E^*) \leq 0$. Because we have $b(E^{**} \cap \overline{U}) \geq 0$, the validity of (4.14) is sufficient to guarantee this. Hence, theorem 2 has been proven.

The case $E^{**} \subseteq U \setminus E^*$ shows that the condition that the expected utility intervals of the considered actions have at least one point in common is a sufficient but not necessary condition for dominance: it holds $\left[E_p[u(E, z^i)], \overline{E}_p[u(E, z^i)] \right] = [a[E], b[E]]$, $E \in \{E^*, E^{**}\}$. From theorem 2, one knows that E^* dominates E^{**} if $a[E^{**}] \leq a[E^*]$. This is a weaker condition than $b[E^{**}] \leq a[E^*]$ is.

Regret With respect to LPI given by $W \subseteq \mathbb{R}^k$, the regret $R_W(a^*)$ for an action $a^* \in A$ is defined to be the maximal deficit (in terms of expected utility) that can arise from the choice of a^*:

$$R_W(a^*) := \max_{a \in A} \max_{p \in W} \left\{ E_p[u(a, z^i)] - E_p[u(a^*, z^i)] \right\} .$$
(4.15)

For the determination of the expected utility intervals and for the checking of the dominance criterion (4.10), it is possible to compute the necessary values of $\tilde{u}(a, z^i)$ with respect to $\overline{U}$ ex ante, i.e., before the focussed posterior distribution is known. For the regret values, this proceeding delivers only an upper bound:

Theorem 5 *If LPI according to W in (4.6) is given, it holds for each $a^* \in A$ that*

$$\mathrm{R}_W(a^*) \leq \max \left\{ \mathrm{R}_{p(z|d,U)}(a^*), \right. \tag{4.16}$$

$$\left. (1-\beta) \max_{a \in A} \max_{1 \leq i \leq M} \left\{ \tilde{u}(a, z^i) - \tilde{u}(a^*, z^i) \right\} + \beta\, \mathrm{R}_{p(z|d,U)}(a^*) \right\}.$$

Thereby, $\mathrm{R}_{p(z|d,U)}(a^*) := \max_{a \in A} \left\{ \mathrm{E}_{p(z|d,U)}[\tilde{u}(a, z)] - \mathrm{E}_{p(z|d,U)}[\tilde{u}(a^*, z)] \right\}$ is the regret in the respective focussed Bayesian model.

PROOF. Except for the notation, the set in (4.15) is equal to the set in (4.11). Therefore, theorem 5 follows from a nearly analogous proceeding as the one applied at the maximization of the set in (4.11): performing an additional maximization with respect to a, noting that this maximization is subadditive, and respecting the definition of $\mathrm{R}_{p(z|d,U)}(a^*)$ directly leads to (4.16). □

Example Let Z be finite, $A = Z$, and $\tilde{u}(z^{**}, z) = \mathbf{1}_{\{z^{**}\}}(z)$ such that $\mathrm{E}_{p(z|d)}[\tilde{u}(z^{**}, z)] = p(z^{**}|d)$. Then, for $z^* \in U$, it holds that

$$\mathrm{R}_W(z^*) = \max_{z^{**} \in U} \left\{ \mathrm{b}(z^{**}) - \mathrm{b}(z^*), \mathrm{a}(z^{**}) - \mathrm{a}(z^*), (1-\beta) - \mathrm{a}(z^*) \right\}.$$

The reader may verify this directly as done as in the proof of theorem 2 or more straightforwardly as done in this section by using the results from Sec. 4.2. Theorem 5 delivers

$$\mathrm{R}_W(z^*) \leq \max_{z^{**} \in U} \left\{ \mathrm{b}(z^{**}) - \mathrm{b}(z^*), (1-\beta) + \mathrm{a}(z^{**}) - \mathrm{a}(z^*) \right\}.$$

4.4 Application and Improvement of the Decision Criteria

At the application of the developed criteria, the decision maker should firstly eliminate the dominated actions from A. Also if no action which maximizes the expected utility with respect to all $p \in W$ is identifiable, the decision maker may be able to make a final decision: considering the expected utility intervals and the regret values (or rather the respective bounds), he may be able to chose an action which is guaranteed to be good enough with respect to the task at hand. Following the principles of Lazy Decision Making [Pre02], the decision maker may render the LPI more precisely in cases in that no action is acceptable in this sense.

He may improve the probability interval scheme by enlarging U. To show this, it is assumed without loss of generality that U is enlarged to $U_{\mathrm{L}} := U \cup \{z^M\}$ and that it holds $p(d|z) \leq \delta_L$ for all $z \in U_L$ with a $\delta_L \leq \delta$. Compare the beginning of Sec. 2.2. By this, in (4.6), the inequality $0 \leq p^M$ gets sharpened to the equality $p^M = p^{M+1} \frac{p(z^M|d,U_L)}{1-p(z^M|d,U_L)}$ and the inequality $p^{M+1} \geq \beta$ gets sharpened to

$$p^{M+1} \geq \frac{\int_U p(d|z)\, p(z)\; \mathrm{d}z}{\int_{U_L} p(d|z)\, p(z)\; \mathrm{d}z + (1 - P(U_L))\delta_L} \quad (\geq \beta)\,.$$

Hence, enlarging U results in LPI which is specified by a subset W_L of the set W in (4.6). This can lead to a shrinking of the expected utility intervals, a larger set of dominated actions and smaller regret values. For the numerical evaluation of the decision criteria, the new LPI can get redrafted: setting $M_L := M - 1$, $Z_D := \{z^1, \ldots, z^{M_L+1}\}$, $\boldsymbol{p} := (p^1, \ldots, p^{M_L+1})$ with $z^{M_L+1} := U_L$, $p^i = p(z^i|d)$ for $i \in \{1, \ldots, M_L\}$, and $p^{M_L+1} := P(U_L|d)$, the results from Sec. 4.2 and Sec. 4.3 are directly applicable by replacing M by M_L.

Making the additional assumption that $P(\overline{U}|d)$ is not concentrated on small parts of $\overline{U}$, the decision maker may alternatively precise the LPI by the inclusion of non-trivial upper bounds for p^i, $i \in \{1, \ldots, M\}$. Obviously, this also leads to a subset of W in (4.6). If he assumes $p^i \leq \frac{1-\beta}{k}$ with a $k \in \{2, \ldots, M\}$, the set of edges $V(W)$ gets changed and formulas (4.8), (4.9), (4.10), and (4.16) must be modified: the minimal and maximal values of the utility and utility differences of actions with respect to $\overline{U}$ get substituted by the arithmetic means of the respective k-th lowest and largest values. We remark that the case $k = M$ corresponds to the assumption that either $P(\overline{U}|d) = 0$ or $p^i = \frac{1-\beta}{M}$, $i \in \{1, \ldots, M\}$, holds.

4.5   Generalization of the derived concept

Analyzing the previous results, it becomes clear how to proceed also in the case that $\overline{U}$ is not a finite set. We will sketch this by deriving exemplarily a lower bound for the expected utility of an action $a \in A$: because of (2.1) and (4.2), we have

$$\mathrm{E}_{p(z|d)}[\tilde{u}(a,z)] = (1 - P(U|d))\, \mathrm{E}_{p(z|d,\overline{U})}[\tilde{u}(a,z)] + P(U|d)\mathrm{E}_{p(z|d,U)}[\tilde{u}(a,z)]\,. \tag{4.17}$$

(4.17) corresponds to a splitting of the expected utility of a with respect to $p(z|d)$ into a weighted sum of two different expected utilities: $\mathrm{E}_{p(z|d,U)}[\tilde{u}(a,z)]$ is the expected utility of a within the focussed model. While the value of this quantity is known, the value of $\mathrm{E}_{p(z|d,\overline{U})}[\tilde{u}(a,z)]$ depends on the completely unknown distribution $p(z|d,\overline{U})$. This means that, to obtain a lower bound for $\mathrm{E}_{p(z|d,\overline{U})}[\tilde{u}(a,z)]$, all distributions on $\overline{U}$ have to be considered. Hence, we must assume that the probability mass is concentrated as well as possible on these elements of Z for that $\tilde{u}(a, z)$ is minimal. Then, to obtain the lower bound for $\mathrm{E}_{p(z|d)}[\tilde{u}(a, z)]$, the weighting factors of the two expected utilities have to be adjusted such that the lower bound for $\mathrm{E}_{p(z|d,\overline{U})}[\tilde{u}(a, z)]$ gets as much weight as possible if it is smaller than $\mathrm{E}_{p(z|d,U)}[\tilde{u}(a, z)]$ and as low weight as possible, otherwise. Thereby, the constraint (2.2) on $P(U|d)$ has to be kept in mind. These observations lead to a lower bound for $\mathrm{E}_{p(z|d)}[\tilde{u}(a, z)]$ which is consistent with (4.8). Of course, a upper bound that is consistent with (4.9) is obtained analogously.

5   Conclusion

The reduction of the probability interval scheme to a unique posterior distribution by the ME method may be reasonable to obtain a comprehensive representation of the posterior knowledge as final result. If the size of U is low compared to the total size of Z, usually, the ME distribution corresponds to the lower bounds in the probability interval scheme. At subsequent (additional) decision making, the direct use of the probability interval scheme makes more sense than its reduction to a unique distribution. In the LPI case, the determination and estimation, respectively, of common decision criteria under partial information is not excessively costly, here–provided that the size of U is moderate and that specific values of the utility function are calculable ex ante. In principle, results that have been easily obtained for the LPI case are generalizable, here.

Bibliography

[Abb05]   Ali E. Abbas. Maximum Entropy Distributions between Upper and Lower Bounds. In *Proceedings of the 25th International Workshop on Bayesian Inference and Maximum Entropy Methods in Science and Engineering*, pages 25–42, 2005.

[Aug98]   Thomas Augustin.   *Optimale Tests bei Intervallwahrscheinlichkeit*.   Vandenhoeck & Ruprecht, 1998.

[BHSG08]   Jürgen Beyerer, Michael Heizmann, Jennifer Sander, and Ioana Gheta. Bayesian Methods for Image Fusion. In Tania Stathaki, editor, *Image Fusion: Algorithms and Applications*, pages 157–192. Academic Press, 2008.

[Bov10]   Luc Bovens. Judy Benjamin is a Sleeping Beauty. *Analysis*, 70(1):23–26, 2010.

[BS04]   José M. Bernardo and Adrian F. M. Smith. *Bayesian Theory*. Wiley, 2004.

[BV05]   Stephen P. Boyd and Lieven Vandenberghe. *Convex Optimization*. Cambridge University Press, 2005.

[DL75]   Uri Dinur and Raphael D. Levine. On the Entropy of a Continuous Distribution. *Chemical Physics*, 9(1-2):17–27, 1975.

[DR09]   Igor Douven and Jan-Willem Romeijn. A New Resolution of the Judy-Benjamin Problem. *Choice Group Working Papers*, 5(7), 2009.

[Fis01]   Gerd Fischer. *Analytische Geometrie*. Vieweg, 2001.

[Fra81]   Bas C. Van Fraassen. A Problem for Relative Information Minimizers in Probability Kinematics. *The British Journal for the Philosophy of Science*, 32(4):375–379, 1981.

[Kap93]   Jagat N. Kapur. *Maximum-Entropy Models in Science and Engineering*. Wiley, 1993.

[KM76]   Eduard Kofler and Günter Menges. *Entscheidungen bei unvollständiger Information*. Springer, 1976.

[NM04]   Klaus Neumann and Martin Morlock. *Operations Research*. Hanser, 2004.

[OA07]   Michael Obermaier and Thomas Augustin. Luceno's discretization method and its application in decision making under ambiguity. In *Proceedings of the Fifth International Symposium on Imprecise Probabilities and their Applications (ISIPTA '07)*, pages 327–336. SIPTA, 2007.

[Pre02]   Gero Presser. *Lazy Decision Making*. Dissertation, Universität Dortmund, 2002.

[Rüg99]   Bernhard Rüger. *Test- und Schätztheorie, Band 1, Grundlagen*. Oldenbourg, 1999.

[Ros77]   Roger D. Rosenkrantz. *Inference, Method and Decision*. Reidel, 1977.

[San09]   Jennifer Sander. Further Investigation of Focussed Bayesian Fusion. Technical Report IES-2009-03, 2009.

[SB08]   Jennifer Sander and Jürgen Beyerer. Decreased Complexity and Increased Problem Specificity of Bayesian Fusion by Local Approaches. In *Proceedings of 11th Conference on Information Fusion 2008 (Fusion 2008)*, pages 1035–1042. IEEE, 2008.

[SHGB09] Jennifer Sander, Michael Heizmann, Igor Goussev, and Jürgen Beyerer. A Local Approach for Focussed Bayesian Fusion. In Belur Dasarathy, editor, *Multisensor, Multisource Information Fusion: Architectures, Algorithms, and Applications, Proceedings of SPIE Vol. 7345*, 2009.

[SHGB10] Jennifer Sander, Michael Heizmann, Igor Goussev, and Jürgen Beyerer. Global Evaluation of Focussed Bayesian Fusion. In Jerome J. Braun, editor, *Multisensor, Multisource Information Fusion: Architectures, Algorithms, and Applications, Proceedings of SPIE Vol. 7710*, 2010.

[SKB10]   Jennifer Sander, Jonas Krieger, and Jürgen Beyerer. The Importance of Statistical Evidence for Focussed Bayesian Fusion. In Rüdiger Dillmann, Jürgen Beyerer, Uwe D. Hanebeck, and Tanja Schultz, editors, *KI 2010: Advances in Artificial Intelligence*, volume 6359, pages 299–308. Springer, 2010.

[UA05]   Lev Utkin and Thomas Augustin. Powerful Algorithms for Decision Making under Partial Prior Information and General Ambiguity Attitudes. In *Proceedings of the Fourth International Symposium on Imprecise Probabilities and their Applications (ISIPTA '05)*, pages 349–358. SIPTA, 2005.

[UD09]   Lev Utkin and Sebastien Destercke. Computing Expectations with Continuous P-Boxes: Univariate Case. *International Journal of Approximate Reasoning*, 50(5):778–798, 2009.

[Wal91]   Peter Walley. *Statistical Reasoning with Imprecise Probabilities*. Chapman and Hall, 1991.

[Wei01]   Kurt Weichselberger. *Elementare Grundbegriffe einer allgemeineren Wahrscheinlichkeitsrechnung, Band 1, Intervallwahrscheinlichkeit als umfassendes Konzept*. Physica, 2001.

Interoperability of Process Visualization as Interface from Human to Production Monitoring and Control System

Miriam Schleipen

Vision and Fusion Laboratory
Institute for Anthropomatics
Karlsruhe Institute of Technology (KIT), Germany
miriam.schleipen@kit.edu

Technical Report IES-2010-04

Abstract: The engineering of production monitoring and control systems has to be done before it can be taken into operation. This engineering splits up into different tasks: engineering of plant components, engineering of I/O, and engineering of process visualization. Today, these tasks are mainly processed manually, are time- and cost-intensive and error-prone.

The project IDA deals with interoperable semantic data fusion for the automated provision of view-based process visualization. Its goal is to increase efficiency in the engineering process and to simplify and improve the subsequent operation phase. This contribution provides an overview about the general architecture developed in the project and highlights several aspects of the developed methods and tools.

1 Introduction

Process visualization forms part of a production monitoring and control system. It component visualizes the monitored and controlled production process. One example is depicted in Figure 1.1. Each of the images in a process visualization shows another process step or provides a specific view on process data. The process visualization serves not only for monitoring the production process, but also for manual intervention. It bridges the gap between men and machine, and provides the following functionality:

- Static and dynamic representation of values of the process signals and production monitoring and control system variables

- Manipulation of values of the process signals and production monitoring and control system variables
- Representation and confirmation of alarms
- Representation and archiving of measured values
- Switch between different representation types or images

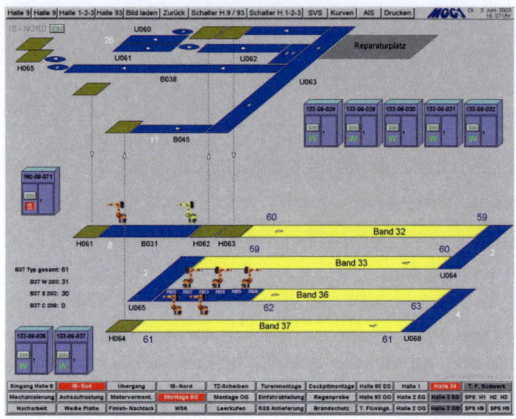

Figure 1.1: Example image of a process visualization

1.1 Motivation

The engineering of production monitoring and control systems aims for connecting at the level of automation components, such as PLCs, with the production monitoring and control system. Normally, the engineering of the corresponding process visualization takes place as follows:

- The engineer specifies the production process, including plant and cell layout, material flow and control equipment. Plant and control equipment is represented either by graphical objects or by I/O fields. In this step, the type (overview, topology, detail) and number of images and the navigation through them is determined.
- The engineer connects the real process signals with specific elements of the configured plant and control equipment. In this step, selected objects of the process image are dynamized to change their appearance dependant on the process values or react on user interaction.
- Before the real startup and test at the plant, there is more and more often a simulation-based virtual startup and test.

This is done mainly manually and it is time-/cost-intensive and error-prone. The information processing depends highly on the abilities and preference of the engineer, as there are no standards for the discrete production industry. The process visualization shall be as standardized as possible, but as individually as necessary.

1.2 Goals and Innovation

The approach tries to achieve different goals:

- Process visualization shall be generated automatically using already existing information and its interpretation by semantic relations.
- The manual and error-prone part of the work shall be reduced.
- The quality of the solution shall be increased. This shall be done by the provision of different views independent of system and application.
- The work of the plant operator shall be simplified by additional visualization.
- Errors shall be avoided by more ergonomic visualization

1.3 Approach

An overview about several basic parts developed in the project is given in Figure 1.2. One part deals with the model-specific data interpretation and the interpretation of the fusioned data. Challenges are to design the data model being able to integrate all examined information in one data format and to introduce semantic. Another part deals with the development of data models, their semantic fusion, and the algorithms for view generation. The export of the acquired information in different visualization systems is also one of the key tasks. All developed methods have to be easily adaptable to future views and interfaces.

2   AutomationML as Integrated Data Exchange Format

AutomationML [Dra09, Aut10, SD09, DLPH08] is an open, independent, XML-based data format for the exchange of plant planning data. It tries to bridge the gap between product development and production. It aims to enhance the interoperability of production-related IT tools and can be used for all phases of engineering. The general architecture is depicted in Figure 2.1. The topology of objects and relations between them is described by means of the format CAEX (Computer Aided

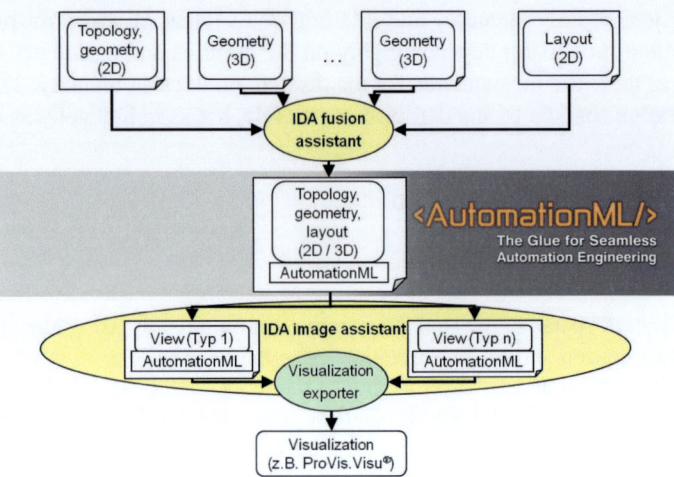

Figure 1.2: Approach of IDA

Engineering Exchange) [FEDF03]. For geometry and kinematics, Automation ML
integrates COLLADA (COLLAborative Design Activity) [AB06]. Logic and behavior is introduced by means of PLCOpenXML [PLC10]. The combination of
these standards and their linkage using CAEX opens up completely new possibilities for applications, such as the integrated process description. Furthermore, it is
designed to integrate further relevant XML based data exchange formats for relevant topics. The current model is scalable. For the IDA goals, only the top-level
format CAEX and the geometry area with Collada are important.

2.1   CAEX

CAEX [FEDF03, FD05] has been developed in cooperation with the Department
of Process Control Engineering of the RWTH Aachen and the ABB Research Center in Ladenburg. It is defined in the IEC62424 standard. CAEX is a semi-formal
data description language, which is based on XML. It contains an XML meta
model for describing the setup and structure of plant data. First and foremost,
the format supports library concepts and object-oriented approaches. It is possible
to integrate libraries from users and suppliers as well as project-specific libraries.
In addition, both a top-down and a bottom-up system design are supported. The
technical innovation of this approach is the syntactic and semantic unification of
the data. This allows the required configuration algorithms to be decoupled from

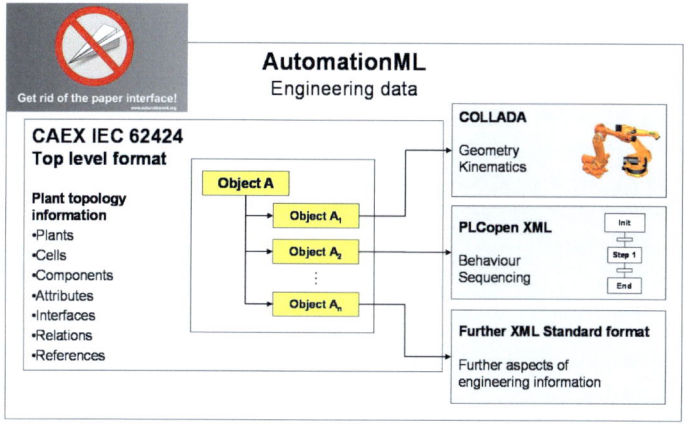

Figure 2.1: General architecture of AutomationML [DLPH08]

the data sources. [SDS08] CAEX consists of three types of libraries: Interface-ClassLibraries, RoleClassLibraries and SystemUnitClassLibraries. In addition to these libraries, there is the InstanceHierarchy which models the specific plant. An InterfaceClassLibrary consists of one or many InterfaceClasses. They are used to model interfaces for communication or the topology, or, briefly, to create relations between elements within the CAEX model. The interfaces themselves do not include any connection; rather, they are mere connection points. The functional RoleClasses are described within the RoleClassLibraries. The roles are used to describe the semantics of elements. Examples of roles include conveyors, turntables, or robots. Roles do not contain information about the internal structure of elements. They define general attributes and interfaces for these objects. SystemUnitClassLibraries consist of the description of complex plant components, the SystemUnitClasses. They contain specific information about their functionality and structure. The semantic is then introduced by assigned RoleClasses. Instances serve for the modelling of concrete real-world plant objects in an InstanceHierarchy. In the described approach, the InternalElements are always instances of SystemUnitClasses. In this part of the data model, planning data and parameters are stored. These main components of CAEX form the basis for a CAEX file. In addition, there are further elements, which serve the purpose of detail specification or definition of links between the elements.

2.2 Collada

Collada is an exchange format for interactive three-dimensional contents. It describes the geometric shape of an object. One advantage of Collada are precise object descriptions which are represented by meshes. But there are still other types of information which can be integrated: information about kinematic, material and structure. The information within a Collada XML file is easily readable for men and machine. [AB06]

3   General Architecture Developed in the Project IDA

As already shown in Figure 1.2, the general architecture (developed in the project IDA) is divided into the IDA fusion assistant and the IDA image assistant.

3.1 Import and Merge

Import and merge of data is done in the IDA fusion assistant (see Figure 3.1). Several possible data formats can be imported. CAEX describes the topology and I/O connection. This can be handled by the EA importer developed in the ProduFlexil research project [SBO+09, EOB07]. The 2D topology and geometry can be handled by a CAEX importer. The Collada importer deals with the three dimensional geometry or layout. One additional data format used for hall layout is DXF. This format is integrated by a DXF2COLLADA converter. In the end, a data merger integrates all these information and builds up one single description.

Figure 3.2 shows the integration of AutomationML and Collada used in IDA. Topology and I/O connections are described in CAEX. 3D geometry is described in Collada. The 2D data of the hall layout serves for the positioning of the specific 3D geometries. All this forms part of an AutomationML model which acts as provider for the generation of the process visualization.

The Drawing Interchange Format (DXF, [Wik10]) is an ASCII-based standard, which was specified by Autodesk. DXF describes a CAEX model as vector graphic. Supported geometry elements are point, line, circle, spline, etc. In Figure 3.3, the relation between a 2D hall layout, an AutomationML model, 3D detail information, and the generated process visualization can be seen. The DXF layout is used to determine the position and orientation of the plant component (in

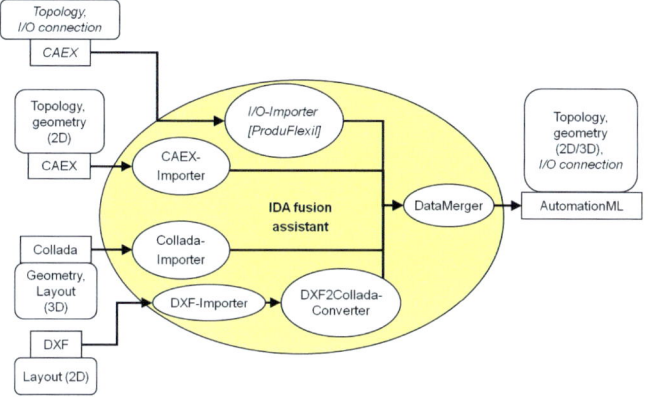

Figure 3.1: IDA fusion assistant

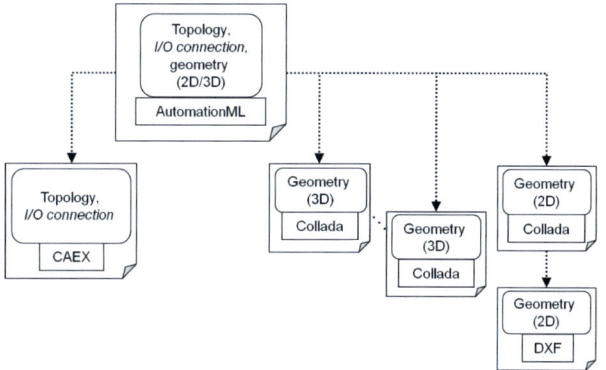

Figure 3.2: Data integration with AutomationML

this case: a robot) in the production cell, line or hall. This position and orientation is introduced in an AutomationML-CAEX-frame attribute which consists of the 3D position coordinates and Roll-Pitch-Yaw angles. The frame forms part of the AutomationML object of the robot in the InstanceHierarchy. At the same AutomationML object, the Collada 3D geometry is linked in by an ExternalInterface of type ColladaRepresentationInterface. The DXF data can be used additionally by transforming it to Collada geometry data. A complete AutomationML scene consists of different AutomationML objects in the InstanceHierarchy. They are derived from SystemUnitClasses, and have a corresponding RoleClass to define their semantic. Furthermore, they posses different interfaces which connect them to other AutomationML objects.

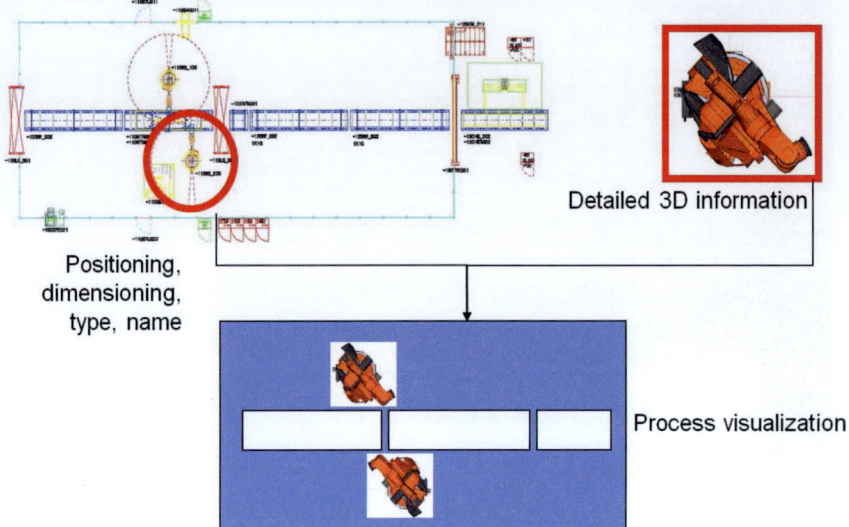

Figure 3.3: IDA information fusion

One of the application examples is a transport line consisting of six conveyors, four turntables and a test station. Every conveyor is an InternalElement (AutomationML object) in the InstanceHierarchy. It is derived from a SystemUnitClass Bidirectional conveyor and posseses the role conveyor. It has different External-Interfaces such as the ColladaRepresentationInterface for linking corresponding 3D geometry to the object and Order to describe the material or process flow. By means of the frame attributes at each of the InternalElements, a complete scene of this production cell can be built up. This scene is shown in Figure 3.4.

3.2   Processing and Projection

After merging all information into one consisting AutomationML model, there are still several problems concerning the representation of the objects in the process visualization. First of all, many of the process visualization at the market support only two dimensional. Furthermore, these systems would be overextended by the detailed geometries of the CAD because they do not concentrate on one specific plant component, but often deal with up to 50 components in one image. The difference is outlined in Figure 3.5.

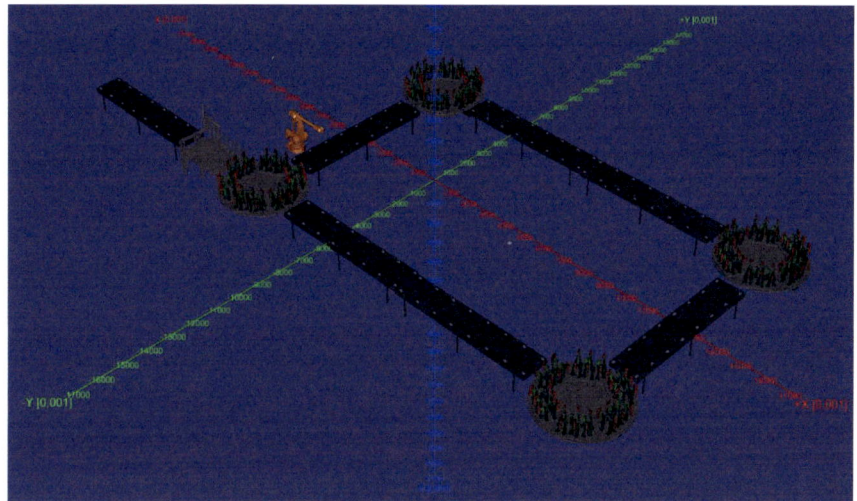

Figure 3.4: IDA application example - demo line

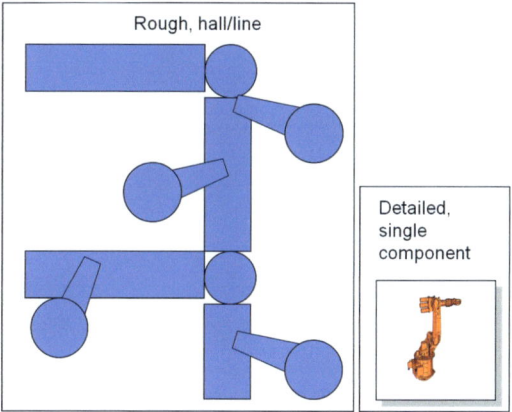

Figure 3.5: Abstraction problem

The problems by breaking down three dimensions into two are various. Figure 3.6 shows that depending on the point of view on the object (here: top), the underlying object cannot be determined unambiguously. In the figure, both objects at the left have the same top view.

The silhouette of an object is also problematic. It can falsify the look of the object of the user. One essential point for process visualizations is that users recognize

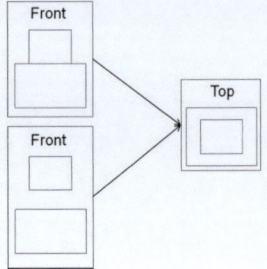

Figure 3.6: Representation problem

the depicted objects and their types easily. Therefore, this is a problem. Figure 3.7 depicts how a cuboid or a robot can look like as silhouette. It is not always possible to recognize this as cuboid or robot without any additional information. The visible edges in contrast to this are rich of information. The problem there is that the objects remain very complex in this representation.

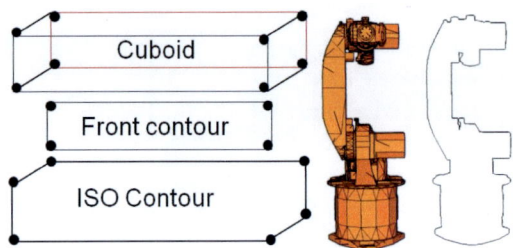

Figure 3.7: Contour problem

For the processing and projection of the geometries/the representation there are several steps and complexity levels.

3.2.1 Projection Level One

On level one, bitmaps are used for every objects. That means that the three dimensional geometries are screen captured from different point of view like top, front, back, side,iso (see Figure 3.8). These bitmaps can then be imported in the process visualization. The disadvantage of this case is the dynamization of the objects. If the state of a plant component connected to this object is erroneous, the whole object blinks in red for example. If there are overlapping objects, this becomes very quickly confusing. One possible extension or improvement can be made by generating bitmaps for each part of the plant components itself. This concept is integrated as on-top-plugin in an existing layout manager for the visualization system (see [SS08, SS09]).

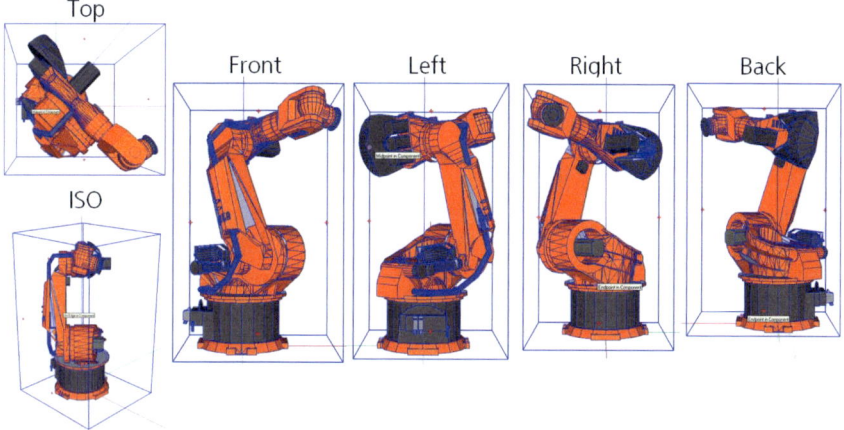

Figure 3.8: Views

3.2.2 Projection Level Two

The level two approach in IDA is to take a Bitmap and generate an overlaying contour element (Figure 3.9). Advantages are the easy structure (bitmap) of the object and that there is no need to reduce information in this case.

3.2.3 Projection Level Three

The level three approach deals with the handling of complex objects (see left side of Figure 3.10). The first step the projection from 3D to 2D. This is in this case done by a parallel projection (instead of for example a central projection or an intersection). Therefore, every point coordinates in the Collada description is projected to the x-z-, y-z-, x-y-, or ISO-layer. Before that, the visible contours are extracted by a calculation via the normals of the triangles. If a normal of a surface triangle 'looks into the direction of the camera', it is visible and in the foreground and is extracted for the whole projection. This can be calculated by proving, if the normal multiplied with the unit vector and normalized is greater than zero. After having generated such a two dimensional, geometry in the three dimensional space

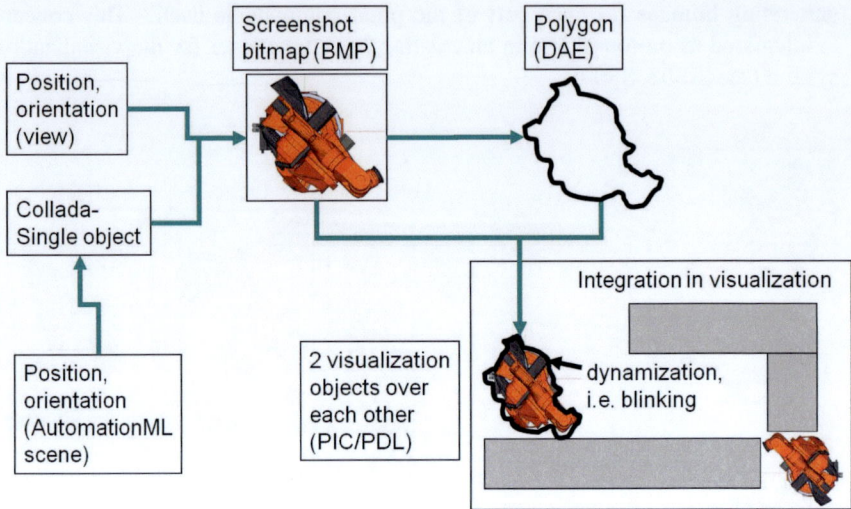

Figure 3.9: Silhouette and bitmap fusion

(as on the right hand of Figure 3.10), the complexity has to be reduced, because visualization systems have to process a big amount of such objects in an acceptable timeslot.

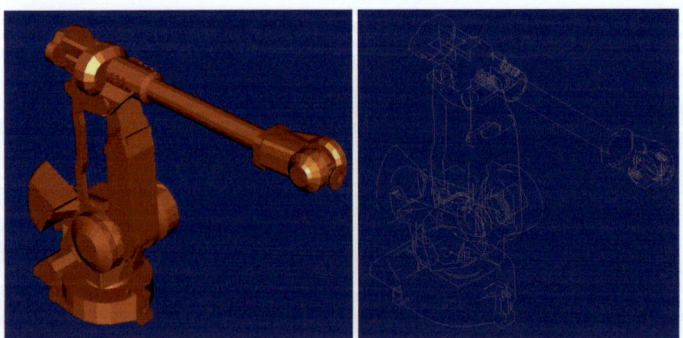

Figure 3.10: Contour extraction and reduction

3.3 View Generation

The view generation consists of several steps and is highly related to the export (both are depicted in Figure 3.11). Altogether they build up the IDA image assistant.

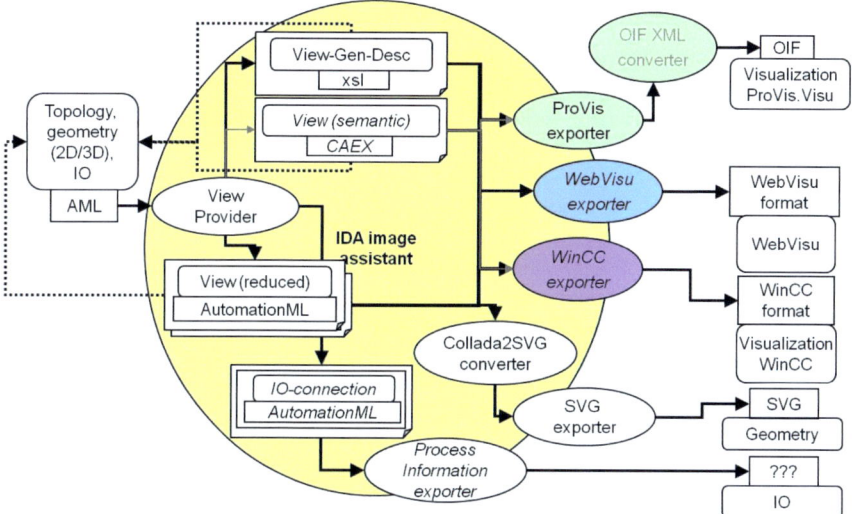

Figure 3.11: IDA image assistant

The user can configure how the views and images shall be generated. The user defines representations, image grouping and configures in this way his personal view. Figure 3.12 shows how the components work together. The user gets an AutomationML file consisting of topology and geometry. He defines or has already defined which views shall be generated. This information is given altogether with the AutomationML file to the view provider. The view provider generates with the information or list of actions a reduced view. The configuration can be seen as manual for view generation.

3.4 Export

In the end of the process (see Figure 3.11), the reduced view has to be exported to the process visualization system. Therefore, the data is in the case of ProVis.Visu® converted to OIF which is a proprietary XML based data format.

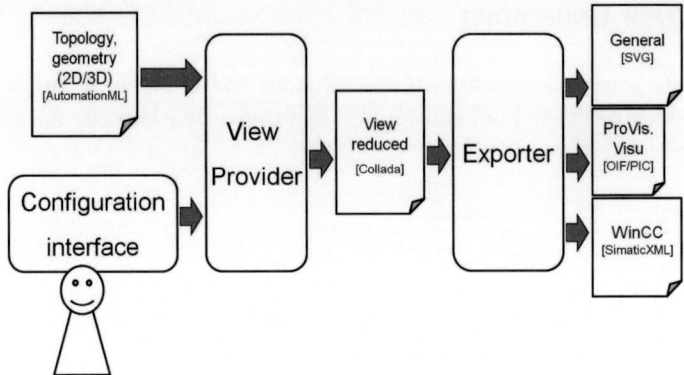

Figure 3.12: View generation

This interface helps to import and manipulate the system-specific data. For each visualization system a specific exporter has to be developed.

4   Summary

In this contribution, the general architecture developed in the research project IDA was explained. Figure 4.1 depicts the sample process through all developed methods and tools. Starting with the import of data from different sources, the acquired data is then fusioned. After that, the data is processed, and projections from three to two dimensions are created. The views on these data are applied and these will be exported to the proprietary process visualization format. All concepts were tested by means of the mentioned application example. In the field of view generation and processing/projection there is still a big range of open questions and research topics.

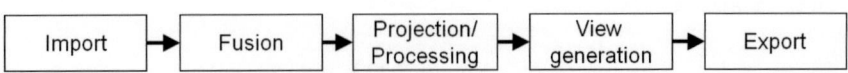

Figure 4.1: IDA process

5   Acknowledgments

The project underlying this paper is funded by the Federal Ministry of Economics and Technology using the KF2074702ED9 funding code. The author assumes the responsibility for the contents of this paper.

Bibliography

[AB06]   Remi Arnaud and Mark C. Barnes, editors. *Collada: Sailing the Gulf of 3D Digitial Content Creation.* A K Peters, Ltd., Wellesley, Massachusetts, USA, 2006.

[Aut10]   AutomationML. AutomationML Website. www.automationml.org, 2010.

[DLPH08]   Rainer Drath, Arndt Lueder, Jörg Peschke, and Lorenz Hundt. AutomationML – the glue for seamless Automation Engineering. In *Proceedings of IEEE International Conference on Emerging Technologies and Factory Automation (ETFA)*, Hamburg, September 2008.

[Dra09]   Rainer Drath, editor. *Datenaustausch in der Automatisierungsplanung mit AutomationML.* Springer Verlag, Berlin, 2009.

[EOB07]   Miriam Ebel, Michael Okon, and Michael Baumann. ProduFlexil Flexible Produktion mit SOA-Architektur und Plug-and-Work-Mechanismus. In *Proceedings of Stuttgarter Softwaretechnik Forum (Science meets business)*, pages 65–74, Stuttgart, December 2007.

[FD05]   Murat Fedai and Rainer Drath. CAEX - a neutral data exchange format for engineering data. *atp/international*, (1/2005):43–51, 2005.

[FEDF03]   Murat Fedai, Ullrich Epple, Rainer Drath, and Alexander Fay. A Metamodel for generic data exchange between various CAE Systems. In *Proceedings of 4th Mathmod Conference), Edition 24 of ARGESIM Report*, pages 1247–1256, 2003.

[PLC10]   PLCOpen. PLCopen XML Website. http://www.plcopen.org/pages/tc6_xml/, 2010.

[SBO⁺09]   Miriam Schleipen, Michael Baumann, Michael Okon, Martin Neukäufer, Christian Fedrowitz, Martin Feike, Natalya Popova, Markus Nick, Sören Schneickert, and Martin Wessner. Design and engineering processes in highly adaptive plants with ambient intelligence techniques. In *Proceedings of CIRP International Conference on Manufacturing Systems (ICMS)*, Grenoble, June 2009.

[SD09]   Miriam Schleipen and Rainer Drath. Three-View-Concept for modeling process or manufacturing plants with AutomationML. In *Proceedings of IEEE International Conference on Emerging Technologies and Factory Automation (ETFA)*, Palma, September 2009.

[SDS08]   Miriam Schleipen, Rainer Drath, and Olaf Sauer. The system-independent data exchange format CAEX for supporting an automatic configuration of a production monitoring and control system. In *Proceedings of IEEE International Symposium on Industrial Electronics (ISIE)*, pages 1786–1791, June 2008.

[SS08]   Miriam Schleipen and Klaus Schick. Self-configuring visualization of a production monitoring and control system. In *Proceedings of CIRP International Conference on Intelligent Computation in Manufacturing Engineering (ICME)*, July 2008.

[SS09]   Miriam Schleipen and Olaf Sauer. Usage of dynamic product and process information in a production monitoring and control system by means of CAEX and OPC-UA. In *Proceedings of CIRP International Conference on Changeable, Agile, Reconfigurable and Virtual Production (CARV)*, München, October 2009.

[Wik10]   Wikipedia. Drawing Interchange Format. http://de.wikipedia.org/wiki/ Drawing_Interchange_Format, 2010.

Side-Scan Sonar Based SLAM for the Deep Sea

Philipp Woock

Vision and Fusion Laboratory
Institute for Anthropomatics
Karlsruhe Institute of Technology (KIT), Germany
woock@ies.uni-karlsruhe.de

Technical Report IES-2010-05

Abstract: In order to robustly perform SLAM (Simultaneous Localization and Mapping), places need to be recognized when they are visited again. In the deep-sea environment SLAM-assisted navigation based on side-scan sonar data benefits from using three-dimensional features of the environment as they are much less view-dependent than classic 2D features. Obtaining these features requires processing of the sonar data as the side-scan sonar sensor readings contain three dimensional information only indirectly. To extract that information the ensonification process needs to be inverted. This inversion is an ill-posed inverse problem and therefore regularization is needed before a unique solution can be found. Once the true seabed shape is reconstructed, wide area SLAM techniques can be applied.

1 Introduction and Existing Work

The process of robustly navigating an autonomous underwater vehicle (AUV) through unknown terrain using side-scan sonar data and an inertial measurement unit (IMU) is a multi-layered process. The first stage involves transforming the side-scan sonar data to a 3D representation of the environment. Afterwards, significant features of the environment have to be identified. Using the extracted features and the data of the inertial sensors a SLAM method can be employed.

The paper is structured as follows. First, related work to underwater SLAM is presented. In Section 2 the challenge in side-scan sonar reconstruction is explained and it is shown how data is preprocessed for the regularization steps (Section 3.1) where a state-of-the-art method to tackle the problem is explained. Section 4 shows a hybrid SLAM concept that is suitable for deep-sea applications and gives an outlook to further developments. In Section 5 a short peek of the used hardware is given.

1.1 Loop-closing

An essential task of every SLAM system is the closing of trajectory loops, e.g., detecting that exactly the same spot has been visited before. Johnson-Roberson et al. [JPWM10] perform loop closing in a shallow water environment with a stereo camera. With the great amount of information obtained by high resolution color camera images, the resulting loop closures are very reliable and accurate.

For a similar approach in the deep-sea it would be necessary to artificially illuminate the environment. However, turbid water and energy constraints make classic lighting impossible. In the future, gated viewing solutions using a very short laser pulse and precise camera shutter timing may enable image-assisted loop-closing also in the deep sea.

It is difficult to apply this technique to side-scan sonar data only as the side-scan sonar provides gray level image lines which contain much less information compared to high-resolution 2D color images.

1.2 Dead-reckoning

In order to build a robust SLAM solution one has to deal with cases where the AUV is unable to detect features in the environment either because of sensor error or simply because the environment is lacking significant features. Without environmental features the dead-reckoning navigation of the vehicle is the only source of ego-motion estimation and therefore has to be calibrated carefully.

Jakuba et al. show in [JPW10] that with sophisticated calibration methods very small navigation errors can be achieved. To correctly calibrate the compass they performed star-shaped test dives. The trajectory obtained through camera-based visual SLAM served as ground truth. That way they could calibrate the compass readings according to that ground truth. With their calibration they can bridge several minutes without observing external features. They also investigated the influences of the tides on the depth measurements.

1.3 SLAM in Man-made Environments

SLAM for underwater man-made environments (e.g., a marina) using sonar sensors was investigated in [?]. They use a mechanically scanning imaging sonar sensor (MSIS) that is rotating while taking measurements. That way the vehicle repeatedly gains a full 360° view of the environment. Depending on the sensor settings it takes only several seconds for a full 360° scan. Due to the sensor principle the measurements are carried out in a polar coordinate frame. Applying the Hough-Transform to the data, they are able to detect lines that correspond to the man-made walls. Eventually, their environment map in which the vehicle localizes itself and navigates consists of these lines.

The approach was refined to a scan matching approach in [MRRH10] that does not rely on line-shaped structures any more.

2   Data Preprocessing

The main difficulty in performing SLAM on side-scan sonar data is the ambiguity in the sensor readings itself: the side-scan sonar records an echo amplitude over time, i.e., with no spatial information *where* that echo came from but only *when* it arrived (two-way travel time). Furthermore, a certain echo tells only whether there is a reflector or not and how strong the reflectance is. Unfortunately, the reflectance strength is only partially linked to the reflector's geometry. Amongst other things the echo strength is also dependent on the sediment material, water absorption and the grazing angle (denoted β in Figure 2.3). More information about this problem and related research in that field is given in [WF10].

Before the three-dimensional reconstruction of the environment based on the side-scan sonar data can take place the sonar data has to be pre-processed: The first bottom return has to be found and the sonar data is mapped to ground coordinates (slant range correction).

2.1   First Bottom Return

Before the side-scan sonar pulses reach the ground they propagate through the water beneath the AUV which results in a silent period after the sending peak at the beginning of each line as water does not produce an echo. After the silent period the first echo is received. The time until the first echo arrives is the two-way travel time of the sonar signal and thereby gives information about the distance to the nearest reflecting object which is assumed to be the seabed perpendicularly below the vehicle. That assumption does not always hold as can be seen in Figure 2.1. This fact is mostly neglected as the seafloor shape can often be approximated by a plane and the error is usually not too large. Hence, this first echo is called the First Bottom Return (FBR) and its detection can be seen as an additional altitude sensor which can be combined with altitude measurements of another sensor.

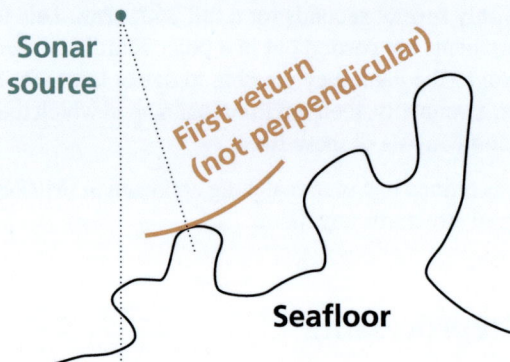

Figure 2.1: The FBR is not necessarily an echo from perpendicularly below the vehicle and therefore not always equal to the altitude of the vehicle. However, in a deep-sea environment it is assumed to be the case most of the time.

Before the detection of the FBR the sonar line is filtered by a median filter to reduce the influence of speckle noise while preserving discontinuities for a more robust detection. Speckle noise stems from the side-scan sonar being a coherent recording method. Rank value filters, for example a median filter, are very effective against this type of noise [RVRV95].

In Fig 2.2 the FBR is detected as the first occurrence of two adjacent sonar samples that are more than 1.7 standard deviations apart from the mean value of the sonar line. The threshold value is determined empirically for every sensor configuration in advance. However, an automatic derivation and adaptive behavior of the threshold is possible and will be added in the future.

The FBR detection applied is strictly per-line. Under the assumption that the first return always stems from perpendicularly beneath and that the surface geometry is not changing too quickly one could also apply Kalman filtering in time to smooth the detection and limit the influence of outliers as occasionally a stronger echo that arrives later could be mistaken for the FBR.

2.2   Slant Range Correction

In order to obtain ground coordinates (e.g., to perform the aforementioned regularization) the sonar image has to be slant range corrected when the sonar altitude is known either from detection of the FBR or from additional sensor readings. The geometric configuration is depicted in Figure 2.3. The original data can be thought

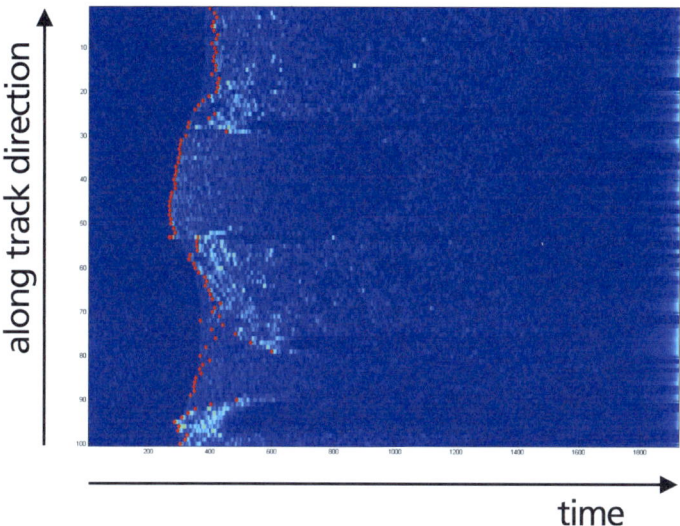

Figure 2.2: Per-line detection of the FBR (red) on side-scan sonar data. The plot shows the echo intensity over time.

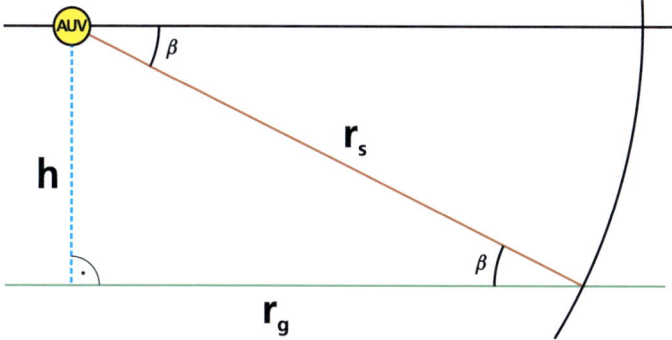

Figure 2.3: Geometry of slant range correction

of lying on the r_s ray (brown). The data of the water column (before the FBR) is mapped to the height h and the part starting at the FBR until the end is mapped to the ground r_g (green).

This correction is a non-linear distortion and its effect on a sonar image is depicted in Figure 2.4 where the signal part from the FBR to the end are shown. The strongest effect is seen for the near-nadir parts of the sonar image (left hand side

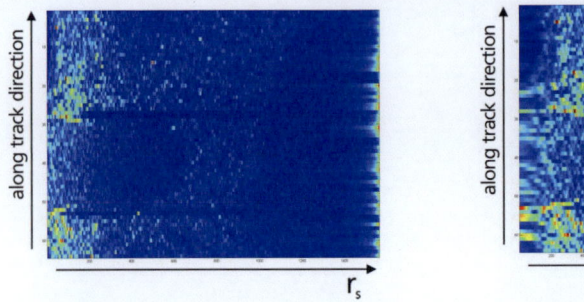

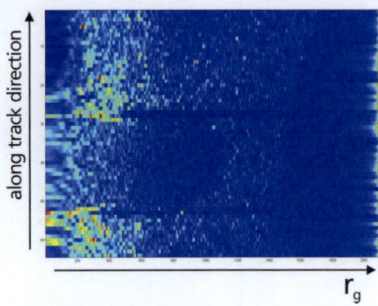

(a) Before slant range correction.   (b) After slant range correction.

Figure 2.4: Sonar image slant range correction. The part containing the water column up to the FBR has been removed.

in Figure 2.4b)). For longer ranges the difference between slant range and ground range diminishes as the grazing angle β is decreasing.

All sonar lines in the image are corrected with the same depth value, derived from the median of the FBR detections in the whole observation window, assuming constant altitude and a flat seabed. This is necessary to apply the regularization process of [CPL07] which is detailed in Section 3.1.

$$r_g = \sqrt{r_s^2 - h^2}$$
$$\cos \beta = \frac{r_g}{r_s}$$

In Figure 2.3 and in the above equation r_s denotes the slant range, r_g denotes the ground range and h the sensor altitude.

3 Estimating Seabed Shape from Side-Scan Sonar Data

To obtain the seabed shape that created a particular echo one has to *invert* the ensonification process. As it is known how sonic waves propagate in water and how they are reflected on objects, inverting that process means estimating what kind of shape may be responsible for a certain echo. This is done through a so-called forward model that performs a simulation of the ensonifying process and the echo generation.

However, there is a multitude of environmental parameters that alter a sonic echo, e.g., sediment type, water temperature, salinity, sonar beam form, etc. It is not feasible to incorporate all of them into such a forward model as there are only few measurements and infinitely many possibilities to adjust parameters. Besides, computation time restrictions call for a simple but sufficiently accurate model.

An overview over different sonar simulation models is given in [CPL07].

3.1   Iterative Optimization

Incorporation of a priori knowledge or assumptions about the seabed to make the problem invertible are called regularization. Coiras et al. proposed a powerful method for the inversion process, where they investigated different regularization strategies ([CPL07] and [CG09]).

Their inversion method is an iterative approach, the basic principle is shown in Figure 3.1. Initially, in [CPL07] a flat seabed is assumed and the sonar data is slant range corrected (see Section 2.2) before the estimation starts. Within an Expectation-Maximization (EM) framework they optimize the seabed shape to be close to the truth. With a forward model they simulate an echo response for a given seabed shape and compare it to the measurements taken. The difference between simulation and measurement indicates whether the model represents reality already correctly and where it needs further adaptation. Then, parameters are adjusted accordingly. Then, the simulation with the forward model is done with the updated parameter set and the difference is examined again. This is repeated until the difference between the simulated echo and the measured echo falls below an error threshold or until the model is unable to diminish the difference further.

3.2   Regularization Techniques

In this iterative cycle the regularization is performed after each iteration step: For example in [CPL07] it is assumed that the sensor's beam form is constant over time. That means that every surface patch pointing to the sensor at a certain angle is subject to the same beam form model parameter even across sonar scan lines.

In [Woo10] it was illustrated that no information about the surface shape is obtained in areas that are not reached by the sonic waves (so-called sonar shadows). It is assumed that in such areas the seabed does not behave differently than in the directly adjacent areas. It is therefore plausible to assume the model parameters describing the reflectance properties of the sediment are similar both in the shadowed areas and the surrounding non-shadowed areas.

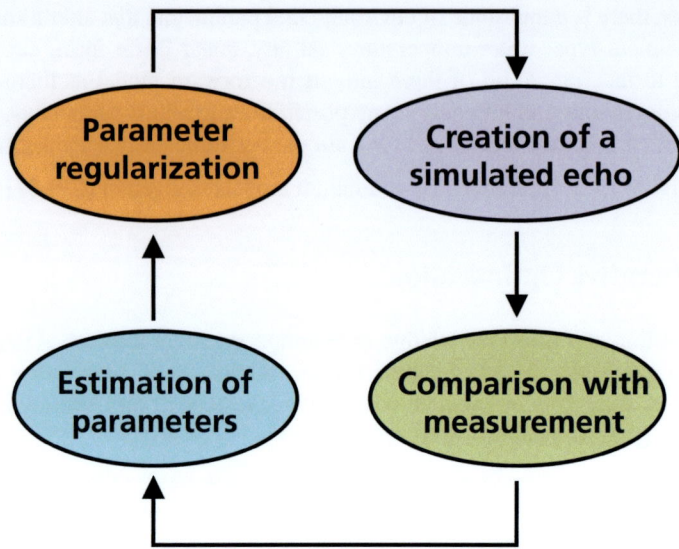

Figure 3.1: Iterative estimation process of the seabed surface shape.

Additionally, as another regularization restriction it could be assumed that sediment composition in general changes rather slowly and not with each sonar sample which corresponds to smoothing the reflectance map.

It is also possible to introduce smoothness constraints to be imposed on the reconstructed surface. The rationale is that between two scan lines and two sonar samples the changes of the surface height are assumed to be minor (i.e., no needle-shaped seafloor). Thus, the connection between the surface points should also be continuous and may have matching derivatives (first and higher derivatives, depending on the level of intended smoothing). However, this method is prone to smooth out interesting surface details. Coiras et al. try to avoid this effect using different surface constraints, e.g., based on a deformable mesh with forces between the mesh points [CG09].

Further, Coiras et al. achieved much better reconstruction results with a hierarchical approach using an image pyramid. That way, the coarser surface parts are reconstructed first while the details are recovered later in the stages with finer resolution. This helps to avoid local minima in the optimization process. In addition, the subsampling reduces the image noise which helps the optimization process to converge quicker in the low resolution stages.

Using synthetic aperture sonar (SAS) data the method can be modified [CG09] to work in polar coordinates. With SAS it is not necessary to estimate the beam form of the sonar sensor in contrast to the side-scan approach [CPL07] as it can be assumed as being uniform. In the procedure for SAS data the surface is modeled as a deformable elastic mesh where forces between the grid points make sure that smoothness requirements are met.

The method in [CPL07] is related to [LH91] who worked their way from nadir towards the peripheral areas by summing up differential surface patches. A detailed description of this Propagation Shape-from-Shading and a comparison to a Fourier-based approach is done by [DBL04].

3.3   Extension

In order to perform SLAM with the reconstructed seabed surface, the mentioned inversion methods need to be extended so that curved trajectories and varying AUV altitudes may be also considered as AUVs drive turns and are unable to perfectly maintain a constant flying altitude. With an ego-motion estimation based on inertial sensors the reconstruction may be modified accordingly to obtain an undistorted map.

4   SLAM Concept

4.1   3D Features

SLAM approaches that use higher-level landmarks opposed to plain point cloud data feature a more robust recognition and distinction. Spline features ([PDM$^+$07] [PRLM$^+$09]) are an example for such landmarks. They are more robust because formulated as a spline one landmark comprises multiple points and as a result small variations of the input points in general do not alter the overall shape of the spline much. Three-dimensional landmarks may be compiled of several one-dimensional splines in space that have one point in common or may even consist of full spline surface patches.

A comprehensive overview of other features that may be used for three-dimensional SLAM applications is given in [Run10].

4.2   Hybrid SLAM Concept

In order to achieve long underwater mission durations, the used SLAM algorithm needs to be carefully chosen. Furthermore, it is important to balance computing requirements and the stability of the SLAM solution.

In [BB08] Brooks and Bailey propose a combined EKF/FastSLAM framework termed HybridSLAM. It tries to retain the best of both SLAM approaches while mitigating their respective weaknesses. FastSLAM works by approximating the true probability distribution of the vehicle paths and maps by particles and can therefore inherently track multiple hypotheses about the path taken and the respective map of the environment. However, the approach suffers from so-called *particle depletion* which means that the longer the filter runs the more certain it becomes about the beginning of the path trajectory and the oldest parts of the map. It more and more "forgets" about other possibilities in the past. On the other hand, the EKF can only maintain a single hypothesis and wrong associations between measurements and landmarks are "remembered" forever and may eventually lead to divergence of the filter. The idea is to use a FastSLAM front-end and an EKF back-end. The rationale behind the concept is that for the most recent measurements the FastSLAM algorithm can deal better with wrong associations by maintaining multiple path and map hypotheses. The parts of the map about which the FastSLAM filter has become "more confident" over time are placed inside an EKF as submaps. Until then the risk of wrong submap associations has become very low and the EKF will most probably remain stable.

Other submapping approaches that tackle the same problem are Fairfield's SegSLAM [Fai09] and Bosse's ICP-based map matching [BZ08].

5   Hardware

The computing devices are placed inside a glass sphere that can withstand water pressure up to 10000 m. The main difficulty is to integrate a powerful processing unit while at the same time managing heat transfer and placing all components in the small volume of the sphere. For the on-board sonar data processing, feature extraction and the SLAM algorithm we will use an embedded PCI/104 board using an Intel Core2Duo^{TM} SP9300 processor. The inertial measurements are provided by an Xsens MTi. Data logging is done with an Intel 1,8″ Postville SSD as SSD technology provides high speed and shock resistance. The hardware is pictured in Figure 5.1. Not shown are the two side-scan sonar sensors that are connected via USB.

(a) View from below: PCI/104-Module with heat spreader baseplate.

(b) Top view: inertial measurement unit and SSD data storage.

(c) Pressure hull made of glass resistant to 10,000 m water depth.

Figure 5.1: Hardware of the sensor data processing module.

The cooling solution consists of an aluminum baseplate that serves as heat spreader to conduct the heat to the titan flange of the sphere which in turn is cooled by the surrounding seawater. All metal-metal connections have thermal grease applied to feature better thermal conductance.

6 Conclusion

The systematic process of creating an underwater SLAM solution that is suitable for deep-sea applications has been shown using inertial measurements and side-scan sonar. The challenge to invert the side-scan sonar image creation into a 3D representation has been discussed. A suitable SLAM architecture for long deep-sea missions and the chosen hardware layout have been outlined.

Bibliography

[BB08]   Alex Brooks and Tim Bailey. HybridSLAM: Combining FastSLAM and EKF-SLAM for reliable mapping. In *WAFR 2008: The Eighth International Workshop on the Algorithmic Foundations of Robotics*, 12 2008.

[BZ08]   Michael Bosse and Robert Zlot. Map matching and data association for large-scale two-dimensional laser scan-based slam. *I. J. Robotic Res.*, 27(6):667–691, 2008.

[CG09]   Enrique Coiras and Johannes Groen. 3D target shape from SAS images based on a deformable mesh. In *Proceedings of the 3rd International Conference on Underwater Acoustic Measurements (UAM), Nafplion, Greece*, 2009.

[CPL07]   Enrique Coiras, Yvan Petillot, and David M. Lane. Multiresolution 3-D Reconstruction From Side-Scan Sonar Images. *IEEE Transactions on Image Processing*, 16(2):382–390, February 2007. Heriot-Watt University Edinburgh.

[DBL04]   Esther Durá, Judith M. Bell, and David M. Lane. Reconstruction of textured seafloors from side-scan sonar images. *IEE Proceedings – Radar, Sonar and Navigation*, 151(2):114–126, April 2004.

[Fai09]   Nathaniel Fairfield. *Localization, Mapping, and Planning in 3D Environments*. PhD thesis, Robotics Institute, Carnegie Mellon University, Pittsburgh, PA, January 2009.

[JPW10]   Michael V. Jakuba, Oscar Pizarro, and Stefan B. Williams. High resolution, consistent navigation and 3D optical reconstructions from AUVs using magnetic compasses and pressure-based depth sensors. In *Proceedings of MTS/IEEE OCEANS 2010, Sydney, Australia*, 2010.

[JPWM10]   Matthew Johnson-Roberson, Oscar Pizarro, Stefan B. Williams, and Ian Mahon. Generation and visualization of large-scale three-dimensional reconstructions from underwater robotic surveys. *Journal of Field Robotics*, 27(1):21–51, 2010.

[LH91]   Dirk Langer and Martial Hebert. Building Qualitative Elevation Maps From Side Scan Sonar Data For Autonomous Underwater Navigation. In *Proc. IEEE International Conference on Robotics and Automation*, pages 2478–2483, April 9–11, 1991.

[MRRH10]   Angelos Mallios, Pere Ridao, David Ribas, and Emili Hernàndez. Probabilistic sonar scan matching SLAM for underwater environment. In *Proceedings of the Oceans IEEE*, Sydney, Australia, May 2010.

[PDM⁺07]   Luis Pedraza, Gamini Dissanayake, Jaime Valls Miró, Diego Rodríguez-Losada, and Fernando Matía. Bs-slam: Shaping the world. In Wolfram Burgard, Oliver Brock, and Cyrill Stachniss, editors, *Robotics: Science and Systems*. The MIT Press, 2007.

[PRLM⁺09]   Luis Pedraza, Diego Rodriguez-Losada, Fernando Matía, Gamini Dissanayake, and Jaime Valls Miró. Extending the limits of feature-based slam with b-splines. *Trans. Rob.*, 25(2):353–366, 2009.

[Run10]   Adrian Runte. Robuste Merkmale auf 3D-Daten. Term Paper, Vision and Fusion Laboratory (IES), Karlsruhe Institute of Technology, July 2010.

[RVRV95]   P. V. Narasimha Rao, M. S. R. R. Vidyadhar, T. Ch. Malleswara Rao, and L. Venkataratnam. An adaptive filter for speckle suppression in synthetic aperture radar images. *International Journal of Remote Sensing*, 16(5):877–889, 1995.

[WF10]   Philipp Woock and Christian Frey. Deep-sea auv navigation using side-scan sonar images and slam. In *Proceedings of the IEEE Oceans Conference 2010*, may 2010.

[Woo10]   Philipp Woock. Deep sea navigation using SLAM. *Proceedings of the 2009 Joint Workshop of Fraunhofer IOSB and Institute for Anthropomatics, Vision and Fusion Laboratory*, 4, 2010.

A Comparison of Algorithms for Planning Cooperative Motions of Cognitive Automobiles

Christian Frese

Vision and Fusion Laboratory
Institute for Anthropomatics
Karlsruhe Institute of Technology (KIT), Germany
frese@ies.uni-karlsruhe.de

Technical Report IES-2010-06

Abstract: Planning cooperative motions of multiple vehicles is a task of high computational complexity. However, real-time performance is required in applications such as cooperative collision avoidance for road vehicles, enforcing a trade-off between computing time and solution quality. In this report, several motion planning algorithms are compared with respect to these criteria. The considered algorithms are a tree search algorithm relying on precomputed lower bounds, the elastic band method, mixed-integer linear programming, and a priority-based approach.

1 Introduction

In recent years, an increasing number of vehicles has been equipped with sensor-based driver assistance systems and drive-by-wire actuators [Bis00]. Furthermore, many researchers have shown the feasibility of vehicle-to-vehicle communication [HL08]. Taken together, these technologies offer the foundations for the development of a cooperative collision avoidance and mitigation system. In dangerous situations involving multiple vehicles, automatic intervention of this assistance system might prevent accidents. Human drivers are often unable to initiate the appropriate actions, as they have a considerable response time and few possibilities to coordinate their actions with other drivers [BWB09].

Planning cooperative maneuvers which avoid or mitigate accidents is an important requirement for the proposed system. Previous work has considered cooperative motion planning mainly in the context of robotics, and decoupling strategies like

path-velocity decomposition and prioritized planning prevail. However, the requirements in robotics are somewhat different from dangerous traffic situations in
which the vehicles have significant dynamics.

1.1   Contributions

This report investigates different algorithms for planning cooperative motions in
dangerous traffic situations. The algorithms are examined by simulating several
scenarios. Both computing times and success rates are compared. It is shown that
the suitability of the algorithms varies with the scenario.

1.2   Structure

The paper is structured as follows. In Section 2, the cooperative motion planning
problem is formalized. Section 3 presents the four algorithms considered: a tree
search algorithm, mixed-integer linear programming, the elastic band method, and
a prioritized approach. Results of the comparison are reported in Section 3, and
Section 6 presents some conclusions.

2   Problem Formulation

The configuration of a vehicle c_i is denoted $\mathbf{q}_i \in \mathcal{Q}_i$. A motion planning algorithm
has to compute a motion trajectory, which is a continuous function from time into
configuration space, $[0, t_{\max}] \to \mathcal{Q}_i$. The configuration of a vehicle is a parametric
specification of its entire geometric position [LP83]. A common approximation is
a rectangular vehicle geometry and a configuration restricted to the position and
orientation on the road plane, $\mathbf{q}_i = (x_i, y_i, \phi_i)^{\mathrm{T}}$. The resulting configuration space
is the manifold $\mathcal{Q}_i = \mathbb{R}^2 \times \mathbb{S}$, where $\mathbb{S}$ denotes the unit circle [LaV06].

The motion plan has to respect several constraints, caused by static and moving
obstacles, road boundaries and the kinodynamic capabilities of the vehicle.

Cooperative motion planning involves multiple vehicles which have to avoid collisions among each other. For M vehicles, the composite configuration space
$\mathcal{Q} = \mathcal{Q}_1 \times \ldots \times \mathcal{Q}_M$ results.

Altogether, the motion planning task for M vehicles can be formalized as follows:
compute a continuous trajectory $[0, t_{\max}] \to \mathcal{Q} = \mathcal{Q}_1 \times \ldots \times \mathcal{Q}_M$ which

1. starts at the initial states of the vehicles,

2. avoids collisions among the M cooperative vehicles, considering their geometric models,

3. avoids collisions with both static and moving obstacles,

4. keeps the vehicles on the road area, and

5. respects the kinematic and dynamic constraints of the vehicles.

Additionally, a goal region is specified usually. This has been omitted here because collision avoidance is the main objective in dangerous situations. Motion planning is required in this application due to the multi-vehicle coordination problem, the moving obstacles and the dynamic constraints. This cannot be achieved with path planning algorithms which neglect the velocities along the path.

3   Algorithms for Cooperative Motion Planning

In this section, four different algorithms for planning cooperative motions are described. Specific advantages and drawbacks of each method are pointed out. Three of the algorithms try to exploit the full potential of cooperative actions. Table 3.1 summarizes the characteristics of these methods. The fourth method is a state-of-the-art prioritized planner, which is used as a baseline in the comparison.

3.1   Tree Search

The tree search method has been proposed in [Fre10, FB10] and is only sketched briefly here. A set $\mathcal{A}_i$ of actions like maximum braking, steering, etc. is defined for each vehicle. The execution of an action by vehicle c_i can be simulated by means of a state-space model f_i. An action is performed for a predefined interval of time before the next decision is made. Therefore a tree of possible action sequences results. The tree has A^T leaves for a single-vehicle motion planning problem and $A^{M \cdot T}$ leaves for cooperative motion planning, where A is the number of actions considered per vehicle and T is the number of decision points. Action sequences are rated using a loss functional which penalizes violations of the constraints listed in Section 2. The algorithm has to find the action sequence having minimum accumulated loss within the tree.

Even for moderate values of A, M, and T, the tree grows too large to be constructed entirely. Therefore pruning techniques are applied in order to avoid searching subtrees which cannot contain the optimal solution. The pruning relies on lower bounds for the loss values. If the loss within a subtree is guaranteed to be higher than the minimum loss found so far, the subtree can safely be discarded. The bounds are obtained in a precomputation stage by evaluating all action sequences of each single vehicle. This approach is effective because many components of the loss functional only depend on the decisions of one vehicle. Different search strategies may be used within the cooperative tree, including branch and bound search and A* search.

An important advantage of the tree search formulation is the use of explicit vehicle, loss and action models, which can be chosen in the level of detail appropriate for the task under consideration. By shifting most of the computational effort into the precomputation stage, running times become more predictable, increasing the real-time capability of the algorithm. The algorithm offers good parallelization potential, e.g., the precomputation can be distributed by assigning one processor core for each vehicle. The main drawback of the tree search method is the coarse discretization of actions and time which is required in order to achieve computational feasibility.

3.2 Mixed-Integer Linear Programming

A linear program consists of an objective function, equality and inequality constraints, all of them being linear in the real-valued variables. An extension is mixed-integer linear programming (MILP) which constrains some of the variables to be integer, or—as a special case—binary. As standard software is available for solving MILPs, it is appealing to formulate cooperative motion planning in this framework. In recent years, there has been some research in this direction, with focus on the air traffic domain [SDMFH01, BSRB06, RH02].

Variables $\mathbf{p}_{i,k} = (x_{i,k}, y_{i,k})^{\mathrm{T}}$ denote the position of vehicle c_i at time $t = k \cdot \Delta t$ within a planning horizon $k = 0, \dots, T$. Further variables $\mathbf{v}_{i,k}$, $\mathbf{acc}_{i,k}$ are introduced for velocity and acceleration vectors, together with appropriate inequality constraints based on vehicle dynamics. They are coupled by equations describing a linearized version of a state-space vehicle model:

$$\mathbf{v}_{i,k+1} = \mathbf{v}_{i,k} + \Delta t \cdot \mathbf{acc}_{i,k}$$
$$\mathbf{p}_{i,k+1} = \mathbf{p}_{i,k} + \Delta t \cdot \mathbf{v}_{i,k}$$

Binary variables $b_{i,j,k,l}$, $1 \leq i < j \leq M$ are required for the collision avoidance constraints:

$$x_{i,k} - x_{j,k} + b_{i,j,k,1} \cdot C > d_{i,j}$$
$$y_{i,k} - y_{j,k} + b_{i,j,k,2} \cdot C > d_{i,j}$$
$$-x_{i,k} + x_{j,k} + b_{i,j,k,3} \cdot C > d_{i,j} \qquad (3.1)$$
$$-y_{i,k} + y_{j,k} + b_{i,j,k,4} \cdot C > d_{i,j}$$
$$\sum_{l=1}^{4} b_{i,j,k,l} \leq 3$$
$$b_{i,j,k,l} \in \{0,1\} \qquad k = 1, \dots, T$$

Therein, $d_{i,j}$ is the minimum distance to be enforced between the vehicle reference points $(x_{i,k}, y_{i,k})^{\mathrm{T}}$ and $(x_{j,k}, y_{j,k})^{\mathrm{T}}$ at time $k \cdot \Delta t$, and $C \gg 0$ is a large constant. This formulation makes use of a well-known modeling technique to transform a disjunction of inequalities into a conjunction, which is the standard semantics of MILP constraints [Sie96]. Only one of the first four inequalities has to be active, while the others can be trivially satisfied with $b_{i,j,k,l} = 1$. The binary variables thus describe on which side the vehicles pass each other. It may be necessary to discretize the space of directions into more than the four paraxial directions of (3.1). This can be accomplished by additional separating half-planes [ED07]. Obstacle avoidance is modeled in the same way, the only difference being that the position of the second object is no longer variable. Complex obstacles may be represented by a covering of several geometric primitives.

The constraints (3.1) turn out to be too restrictive for road traffic applications: if $d_{i,j}$ is chosen large enough to ensure collision avoidance, vehicles can no longer pass each other on neighboring lanes. An accurate modeling of a vehicle as an oriented rectangle is impossible because of the nonlinearity of rotation equations. Therefore the following workaround is chosen: collision avoidance constraints are imposed not only on the positions of the same time index k, but also on the positions of the time indices $k - 1$ and $k + 1$ which immediately precede and follow the reference time k, respectively:

$$x_{i,k} - x_{j,k-1} + b_{i,j,k,5} \cdot C > d_{i,j}$$
$$y_{i,k} - y_{j,k-1} + b_{i,j,k,6} \cdot C > d_{i,j}$$
$$-x_{i,k} + x_{j,k-1} + b_{i,j,k,7} \cdot C > d_{i,j}$$
$$-y_{i,k} + y_{j,k-1} + b_{i,j,k,8} \cdot C > d_{i,j}$$
$$\sum_{l=5}^{8} b_{i,j,k,l} \leq 3$$
$$b_{i,j,k,l} \in \{0,1\} \qquad k = 2, \dots, T$$

$$x_{i,k} - x_{j,k+1} + b_{i,j,k,9} \cdot C > d_{i,j}$$
$$y_{i,k} - y_{j,k+1} + b_{i,j,k,10} \cdot C > d_{i,j}$$
$$-x_{i,k} + x_{j,k+1} + b_{i,j,k,11} \cdot C > d_{i,j}$$
$$-y_{i,k} + y_{j,k+1} + b_{i,j,k,12} \cdot C > d_{i,j}$$
$$\sum_{l=9}^{12} b_{i,j,k,l} \leq 3$$
$$b_{i,j,k,l} \in \{0,1\} \qquad k = 1, \ldots, T-1$$

Thereby the passing distance $d_{i,j}$ can be lowered. This approximation works quite well due to the nonholonomic kinematics of the vehicle: the position of the back of the vehicle at time index k is approximately where the reference point has been at $k - 1$, and the front at k is approximately at the place where the vehicle reference point will be at $k + 1$. However, this requires the distances $d_{i,j}$ and the time discretization Δt to be chosen according to the velocities of the vehicles.

Road boundaries introduce additional constraints which do not occur in the air traffic domain. A single straight road is easily modeled by two inequality constraints. Curves and intersections, however, have a nonconvex geometry. To model this in a MILP, a decomposition into R convex polygons is performed. A polygon is described by the equations of its E_r edges, $n_x \cdot x + n_y \cdot y \leq d$. Additional binary variables ensure that the vehicle is within one of the road polygons:

$$n_{r,l,x} \cdot x_{i,k} + n_{r,l,y} \cdot y_{i,k} - b_{i,k,r}^{\text{road}} \cdot C \leq d_{r,l} \qquad l = 1, \ldots, E_r$$
$$\sum_{r=1}^{R} b_{i,k,r}^{\text{road}} \leq R - 1 \qquad (3.2)$$
$$b_{i,k,r}^{\text{road}} \in \{0,1\} \qquad k = 1, \ldots, T, \quad r = 1, \ldots, R$$

As collision avoidance and road boundaries are enforced by hard constraints, a suitable objective function to be minimized is the sum of absolute accelerations,

$$\min \sum_{k=1}^{T} \sum_{i=1}^{M} (accabs_{i,k,x} + accabs_{i,k,y}),$$

with the following constraints for defining the absolute accelerations,

$$accabs_{i,k,x} > acc_{i,k,x}$$
$$accabs_{i,k,x} > -acc_{i,k,x}$$

$$accabs_{i,k,\text{y}} > acc_{i,k,\text{y}}$$
$$accabs_{i,k,\text{y}} > -acc_{i,k,\text{y}}$$
$$k = 1, \dots, T.$$

Some constraints of the MILP model can be eliminated by simple reachability considerations. For example, when two vehicles cannot reach each other within $k \cdot \Delta t$ even if maximum acceleration is applied, a collision at time index k is impossible and (3.1) can safely be removed from the model for this k. In other cases, certain constellations of the objects relative to each other are impossible to reach, which then reduces the number of equations and binary variables in (3.1). Concerning the road boundary constraints, usually most of the road polygons are not reachable, which means that much less than R binary variables are necessary in (3.2). These techniques can considerably reduce the number of constraints and especially binary variables. Experiments show that the reduced MILP models are solved much faster than the original ones.

Paralleling the tree search approach of the previous section, MILP solvers often employ branch and bound methods. However, in the tree search formulation, the branching occurs over the vehicle actions and collisions are tested depending on the selected actions, whereas in the MILP formulation, the binary decision variables describe collision avoidance constraints and the vehicle actions are optimized given the collision avoidance decisions. As a consequence, time discretization is tightly coupled with passing distances and cannot be coarsened without impairing collision avoidance. By contrast, in the tree search method, the number of decision points can be reduced without any difficulty in order to improve computational efficiency. Furthermore, adding obstacle and road constraints can cause a dramatic increase in MILP computing time, while it has minor influence in other planning algorithms. This may be an explanation for the observed running times of the MILP approach, which seem to question a real-time usage at present. Another drawback of the MILP method is the restriction to linear models and objective functions. An important advantage is the utilization of an established framework with available tool support, which facilitates modeling and implementation.

3.3   Elastic Bands

Different variants of the elastic band method have been applied to path adaptation for mobile robots [QK93, Bro99, KJCL97] and to path planning for cars [HHBH03, BSW05, HS07, GS07]. Recently, the method has been extended to cooperative motion planning in dangerous situations [FBB08, FBB09].

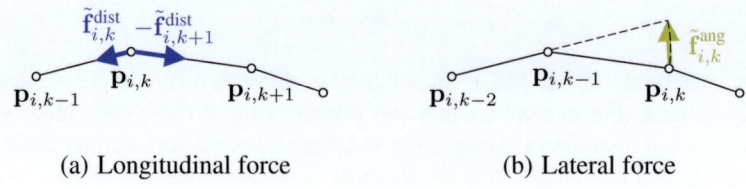

(a) Longitudinal force   (b) Lateral force

Figure 3.1: Illustration of internal forces.

Once again, nodes $\mathbf{p}_{i,k} = (x_{i,k}, y_{i,k})^{\mathrm{T}}$ describe the vehicle positions at discrete points in time. Consecutive nodes of one vehicle are connected to form an elastic band. Orientation and velocity of the vehicle are implicitly represented by the sequence of nodes.

Virtual forces are designed to represent the constraints described above in Section 2. The resulting elastic band can be interpreted as a combination of point masses and springs [BSW05]. The virtual forces show some similarities with potential field path planners, as forces can be interpreted as derivatives of potential fields. However, potential field planners only have a local view of the environment [Lat91], while elastic bands allow collision avoidance forces to propagate along the band. Internal forces can be designed to represent the dynamic and kinematic constraints of the vehicle.

The total force vector applied to node $\mathbf{p}_{i,k}$ is denoted by $\mathbf{f}_{i,k}$. It is additively composed of several force terms. The internal forces $\mathbf{f}^{\mathrm{dist}}$ and $\mathbf{f}^{\mathrm{ang}}$ implement the dynamic and kinematic constraints of the vehicle in longitudinal and lateral direction, respectively. They correspond to springs between consecutive nodes of one band, $\mathbf{p}_{i,k}$ and $\mathbf{p}_{i,k+1}$ (Figure 3.1):

$$\mathbf{f}_{i,k}^{\mathrm{dist}} := \tilde{\mathbf{f}}_{i,k}^{\mathrm{dist}} - \tilde{\mathbf{f}}_{i,k+1}^{\mathrm{dist}}$$

$$\tilde{\mathbf{f}}_{i,k}^{\mathrm{dist}} := w^{\mathrm{dist}}(i,k)(\mathbf{p}_{i,k} - \mathbf{p}_{i,k-1})$$

$$\mathbf{f}_{i,k}^{\mathrm{ang}} := \tilde{\mathbf{f}}_{i,k}^{\mathrm{ang}} - \tilde{\mathbf{f}}_{i,k+1}^{\mathrm{ang}}$$

$$\tilde{\mathbf{f}}_{i,k}^{\mathrm{ang}} := w^{\mathrm{ang}}(i,k)\left(\mathbf{p}_{i,k-1} + \frac{\|\mathbf{p}_{i,k} - \mathbf{p}_{i,k-1}\|}{\|\mathbf{p}_{i,k-1} - \mathbf{p}_{i,k-2}\|}(\mathbf{p}_{i,k-1} - \mathbf{p}_{i,k-2}) - \mathbf{p}_{i,k}\right)$$

These forces act in an anti-symmetric way on both nodes. The scalar weighting functions w^{dist} and w^{ang} prefer the vehicle to drive straight ahead at constant speed and penalize the violation of dynamic constraints with a sharp increase.

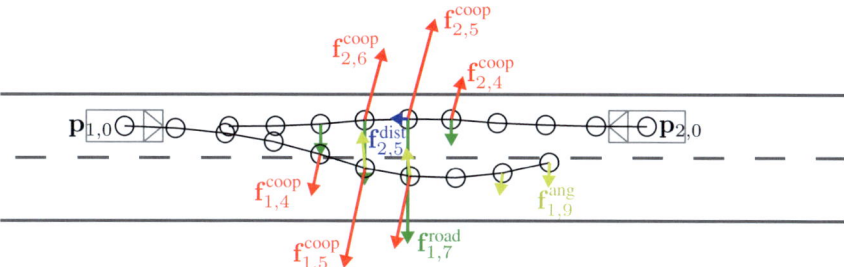

Figure 3.2: Visualization of the elastic bands of two oncoming vehicles. The force components are depicted in different colors.

External forces repel the band from obstacles, other vehicles and the road boundary. For example, the force $\mathbf{f}^{\text{coop}}$ acts between nodes of different bands having the same time index, $\mathbf{p}_{i,k}$ and $\mathbf{p}_{j,k}$:

$$\mathbf{f}_{i,k}^{\text{coop}} := \sum_{j=1,\ldots,M,\, j\neq i} e^{-\|\mathbf{p}_{i,k}-\mathbf{p}_{j,k}\|} \sum_{l=0}^{T} e^{-\|\mathbf{p}_{i,l}-\mathbf{p}_{j,l}\|} \left(\mathbf{p}_{i,l} - \mathbf{p}_{j,l}\right)$$

The direction vectors of the cooperative force are averaged in order to obtain an unambigous direction of evasion and to avoid the forces of neighboring nodes to cancel each other out. In a similar way, the force $\mathbf{f}^{\text{obst}}$ repels the nodes from obstacles:

$$\mathbf{f}_{i,k}^{\text{obst}} := \sum_{j} \left(e^{-\|\mathbf{p}_{i,k}-\mathbf{p}_{j,k}^{\text{obst}}\|+r_j^{\text{obst}}} \sum_{l=0}^{T} e^{-\|\mathbf{p}_{i,l}-\mathbf{p}_{j,l}^{\text{obst}}\|+r_j^{\text{obst}}} \left(\mathbf{p}_{i,l} - \mathbf{p}_{j,l}^{\text{obst}}\right) \right)$$

The elastic band framework uses a circular object model: obstacles are characterized by their center $\mathbf{p}_{j,k}^{\text{obst}}$ at time index k and their radius r_j^{obst}. Other object shapes are approximated by a covering of circles [HHBH03].

Road boundary constraints can be modeled by a force $\mathbf{f}^{\text{road}}$:

$$\mathbf{f}_{i,k}^{\text{road}} := w^{\text{road}}(\mathbf{p}_{i,k})\mathbf{n}(\mathbf{p}_{i,k})$$

Therein, $w^{\text{road}}(\mathbf{p})$ is a scalar function of the distance from $\mathbf{p}$ to the road boundary and $\mathbf{n}(\mathbf{p})$ is the normal vector of the road at point $\mathbf{p}$.

A visualization of elastic bands and virtual forces is shown in Figure 3.2.

The nodes of an elastic band have to be initialized in a meaningful way, e.g., corresponding to a lane-keeping behavior of the vehicle. The virtual forces are applied to the band iteratively until an equilibrium is reached in which the resulting forces vanish for every node: $\forall i \; \forall k \; \mathbf{f}_{i,k} \approx 0$. A continuous state and control trajectory is obtained from the discrete sequence of nodes using, e.g., cubic spline interpolation [HHBH03].

Elastic bands exhibit potential for real-time implementation and a good scalability with the number of cooperative vehicles, even when a comparatively fine time discretization is chosen. However, the method can only find a local optimum, unlike the tree search and MILP approaches. This means that the result depends on the initialization of the elastic bands.

3.4 Prioritized Motion Planning

The algorithms described so far try to exploit the possibilities of combined cooperative actions in the composite configuration space Q as much as possible. While it has been known that planning in the composite configuration space is possible [CLH$^+$05, LaV06], this method has rarely been applied in practice because the computational complexity of motion planning algorithms usually increases exponentially with the dimension of the configuration space [Lat91]. Instead, decoupling approaches are state of the art for multi-robot motion planning problems. These methods make certain simplifying assumptions. Thereby the planning problem is decomposed into multiple planning problems in lower-dimensional configuration spaces, usually one associated with each vehicle. This decreases computational complexity, but also restricts the solution space because not all combinations of actions remain possible.

One of the two common decoupling methods is the path-velocity decomposition [KZ86, PA05, GL06]. Path planning is performed separately for each vehicle, and subsequently the velocities are coordinated in order to obtain a collision-free motion. As mentioned in Section 2, path planning is not suitable for cooperative collision avoidance systems. Therefore the path-velocity decomposition is not considered further in this report.

The other decoupling strategy is prioritized motion planning [ELP87, BTK07]. The motions are planned separately for each vehicle in the order of priorities. Each vehicle considers the plans of the higher-priority vehicles as moving obstacles, but ignores the lower-priority vehicles.

More formally, the priorities can be described by a permutation $\sigma \in \mathcal{S}_M$. The symmetric group $\mathcal{S}_M$ consists of all bijections from a set having M elements to itself. As the planning result depends on the choice of the permutation, two variants of prioritized planning are considered: the permutation is either chosen at random,

	Tree Search	Elastic Bands	MILP
Actions	coarse discretization	continuous	continuous
Time discretization	coarse	fine	fine
Optimization	global	local	global
Models	explicit	implicit	explicit
	arbitrary		linear
Collision mitigation	yes	no	restricted

Table 3.1: Comparison of cooperative motion planning algorithms according to certain evaluation criteria. The prioritized method is not shown because it inherits its properties from the underlying single-vehicle planner.

or the result is optimized over all $\sigma \in \mathcal{S}_M$. The latter variant yields the best solution quality possible with prioritized planning. Some strategies for choosing or optimizing the permutation have been proposed in literature [vdBO05, BBT01]. In road traffic applications, criteria based on traffic rules could be used for selecting the permutation. For example, the leading vehicle should have higher priority than the follower when two vehicles are driving on the same lane. Priorities may also be based on the right of way at intersections.

The priority-based approach has been implemented using the tree search method from Section 3.1 as single-vehicle motion planner. As the single-vehicle problems are easier to solve, a finer time discretization may be chosen, resulting in a larger number of decision points T. With regard to time efficiency, this is presumably not the best way to implement prioritized planning. However, results from related work suggest that prioritized planning can achieve real-time performance [vdBO05].

4   Results

The described algorithms have been applied to a multitude of problem instances derived from different scenarios such as cooperative obstacle avoidance, merging, overtaking, and intersection crossing. The scenarios have been created by means of a traffic simulator [VNB+07]. In the following, results on intersection and overtaking scenarios are reported, both of them involving $M = 4$ vehicles. Two variants of the overtaking scenario have been considered, differing mainly in the initial positions of the vehicles. For each scenario, 30-150 problem instances have been generated by periodically starting the planner during the simulation run. An example of a cooperative motion plan is shown in Figure 4.1.

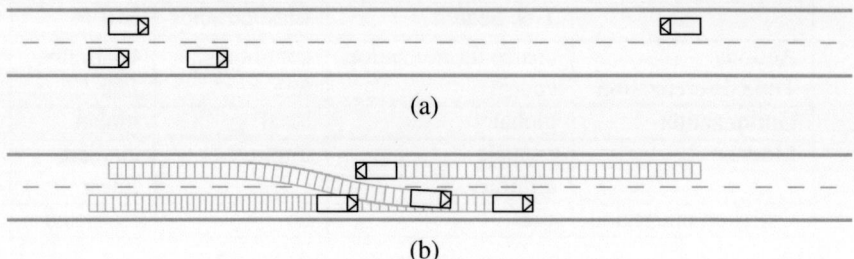

(a)

(b)

Figure 4.1: (a) A problem instance of scenario Overtaking 1. (b) Cooperative motion plan for this instance obtained by the tree search algorithm. A gap is created which allows the overtaking vehicle to merge into the right lane.

Scenario	Tree search		MILP		Elastic bands		Random priorities	
	avg	max	avg	max	avg	max	avg	max
Overtaking 1	0.3	1.1	1.9	17.5	0.4	0.4	0.7	5.0
Overtaking 2	2.5	10.3	443.9	3148.9	0.9	1.1	0.7	4.3
Intersection	0.7	4.3	10.6	382.4	1.5	1.9	1.6	5.6

Table 4.1: Average and maximum computing times in seconds for three different scenarios. For each scenario, averaging and maximization was performed over the problem instances which could be solved successfully by the respective algorithm.

4.1   Computing Times

Table 4.1 shows average and maximum computing times for the different algorithms measured on an off-the-shelf desktop PC. Tree search, elastic bands, and prioritized planning have potential for real-time application: improved implementations should be able to achieve computing times of less than one second on the considered problem instances. The MILP approach is remarkably fast on many problem instances, however it sometimes requires several minutes or even hours on very similar problems. Therefore it seems difficult to obtain real-time performance.

The MILP method has been implemented using the free C library lp_solve 5.5 [BEN08]. Some parameters of the MILP solver significantly influence its performance on cooperative motion planning problems. By changing the bb_rule

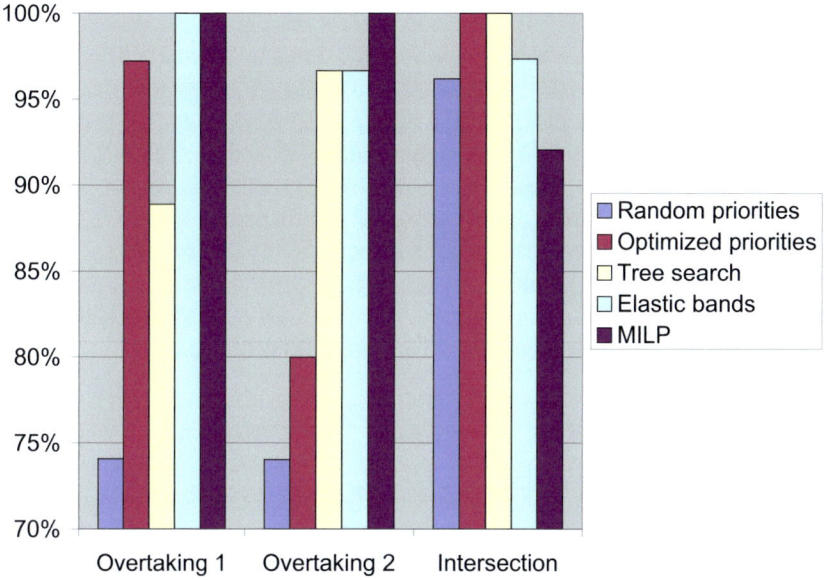

Figure 4.2: Percentage of correct plans obtained by the different algorithms.

parameter, computing times can be decreased by orders of magnitude. The best results are achieved with `fractionselect+branchreversemode`. The computation is stopped as soon as the first feasible solution is found. This solution is
guaranteed to be correct and is usually of good quality. Determining the optimal
solution increases computing times by a factor of about 2.

4.2   Planning Success

Figure 4.2 shows the percentage of problem instances in which the algorithms can
find a correct plan, i.e., a collision-free cooperative motion respecting road boundary and kinodynamic constraints. Surprisingly, the results on the two overtaking
scenarios are quite different, although both scenarios appear very similar at first
glance. However, the merging is the most critical maneuver in scenario 1, while
the collision with the oncoming vehicle is more time-critical in scenario 2 due to
the slight variation of the initial positions. The prioritized planner can deal with the

merging task, but cannot resolve the oncoming situation with a cooperative maneuver. Elastic bands and MILP have good success rates in both scenarios, while the tree search algorithm is a bit worse in scenario 1 due to the coarse discretization.

In the intersection scenario, best results are achieved by the tree search and by the priority-optimizing planner. The elastic band method suffers from its local optimization which prohibits a change of turning direction. The MILP approach fails in some instances because the geometric constellations cannot be modeled exactly with linear models. A conservative approximation is required to ensure collision-free plans, thus narrowing the space of admissible solutions.

Concerning prioritized planning, it becomes clear that the choice of the permutation is crucial for the planning success. But even with optimal priorities, there are scenarios that cannot be solved due to the restricted action space.

5   Conclusions

Different multi-vehicle motion planning algorithms have been evaluated on cooperative collision avoidance tasks. The state-of-the-art prioritized planner cannot solve certain problem instances due to its inherent restriction of the action space. The algorithms which exploit the composite action space of the vehicles have been more successful on these instances. In the intersection scenario, the tree search method performed best, while elastic bands and MILP showed good results in the overtaking scenarios. These observations indicate that either the algorithm should be chosen depending on the traffic scenario, or multiple planners should be executed in parallel to guarantee optimal results.

Tree search and elastic bands clearly have the potential for real-time application. While the MILP method can also solve a lot of problem instances rather fast, its timing behavior appears to be too unpredictable for real-time use.

Another criterion is the possibility to plan collision mitigation maneuvers. The tree search method can handle collision mitigation if the loss functional is modified so that the severity of collisions is minimized. It seems to be difficult to integrate collision mitigation in the elastic band or MILP framework, as these methods do not support arbitrary explicit models.

Acknowledgements

The author gratefully acknowledges support of this work by Deutsche Forschungsgemeinschaft (German Research Foundation) within the Transregional Collaborative Research Center 28 "Cognitive Automobiles". Furthermore, the author would like to thank all project partners contributing to the simulation software.

Bibliography

[BBT01]   Maren Bennewitz, Wolfram Burgard, and Sebastian Thrun. Optimizing schedules for prioritized path planning of multi-robot systems. In *Conference on Robotics and Automation*, Seoul, May 2001.

[BEN08]   Michel Berkelaar, Kjell Eikland, and Peter Notebaert.   lp_solve. http://lpsolve.sourceforge.net/, 2008.

[Bis00]   Richard Bishop. A survey of intelligent vehicle applications worldwide. In *Proceedings of the IEEE Intelligent Vehicles Symposium*, 2000.

[Bro99]   Oliver Brock. *Generating Robot Motion: The Integration of Planning and Execution*. PhD thesis, Stanford University, 1999.

[BSRB06]   Francesco Borrelli, Dharmashankar Subramanian, Arvind Raghunathan, and Lorenz Biegler. MILP and NLP techniques for centralized trajectory planning of multiple unmanned air vehicles. In *American Control Conference*, 2006.

[BSW05]   Thorsten Brandt, Thomas Sattel, and Jörg Wallaschek. On automatic collision avoidance systems. *SAE Transactions*, April 2005.

[BTK07]   Kostas Bekris, Konstantinos Tsianos, and Lydia Kavraki. A decentralized planner that guarantees the safety of communicating vehicles with complex dynamics that replan online. In *Conference on Intelligent Robots and Systems*, pages 3784–3790, 2007.

[BWB09]   Thomas Batz, Kym Watson, and Jürgen Beyerer. Recognition of dangerous situations within a cooperative group of vehicles. In *Proceedings of the IEEE Intelligent Vehicles Symposium*, pages 907–912, Xi'an, China, June 2009.

[CLH+05]   Howie Choset, Kevin Lynch, Seth Hutchinson, George Kantor, Wolfram Burgard, Lydia Kavraki, and Sebastian Thrun. *Principles of Robot Motion*. MIT Press, 2005.

[ED07]   Matthew Earl and Raffaello D'Andrea. Multi-vehicle cooperative control using mixed integer linear programming. In Jeff Shamma, editor, *Cooperative Control of Distributed Multi-Agent Systems*, pages 233–259. Wiley, 2007.

[ELP87]   Michael Erdmann and Tomás Lozano-Pérez. On multiple moving objects. *Algorithmica*, 2:477–521, 1987.

[FB10]   Christian Frese and Jürgen Beyerer. Planning cooperative motions of cognitive automobiles using tree search algorithms. In Rüdiger Dillmann, Jürgen Beyerer, Uwe D. Hanebeck, and Tanja Schultz, editors, *KI 2010: Advances in Artificial Intelligence*, volume 6359 of *Lecture Notes in Artificial Intelligence*, pages 91–98. Springer, September 2010.

[FBB08]   Christian Frese, Thomas Batz, and Jürgen Beyerer. Cooperative behavior of groups of cognitive automobiles based on a common relevant picture. *at – Automatisierungstechnik*, 56(12):644–652, December 2008.

[FBB09]   Christian Frese, Thomas Batz, and Jürgen Beyerer. Kooperative Bewegungsplanung zur Unfallvermeidung im Straßenverkehr mit der Methode der elastischen Bänder. In Rüdiger Dillmann, Jürgen Beyerer, Christoph Stiller, J. Marius Zöllner, and Tobias Gindele, editors, *Autonome Mobile Systeme*, pages 193–200, Karlsruhe, December 2009. Springer.

[Fre10]   Christian Frese. Cooperative motion planning using branch and bound methods. Technical Report IES-2009-13. In Jürgen Beyerer and Marco Huber, editors, *Proceedings of the 2009 Joint Workshop of Fraunhofer IOSB and Institute for Anthropomatics, Vision and Fusion Laboratory*, pages 187–201. KIT Scientific Publishing, 2010.

[GL06]   Robert Ghrist and Steven LaValle. Nonpositive curvature and pareto optimal coordination of robots. *SIAM Journal on Control and Optimization*, 45(5):1697–1713, January 2006.

[GS07]   Stefan Gehrig and Fridtjof Stein. Collision avoidance for vehicle-following systems. *IEEE Transactions on Intelligent Transportation Systems*, 8(2):233–244, June 2007.

[HHBH03]   Jens Hilgert, Karina Hirsch, Torsten Bertram, and Manfred Hiller. Emergency path planning for autonomous vehicles using elastic band theory. In *IEEE/ASME Conference on Advanced Intelligent Mechatronics*, 2003.

[HL08]   Hannes Hartenstein and Kenneth Laberteaux. A tutorial survey on vehicular ad hoc networks. *IEEE Communications Magazine*, pages 164–171, June 2008.

[HS07]   Tobias Hesse and Thomas Sattel. An approach to integrate vehicle dynamics in motion planning for advanced driver assistance systems. In *Proceedings of the IEEE Intelligent Vehicles Symposium*, 2007.

[KJCL97]   M. Khatib, H. Jaouni, R. Chatila, and Jean-Paul Laumond. Dynamic path modification for car-like nonholonomic mobile robots. In *Conference on Robotics and Automation*, pages 2920–2925, April 1997.

[KZ86]   Kamal Kant and Steven Zucker. Toward efficient trajectory planning: The path-velocity decomposition. *Journal of Robotics Research*, 5(3):72–89, 1986.

[Lat91]   Jean-Claude Latombe. *Robot motion planning*. Kluwer, 1991.

[LaV06]   Steven LaValle. *Planning Algorithms*. Cambridge University Press, 2006.

[LP83]   Tomás Lozano-Pérez. Spatial planning: A configuration space approach. *IEEE Transactions on Computers*, 32(2):108–120, February 1983.

[PA05]   Jufeng Peng and Srinivas Akella. Coordinating multiple robots with kinodynamic constraints along specified paths. *Journal of Robotics Research*, 24(4):295–310, April 2005.

[QK93]   Sean Quinlan and Oussama Khatib. Elastic bands: Connecting path planning and control. In *Conference on Robotics and Automation*, 1993.

[RH02]   Arthur Richards and Jonathan How. Aircraft trajectory planning with collision avoidance using mixed integer linear programming. In *American Control Conference*, 2002.

[SDMFH01]   Tom Schouwenaars, Bart De Moor, Eric Feron, and Jonathan How. Mixed integer programming for multi-vehicle path planning. In *European Control Conference*, pages 2603–2608, 2001.

[Sie96]   Gerard Sierksma. *Linear and integer programming: theory and practice*. Dekker, 1996.

[vdBO05]   Jur van den Berg and Mark Overmars. Prioritized motion planning for multiple robots. In *Conference on Intelligent Robots and Systems*, 2005.

[VNB⁺07]   Stefan Vacek, Robert Nagel, Thomas Batz, Frank Moosmann, and Rüdiger Dillmann. An integrated simulation framework for cognitive automobiles. In *Proceedings of the IEEE Intelligent Vehicles Symposium*, pages 221–226, Istanbul, June 2007.

Multi-Sensor Fusion for Localization and Mapping for Mobile Robots

Thomas Emter

Vision and Fusion Laboratory
Institute for Anthropomatics
Karlsruhe Institute of Technology (KIT), Germany.
thomas.emter@iosb.fraunhofer.de

Technical Report IES-2010-07

Abstract: The ability of a mobile robot to localize itself in the environment is a prerequisite for autonomous navigation. This is accomplished by using different sensors. Unfortunately all sensors' measurements are noisy and suffer from errors. Thus it is essential to combine several sensors to reduce the errors and also compensate for the shortcomings of individual sensors by means of multi-sensor fusion and simultaneous localization and mapping (SLAM).

1 Introduction

Due to noisy sensor measurements several sensors have to be used for self localization of a mobile robot. The mobile robot platform of the *Fraunhofer IOSB* and its sensor equipment is shown in Figure 1.1. Motion sensors like odometry and the gyros of the inertial measurement unit (IMU) allow to perform dead-reckoning, i.e., incrementally incorporating their relative measurements from an initially known pose. On the other hand, absolute position and attitude sensors do not depend on an initial pose and their measurements do not suffer from error accumulation. Absolute measuring sensors include for example GPS, compass, and partially the accelerometers of the IMU. The latter are absolute sensors, if used for roll and pitch estimation in contrast to estimation of linear motion by numerical integration of the accelerometers' measurements, in which case the estimates are relative [EFK08].

In addition, sensors which observe the environment like a laser scanner or camera can be used for localization in a map. For navigation, a map is also advantageous as it provides the possibility of path planning beyond the actual sensor coverage.

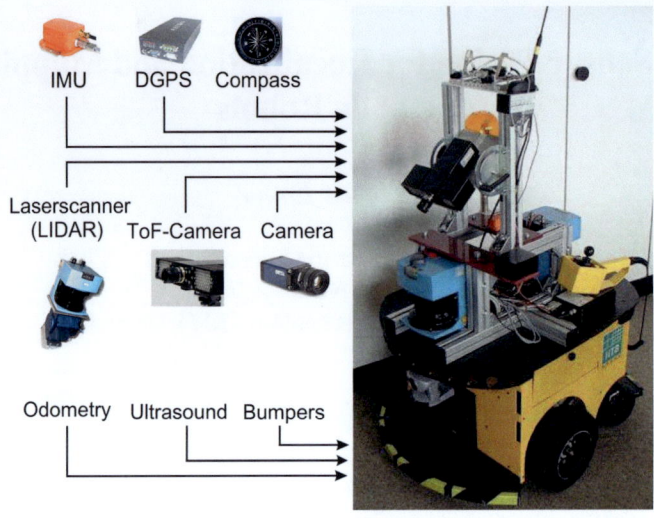

Figure 1.1: System overview.

To build a precise and correct map, the robot has to simultaneously localize itself in the so far registered map which contains errors and has to update it continuously. Consequently, the map built becomes inconsistent unless the dependencies between the uncertainty in the pose and the errors in the map are taken into account. By observing areas or features of the map several times, the uncertainties in the map are decreased and the map converges to a better solution. Several approaches of probabilistic mapping exist to solve this so called simultaneous localization and mapping (SLAM) problem [DWB06a].

For the purpose of combining all mentioned sensors, their individual uncertainties have to be considered in a mathematically and statistically sound way. Therefore, a probabilistic fusion framework has been developed combining methods of multi-sensor fusion to incorporate the motion, position, and attitude sensors with a SLAM algorithm capable of integrating several sensors and corresponding maps.

2   Fusion Framework

The fusion framework is shown in Figure 2.1. In the top left corner the motion, position, and attitude sensors are shown. They are fused in an Extended-Kalman

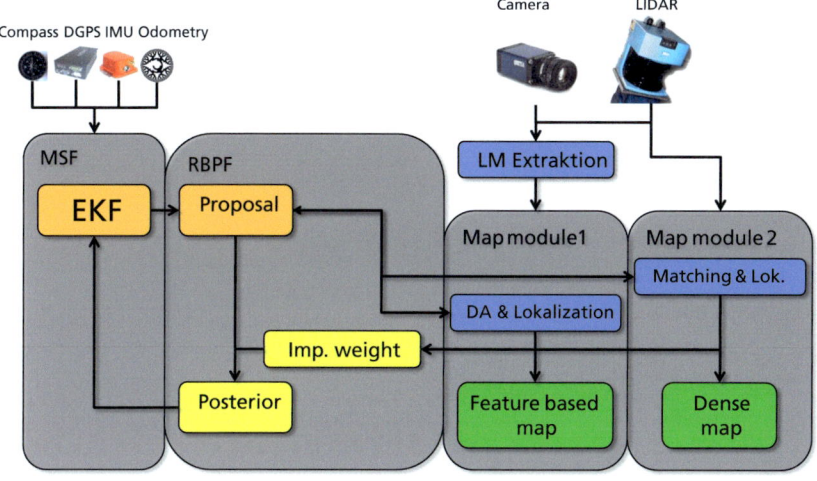

Figure 2.1: Fusion framework.

Filter (EKF), which is explained in in more detail in Section 3. Its estimate serves as prior probability density for the SLAM algorithm. As SLAM algorithm a Rao-Blackwellized particle filter was chosen, due to its property of conditional independence between the landmarks, which enables a straightforward integration of a landmark model comprised of statistically independent attributes as presented in Section 4. Furthermore, it allows to integrate and combine several maps like a dense map as presented in [Emt10] and a feature based map as shown in Figure 2.1 as map modules. A feature map is built of features extracted from the sensor data as distinct landmarks (Section 4). The combination of maps can be seen as map layers with different levels of abstraction of the same area, each one containing data provided by a certain sensor. All landmarks and dense data also could be saved into a hybrid map while ensuring that every type of map data is updated with the appropriate senor data.

A particle filter samples the state space of the robots' path proportional to its probability density. Applying the condition that every particle tracks the hypothesis of the true path, the landmarks become conditionally independent of each other. Every particle tracks its own hypothesis of the robots' path and thus has its own distinct map and dedicated data association hypotheses. Regarding the fusion framework every particle also has its own EKF as the localization estimate is different for each particle. The proposal distribution includes the positioning sensors through the estimates of the EKFs, while the posterior distribution of the particle filter is fed back to the EKFs. The particle filter is based on an instance of the FastSLAM 2.0 algorithm. It incorporates localization by current sensor measurements of the environment into the proposal distribution and is therefore more robust against particle depletion. As the observations of the environment are incorporated into the proposal distribution, convergence of the algorithm with only one particle could be shown [MTKW03]. The proposal distribution is proportional to

$$p(s_k^{[l]}|s^{k-1,[l]}, z^k, u^k, n^{k,[l]})p(s^{k-1,[l]}|z^{k-1}, u^{k-1}, n^{k-1,[l]})$$

and the importance weights are defined by:

$$
\begin{aligned}
w_k^{[l]} &= \frac{\text{target distribution}}{\text{proposal distribution}} \\
&= \frac{p(s^{k,[l]}|z^k, u^k, n^{k,[l]})}{p(s_k^{[l]}|s^{k-1,[l]}, z^k, u^k, n^{k,[l]})p(s^{k-1,[l]}|z^{k-1}, u^{k-1}, n^{k-1,[l]})} \\
&\propto p(z_k|s^{k-1,[l]}, z^{k-1}, u^k, n^{k,[l]}) \cdot w_{k-1} \, .
\end{aligned}
$$

The robots' path per particle $[l]$ is denoted s, while k indicates the time steps. The pose estimate of the EKF is the input u. The measurement z is acquired by sensors observing the environment. The data association is denoted n. A variable with superscripted time step like s^k denotes the set of all its instances up to time step k. The importance weights are calculated by the likelihood of the current observations and the so far recorded landmarks in the map. The higher the resulting importance weight of a particle, the higher the probability that the map of this particle is correct.

The framework was designed for straightforward extensibility and thus is easy to extend with additional position sensors like indoor GPS as well as other mapping sensors like RADAR with according map modules as shown in Figure 2.2.

3   Asynchronous Sensor Fusion

The utilized sensors are not synchronized and the senors' data rates are different. The naïve approach to use the rate of the slowest sensor as estimation rate of the fusion algorithm is not ideal as a lot of information is discarded and the output rate would be restricted. Furthermore, an outage of this sensor would compromise the whole system. Therefore, the fusion algorithm should be capable of incorporating all sensor data at their corresponding clock rate and thus ensuring the highest possible output rate. The fusion algorithm is implemented as an asynchronous

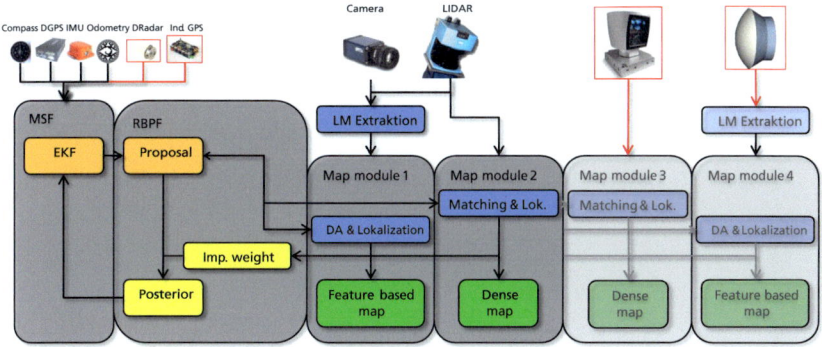

Figure 2.2: Extensibility of fusion framework.

EKF structure to ensure low computational complexity and real-time requirements. The Kalman filter is an optimal estimator for the state of a linear system with a known model from measurements with additive white Gaussian noise. The EKF extends the plain Kalman filter for estimation of non-linear systems by linearization through Taylor-expansion around the current estimate. The asynchronous processing is achieved by a prediction step with the system model for every incoming measurement and a dedicated update step with the according sensor data. The nine sensors of the inertial measurement unit (IMU), i.e., three gyroscopes, three axial accelerometers, and three magnetometers, are pre-processed and fused in a separate Kalman filter to estimate the attitude. Cascading of Kalman filters reduces computational complexity and regarding this mobile robot the assumptions concerning independence between position and attitude subsystems are met because of its comparably low dynamics and restricted pitch and roll movements. The estimated attitude is combined with the sensor data of odometry, compass, and GPS in the main Kalman filter resulting in an estimate of the full 6 DoF. Additional meta-knowledge about the GPS' error characteristics is incorporated by pre- and post-processing combined with an adaptive tuning of the Kalman filter, which is explained in more detail in [ESP10].

Figure 3.1 shows the results of the compensation capabilities of the fusion algorithm in a situation where several short GPS outages occurred. A drawback of the asynchronous processing is the occurrence of sawtooth patterns as shown when zoomed in (Figure 3.2). The relative sensors have higher data rates, and because of the asynchronous fusion technique, for every sensor data a prediction and correction step is performed. Thus, the relative sensor data may cause the position

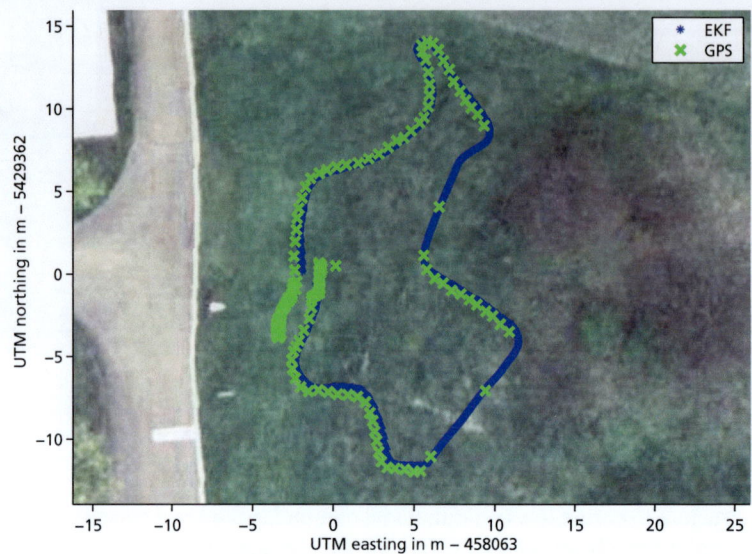

Figure 3.1: Compensation of temporal sensor outages.

estimate to drift somewhat because of the cumulative errors caused by the addition of the relative measurements. The measurements of the absolute sensors arrive less frequently and correct the position, possibly causing the recently filtered position to be slightly away from the previously estimated pose, which causes small skips in the filtered sensor data. This cannot be overcome with a causal filter which is needed for on-line processing.

The integration of the asynchronous EKF in the fusion framework is straightforward as the filter algorithm is capable of computing the density required for the proposal of the particle filter at any required time step.

4   SLAM with an Augmented Landmark Model

A very important prerequisite for the SLAM algorithm to converge is the data association, i.e., the association between an observation and the appropriate landmark in the map. Wrong data associations may lead to wrong or imprecise maps and intensify the particle depletion problem [Emt10]. With a landmark only defined by its position –a point landmark– the data association is particularly prone

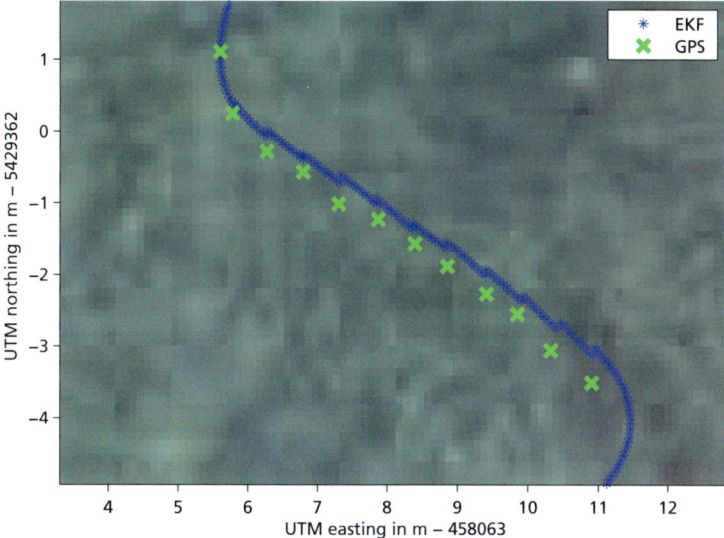

Figure 3.2: Sawtooth pattern of asynchroneous fusion.

to errors in situations where the mobile robot's pose uncertainty is high. How-ever, additional attributes of a landmark model entail a more reliable distinction between landmarks [DWB06b]. Investigations via simulations with point land-marks augmented by an additional signature attribute have shown an improvement in data association and consequently improved convergence of the FastSLAM al-gorithm [Emt10]. In the following paragraph an augmented landmark model and experimental validation of its impact on the convergence of the SLAM algorithm is presented.

4.1   Augmented Landmark Model

To achieve robust data association an augmented landmark model consisting of metric information plus additional features or attributes is utilized. From an object-oriented view a landmark is described by its attributes, whose statistically depen-dency has to be considered. Ideally, some attributes are independent of the position of the landmark so that the data association becomes collectively more independent of the uncertainty of the localization estimate of the mobile robot. The proposed landmark model θ describes vertical cylindrical objects like tree trunks, pillars or

Figure 4.1: Schematic of a landmark and the LIDAR scan in red.

lamp posts and has the feature vector $f(\theta) = (n^{LM}, e^{LM}, r^{LM}, v^{LM})$, which is comprised of metric features (n^{LM}, e^{LM}, r^{LM} for north, east, and radius) and a visual signature (v^{LM}). It augments the simple point landmark model (n^{LM}, e^{LM}) by the additional feature horizontal dimension, expressed as radius r^{LM}, as well as the visual appearance v. The landmark model has been chosen to represent cylindrical objects because their radii do not depend on their position and the visual appearance is mostly invariant under changes of the point of view and thus can also be assumed to be independent of the position (n^{LM}, e^{LM}). Employing SIFT features as augmented landmarks or visual signature has been discarded as it turned out, e.g., in [ESL06], that SIFT is not feasible for real-time applications. Especially in case of particle filter SLAM it is advisable to rather use a straight-forward landmark model described by few parameters combined with an elaborate and robust landmark extraction, as the extraction has to be performed only once, while map processing consisting of data association and fusion is processed multiple times.

To detect and observe these landmarks a hierarchical extraction scheme based on a LIDAR in combination with camera images was used. The LIDAR was used to detect landmark candidates as they appear as distinct local distance minima in the scan as can be seen in Figure 4.1. Within the scan line several objects of the environment like stones are spuriously identified as candidates for landmarks. To eliminate false candidates the camera image regions around the candidates are searched for vertical edges which have to be on the left and right, see Figure 4.2.

Figure 4.2: Laser scan referenced in the camera image.

In the image individual candidates originating from the laser scan are shown as differently colored laser points. The green rectangle depicts the final landmark with its left and right edges detected by the camera. The image content of this rectangle is used as visual signature represented by a normalized HSV-histogram. The distance of the landmark to the robot is obtained from the laser scanner as its measurements are very accurate. Because of the superior angular resolution of the camera compared to the laser scanner the radius is obtained from the image. Thus, the conjunction of these two sensors has the advantage of the accurate distance measurements of the LIDAR combined with the high angular resolution of the camera.

To obtain the position of the landmark (n^{LM}, e^{LM}) in world coordinates transformations have to be applied, cf. Figure 4.3. The radius r of the landmark is half of the width of the aforementioned green rectangle while the distance d and angle ϑ is from the measurement of the LIDAR. The latter are given in the robot coordinate system (x_R^{LM}, y_R^{LM}):

$$\begin{bmatrix} x_R^{LM} \\ y_R^{LM} \\ r^{LM} \end{bmatrix} = \begin{bmatrix} (r+d)\sin(\vartheta) \\ (r+d)\cos(\vartheta) \\ r \end{bmatrix} .$$

The landmark's position has to be transformed into the world coordinate system (n,e) with respect to the robot's position (n^R, e^R) and heading Ψ:

$$\begin{bmatrix} n^{LM} \\ e^{LM} \end{bmatrix} = \begin{bmatrix} n^R + (r+d)\cdot\cos(\vartheta + \Psi) \\ e^R + (r+d)\cdot\sin(\vartheta + \Psi) \end{bmatrix} .$$

At this point it becomes evident that the position of a landmark is dependent of the uncertainty in the pose of the robot.

4.2   Data Association

For the matching of an observation to an existing landmark in the map and for the calculation of the importance weights a statistical distance measure is required.

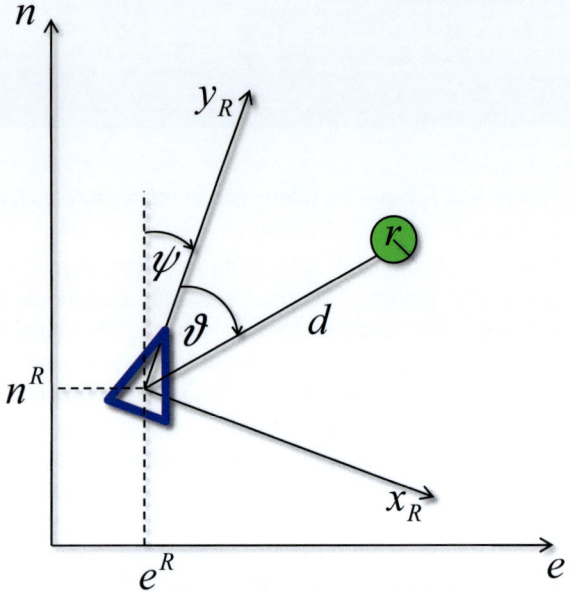

Figure 4.3: Coordinate systems.

One of the most widely used ones is the likelihood. The statistical independence of the visual signature of the mobile robots' pose s is an important characteristic. The likelihood for the observation of the metric features $z_{m^{LM},k}$ is independent of the likelihood for the observation of the visual signature $z_{v^{LM},k}$, so the overall likelihood can be split:

$$p(z_{ges,k}|s^{k-1,[l]}, z_{ges}^{k-1}, u^k, n^{k,[l]})$$
$$= p(z_{m^{LM},k}|s^{k-1,[l]}, z_{m^{LM}}^{k-1}, u^k, n^{k,[l]}) \cdot p(z_{v^{LM},k}|z_{v^{LM}}^{k-1}, n^{k,[l]}) \,.$$

Thus the overall likelihood is calculated by the multiplication of the likelihood of the metric features and the likelihood of the visual signature. While the continuous metric features are assumed to be normally distributed

$$e^{LM}, n^{LM}, r^{LM} \sim \mathcal{N}(\mu_m, \Sigma_m) \,,$$

the discrete multi modal feature v^{LM} is defined by a 2D-histogram q calculated from the earlier mentioned HSV-histogram.

The observation likelihood of the metric features can be calculated by the difference between the observation $z_{m^{LM},n_k^{[l]}}$ and the predicted observation $\hat{z}_{m^{LM},n_k^{[l]}}$ for Gaussian distributions:

$$
p_m = \frac{1}{(2\pi)^{3/2}\sqrt{|Z_{n_k^{[l]},k}|}} \cdot
$$

$$
\exp\left(-\frac{1}{2}(z_{m^{LM},k} - \hat{z}_{m^{LM},n_k^{[l]},k})^T Z_{n_k^{[l]},k}^{-1}(z_{m^{LM},k} - \hat{z}_{m^{LM},n_k^{[l]},k})\right) ,
$$

(4.1)

$Z_{n_k^{[l]},k}$ being the innovation covariance matrix:

$$
Z_{n_k^{[l]},k} = H P_{n_k^{[l]},k-1}^{[l]} H^T + R
$$

composed of the linearized measurement model H, the covariance of the associated landmark $P_{n_k^{[l]}}$, and the covariance of the measurement noise R [MT07]. The likelihood of the histogram matching between an observation $\hat{q}$ and the visual signature of the landmark q can be calculated by:

$$
p(z_{v^{LM},k}|z_{v^{LM}}^{k-1}, n^{k,[l]}) = \exp\left\{-\lambda D(\hat{q},q)\right\} =: p_{v^{LM}}
$$

(4.2)

with $D(\hat{q},q) = 1 - \sum_{b=1}^{B}\sqrt{\hat{q}(b) \cdot q(b)}$, where b denotes the histogram's bins. q is the histogram of the current observation which is compared to the histogram $\hat{q}$ of an already known landmark in the map. The distance D was introduced by [CRM00] who derived it from the Bhattacharyya-distance $D_{\text{Bhattacharyya}}(\hat{q},q) = -\ln\left(\sum_{b\in B}\sqrt{\hat{q}(b)q(b)}\right)$ and proved that it conforms to a metric. The Bhattacharyya-distance itself and the Kullback-Leibler-Divergence for example violate at least one the the distance axioms [PHVG02]. In [CT91] it is stated that the Kullback-Leibler-Divergence is frequently mentioned as distance between two probability densities but it does not fulfill the triangle inequality and the symmetry condition. According to [PHVG02] the likelihood of a histogram matching can be calculated with equation (4.2), in which the parameter λ was chosen to 20 as in [PHVG02].

Thus, the likelihood of an observation to landmark matching can be calculated in closed form and therefore serves directly as a robust data association and can be used as importance weight in the Rao-Blackwellized particle filter.

The data association is performed per particle $[l]$ with the maximum-likelihood estimator:

$$\hat{n}_k^{[l]} = \underset{n_k^{[l]}}{\arg\max}\, p(z_{ges,k}|s^{k-1,[l]}, z_{ges}^{k-1}, u^k, n^{k,[l]})$$

$$= \underset{n_k^{[l]}}{\arg\max}\, p_{m^{LM}} \cdot p_{v^{LM}}\ ,$$

with $p_{v^{LM}}$ for the visual signature from equation (4.2) and $p_{m^{LM}}$ for the metric features from equation (4.1).

4.3 Data Fusion

The hitherto recorded landmarks in the maps have to be updated with the associated observations by fusion. The metric features are assumed to be normally distributed as mentioned before and therefore can be fused with an EKF like update. The visual signature v^{LM} is defined by a 2D-histogram and is updated with a discrete Bayes filter [TBF05].

For all bins b of the histogram a prediction is performed:

$$q_k^-(b) = \sum_i p(x(b)|u_k, x(i))q_{k-1}^+(i)\ .$$

$p(x(b)|u_k, x(i))$ is the transition probability from bin $x(i)$ to bin $x(b)$. In this case $p(x(b)|u_k, x(i))$ is 0 for all $i \neq b$, as the signature is independent of the mobile robots' pose and therefore of the motion u_k. Consequently, the prediction is simplified to $q_k^-(b) = q_{k-1}^+(b)$. The update step is calculated by multiplying the respective bins of the histogram of the landmark with that of the observation $p(z_{v^{LM},k}|x(b))$:

$$q_k^+(b) = \eta p(z_{v^{LM},k}|x(b))q_k^-(b),$$

where η depicts a normalization factor, i.e., the histogram is normalized after every filter step, so that $\sum_{b=1}^{B} \hat{q}(b) = 1$ applies.

4.4 Results

The following results have been accomplished with an implementation of the Fast-SLAM 2.0 algorithm. For the evaluation these scenarios were conducted with and without additional features r^{LM} and v^{LM} for comparison:

1. 1 particle with additional features

2. 1 particle without additional features

3. 25 particles with additional features

4. 25 particles without additional features

The figures show the maps at the end of a course with three loop closures and a traveled distance of about 100m, which was driven by the mobile robot from the left to the right and back. Within the area 12 objects are recognized as landmarks. The blue arrow depicts the mobile robots' pose, which in case of multiple particles is gathered by weighted averaging of the particles. In the scenarios with multiple particles the map shown is the map of the particle possessing the highest importance weight, as it most probably possesses the best map. The landmarks are numbered and their 3σ error interval is shown with blue ellipses. The red line depicts the ground truth. In Figures 4.6 and 4.7 the individual particles are marked as red dots. In the result of scenario 1 (Figure 4.4), it can be seen that the mobile robot is close to the ground truth and the map correctly consists of 12 landmarks,

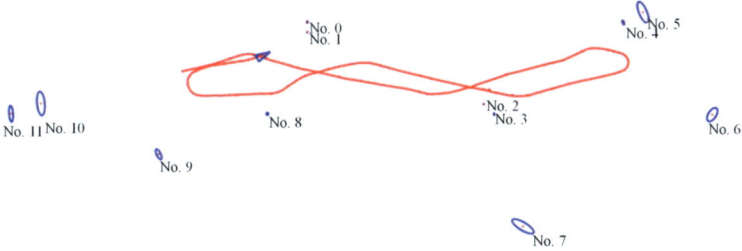

Figure 4.4: Map of one particle with additional features.

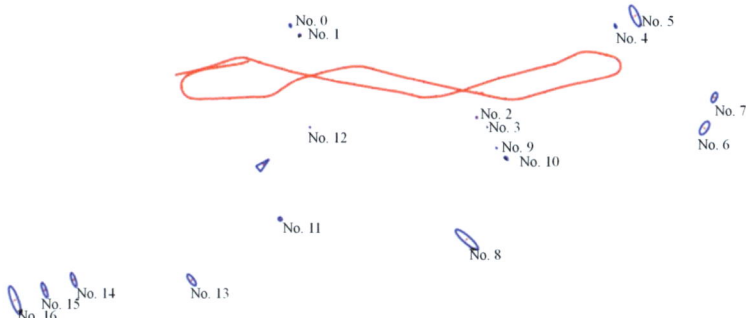

Figure 4.5: Map of one particle without additional features.

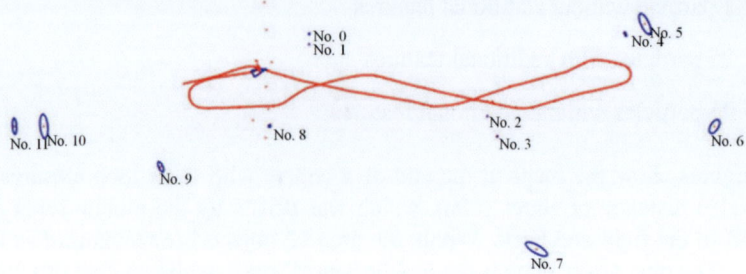

Figure 4.6: Map of 25 particles with additional features.

which all have been recognized properly. In contrast, the result of the second scenario without additional features in Figure 4.5 shows a large offset of the robots' pose to the ground truth and not all landmarks have been properly recognized, but some landmarks have been spuriously instantiated multiple times. Thus, the algorithm did not converge in this case. For example, the right loop could not be successfully closed because landmarks No. 2 and No. 3 were not associated correctly but have been newly instantiated as landmarks No. 9 and No. 10. The same applies for landmarks No. 0 and No. 1. Hence, the additional features improved the data association and loop closure so that the algorithm converges successfully.

The result of scenario 3 (Figure 4.6) is expectedly nearly identical to the result of scenario 1. The landmarks were correctly recognized and the robot is localized quite precisely. The result of scenario 4 (Figure 4.7) shows, that the landmarks were correctly associated and instantiated, but the localization of the mobile robot is set off a little bit compared to the scenarios with additional features (scenarios 1 and 3). One reason for the worse performance of the algorithm without additional features cannot be seen in the figures: Already at the beginning of the course the data association fails several times and cannot correctly associate observations of landmarks No. 0 and No. 1. Thus, additional features also improve the precision of particle filters with a higher number of particles.

The comparisons clearly demonstrate that additional features can improve the quality of the results of the FastSLAM 2.0 mapping algorithm and that less particles are required for robust loop closure. Particularly in case of using only one particle the convergence of the algorithm could only be achieved with additional features.

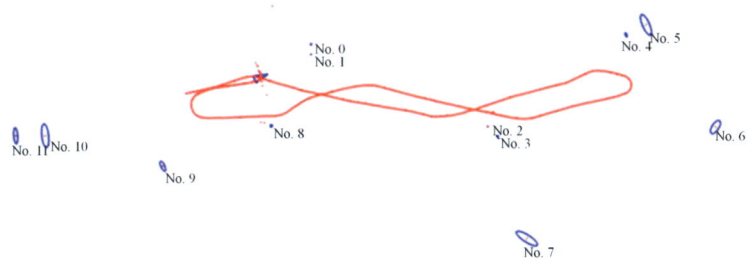

Figure 4.7: Map of 25 particles without additional features.

5 Conclusion & Outlook

A fusion framework has been presented which allows for integration of motion, positioning and attitude sensors combined with ambient sensors by means of multi-sensor fusion and SLAM. An asynchronous EKF-based fusion scheme was designed to integrate unsynchronized sensors with different data rates into the framework. The SLAM algorithm of the fusion framework is based on FastSLAM 2.0 and is capable of using augmented landmark models with additional features for improved data association. This enhances the particle filter with respect to more precise maps or robust convergence with fewer particles.

Future work covers the incorporation of the grid mapping algorithm presented in [Emt10] into the fusion framework in combination with the asynchronous EKF. Further investigations will concentrate on the impact of the sawtooth shaped pattern originating from the asynchronous filter structure on the convergence of the SLAM algorithm.

Bibliography

[CRM00]   Dorin Comaniciu, Visvanathan Ramesh, and Peter Meer. Real-time tracking of non-rigid objects using mean shift. In *Computer Vision and Pattern Recognition, 2000. Proceedings. IEEE Conference*, volume 2, pages 142–149 vol.2, 2000.

[CT91]   Thomas M. Cover and Joy A. Thomas. *Elements of information theory*. Wiley series in telecommunications. Wiley, New York, 1991.

[DWB06a] Hugh Durrant-Whyte and Tim Bailey. Simultaneous localization and mapping: Part I. *IEEE Robotics & Automation Magazine*, 13, June 2006.

[DWB06b] Hugh Durrant-Whyte and Tim Bailey. Simultaneous localization and mapping: Part II. *IEEE Robotics & Automation Magazine*, 13, September 2006.

[EFK08]   Thomas Emter, Christian Frey, and Helge-Björn Kuntze. Multisensorielle Überwachung
           von Liegenschaften durch mobile Roboter - Multi-Sensor Surveillance of Real Estates
           Based on Mobile Robots. *Robotik 2008: Leistungsstand - Anwendungen - Visionen -
           Trends*, June 2008.

[Emt10]   Thomas Emter. Probabilistic Localization and Mapping for Mobile Robots. *Proceedings
           of the 2009 Joint Workshop of Fraunhofer IOSB and Institute for Anthropomatics, Vision
           and Fusion Laboratory*, 2010.

[ESL06]   Pantelis Elinas, Robert Sim, and James J. Little. σSLAM: Stereo Vision SLAM using the
           Rao-Blackwellised Particle Filter and a Novel Mixture Proposal Distribution. In *ICRA*,
           pages 1564–1570, 2006.

[ESP10]   Thomas Emter, Arda Saltoğlu, and Janko Petereit. Multi-Sensor Fusion for Localization
           of a Mobile Robot in Outdoor Environments. *In Proc. VDE-Verlag: ISR/Robotik 2010:
           Visions are Reality.*, June 2010.

[MT07]   Michael Montemerlo and Sebastian Thrun. *FastSLAM - A Scalable Method for the Simul-
           taneous Localization and Mapping Problem in Robotics*, volume 27 of *STAR - Springer
           Tracts in Advanced Robotics*. Springer Verlag, Berlin Heidelberg New York, 2007.

[MTKW03]   Michael Montemerlo, Sebastian Thrun, Daphne Koller, and Ben Wegbreit. Fast-
           SLAM 2.0: An Improved Particle Filtering Algorithm for Simultaneous Localization
           and Mapping that Provably Converges. *Proceedings of the Sixteenth International Joint
           Conference on Artificial Intelligence (IJCAI)*, 2003.

[PHVG02]   Patrick Pérez, Carine Hue, Jaco Vermaak, and Michel Gangnet. Color-Based Probabilistic
           Tracking. In *ECCV '02: Proceedings of the 7th European Conference on Computer
           Vision-Part I*, pages 661–675, London, UK, 2002. Springer-Verlag.

[TBF05]   Sebastian Thrun, Wolfram Burgard, and Dieter Fox. *Probabilistic Robotics*. The MIT
           Press, Cambridge, Massachusetts, 2005.

Anonymization in Intelligent Surveillance Systems

Hauke Vagts

Vision and Fusion Laboratory
Institute for Anthropomatics
Karlsruhe Institute of Technology (KIT), Germany
vagts@kit.edu

Technical Report IES-2010-08

Abstract: Modern surveillance systems collect a massive amount of data. In contrast to conventional systems that store raw sensor material, modern systems take advantage of smart sensors and improvements in image processing. They extract relevant information about the observed objects of interest, which is then stored and processed during the surveillance process. Such high-level information is, e.g., used for situation analysis and can be processed in different surveillance tasks. Modern systems have become powerful, can potentially collect all kind of user information and make it available to any surveillance task. Hence, direct access to the collected high-level data must be prevented. Multiple approaches for anonymization exist, but they do not consider the special requirements of surveillance tasks. This work examines and evaluates existing metrics for anonymization and approaches for anonymization. Even though all kind of data can be collected, position data is still the one with the highest demand. Hence, this work focuses its anonymization and proposes an algorithm that fulfills the requirements for anonymization in surveillance.

1 Introduction

Data protection and (video-) surveillance is an up-to-date topic. Since September 11th, 2001, public space is observed in almost every country. The United Kingdom is still the most observed country and current estimations about installed cameras differ between one million and 4.2 millions, thereof 500,000 in London. These impressive numbers are just estimated, but they point out the need privacy-aware surveillance.

Conventional video systems collect all available information, store it and perform situation analysis on the raw material. With the growing number of cameras and other sensors it is essential to extract required information as soon as possible to reduce the amount of data. In addition, data collected by other sensors (RFID, acoustics, etc.) must be combined with information gained out of the video material. Hence, data must be represented and processed on a high level of abstraction. The abstraction leads to new opportunities for privacy enforcement and a framework for surveillance systems that follows the fair information practice principles [VB09]. If personal data is only stored in conjunction with the corresponding object, anonymization strategies can be applied to the records. It is possible to maximize privacy and efficiently fulfill surveillance tasks at the same time.

Metrics and strategies for anonymization already exist. This work examines to what extent they can be used in the context of surveillance. After a short introduction of the most important metrics for anonymization, metrics useful for surveillance are discussed. In the following the requirements for anonymization in surveillance are pointed out and an algorithm for anonymization of position data in surveillance is presented.

2   Related Work

Multiple architectures for intelligent surveillance systems exist. An overview of them can, e.g., be found in [VV05].

2.1   Intelligent surveillance and privacy

One of the architectures, which is following a task-oriented approach, is NEST [MRV10]. Basically, an architecture of a modern and intelligent surveillance system consists of three parts. These are (smart) sensors that collect all relevant information for a surveillance task, a central storage for data and intelligent modules that process the stored data to fulfill the surveillance task. In NEST data is stored in an object-oriented world model [Bau09], which is a virtual representation of a part of the real world. However, anonymization requires that data is not stored in its raw format (e.g. video), but methods must rather be applied to sets of abstract data, e.g. position data of the observed objects, that contain fused information of all sensors. The anonymization itself is then independent from the data sources.

Existing approaches for privacy in surveillance aim at adding privacy to a the video source itself. This is not sufficient, if different types of sensors are used and systems are working with data on a high level of abstraction. Schiff et al. [SMM+09] propose a system that identifies employees by marks that are applied to the observed objects. However, if the recognition of an objects fails, privacy cannot be enforced. A similar solution is proposed by Senior et al. [SPH$^+$05]. They make use of a "privacy-preserving console" that manipulates a video stream and hides sensitive details. Fleck [SS08b] proposes a more extreme approach that makes use of smart cameras. These cameras do not transmit video data, but rather high-level information, e.g., the position of a human combined with the information, whether he is standing or has fallen to the ground. Fidaleo et al. [FNT04] propose a framework for video surveillance that uses a privacy buffer. According to privacy policies, the information is filtered and presented to the user.

2.2   Metrics for anonymization

Metrics for anonymity have been compared in [AL08] and Kelly2008, but both works do not consider the requirements of surveillance systems. A detailed description of them would go beyond the work. Hence, only k-Anonymity and l-Diversity are roughly introduced.

An explicit identifier is an attribute that can identify an object directly, without other attributes, e.g., an assurance number.

Definition 2 (Explicit Identifier (EI)) Given a population of entities Ω, an entity-specific table $T(A_1, ..., A_m)$, $f_c : \Omega \rightarrow T$ and $f_g : T \rightarrow \Omega'$ with $\Omega \subseteq \Omega'$. An explicit identifier of T, denoted with EI_T, is an attribute $A_i \in \{A_1, ..., A_m\}$ where: $\exists e_i \in \Omega$ such that $f_g(f_c(e_i)[EI_T]) = e_i$.

Besides the EI, also other attributes can be used for identification, but not on there own, they need to be combined with other other attributes.

Definition 3 (Quasi Identifier (QI)) Given a population of entities Ω, an entity-specific table $T(A_1, ..., A_m)$, $f_c : \Omega \rightarrow T$ and $f_g : T \rightarrow \Omega'$ with $\Omega \subseteq \Omega'$. A Quasi-identifier of T, denoted with QI_T, is a set of attributes $\{A_i, ..., A_j\} \subseteq \{A_1, ..., A_m\}$ where: $\exists e_i \in \Omega$ such that $f_g(f_c(e_i)[QI_T]) = e_i$. [Swe02a]
An attribute A_i with $A_i \in QI_T$ is denoted as Quasi Identifier attribute QIA.
The equity of the values in QIA forms an equivalence class over the set of all tuples $t \in T$. A QI equivalence class $QI\text{-}EC$ is a set of tuples $t \in T$ with equivalent QIA values.[WFWP09]

The idea of k-Anonymity is motivated by the observation that QIs can destroy anonymity of a data set. An attacker might use background knowledge to identify objects [SS98]. K-anonymity has weaknesses for numeric values, a solution (k,e)-Anonymity is proposed in [ZKSY07].

Definition 4 (k-Anonymity) Let $T(A_1, ..., A_m)$ be a table and QI_T be the Quasi-identifier associated with it. T is said to satisfy k-Anonymity in relation to QI_T, if and only if each tuple $t \in T$ k-1 other tuples $t_{i_1}, t_{i_2}, ..., t_{i_{k-1}} \in T$ exist, such that $\forall QI \in QI_T : t[QI] = t_{i_1}[QI] = t_{i_2}[QI] = ... = t_{i_{k-1}}[QI]$.

Definition 5 (l-Diversity principle) An equivalence class $QI\text{-}EC$ of a table T is l-diverse, if it contains at least l values for a sensitive attribute SA. A table T is l-diverse, if all of its $QI\text{-}EC$ are l-diverse.

Definition 6 (Entropy l-Diversity) A table T is Entropy l-diverse, if for all $QI\text{-}EC$ of T:

$$-\sum_{s \in SA} p_s \log_2 p_s \geq \log_2(l)$$

with p_s as part of the tuple in the equivalence class with $t[SA] = s$. SA denotes a sensitive attribute.

It follows, because $-x \log_2(x)$ is concave, for Entropy l-Diversity that the entropy of the entire table is at least $\log_2(l)$[MKGV07]. This is a very high requirement, hence Entropy l-Diversity is sometimes too restrictive.

3 Metrics for the anonymization of surveillance

Intelligent surveillance sets a standard for anonymization and the requirements differ depending on the surveillance task. This work focuses on surveillance of a single object.

Position data is still of major importance and has a special characteristic that must be considered during anonymization.

It is important do distinguish between *sensitive* and *non-sensitive* attributes: sensitive attributes of a specific object must be hidden from attackers. It can be estimated that most attributes are QIs. In most work [SS98, MKGV07, ZKSY07], QIs and sensitive attributes are considered not to be disjunct. This assumption cannot be made in the field of surveillance.

3.1 Anonymization of position data

As mentioned above, position data is a sensitive attribute and a QI. In addition, it has its own semantic, which does not allow the use of regular methods for anonymization of numeric attributes. The information content does not change, if the position is altered by a few inches or yards. Hence, position data must be treated in a special manner.

A lot of research has been done in the field of Location Based Services (LBS), but surveillance is a different scenario. In LBS, queries with anonymized position data are send to the LBS service providers. In surveillance, the observers send queries to the systems. Thus, the answer of the system must be anonymized instead and new concepts for surveillance are needed.

In general, k-Anonymity and l-Diversity can be used for the anonymization of position data. It is however essential to consider the special characteristic, respectively, to adapt metrics.

K-Anonymity seems to be a reasonable metric, which was used by Gruteser and Grunwald [GG03] for position data for the first time. A position date must be valid, i. e., must be imprecise enough, for at least k objects. This does not only fulfill the k-Anonymity requirement, but also k-Anonymity, which is different to LBS. Moreover, it matches the original definition of the Anonymity Set. Bettini et al. [BWJ05] follow a similar k-Anonymity approach. They make use of spatio-temporal patterns, which are declared to be identifying for k-Anonymity and at least k persons must be within a pattern. A disadvantage is that these patterns are not known in advance when used in practice.

However, k-Anonymity is not appropriate for position data. If many people are at a small spot, the semantic information of each position is the same, i.e., all tuples of the QI's equivalence class have the same sensitive attribute and a known user attack can be performed. An extension to (k,e)-Anonymity reduces the problems, but the selection of e is random and is based on a global definition, which does not consider the semantic differences.

A solution is to decouple the aspects of being a QI and a sensitive attribute for position data. For this reason the attribute *region* is introduced, as well as a function f_h of a position (x,y) to a region r: $f_h : (x,y) \rightarrow r$. Region contains now the sensitive information and the exact arrangement is depending on the specific context. As a consequence, position data is a QI only. The differentiation of the semantic information is performed in the attribute region.

Two metrics can be used to measure the differentiation of the sensitive aspect, l-Diversity and t-Closeness. T-Closeness is based on distributions and is therefore matching the requirements for anonymization metrics, but has several disadvantages when used in surveillance. When observing a single object exactly one equivalence class, which contains the object, is created. Hence, t-Closeness is trivially fulfilled. Even when collecting data for statistical investigation with multiple objects, t-Closeness cannot be used, unless a critical amount of data is collected. Moreover the measure of distance is depending on the attribute, hence it cannot be flexibly used for different attributes.

The last remaining metric is l-Diversity. Here, a trade-off between the level of anonymization and usability of the data can be made. The highest anonymization with the best theoretical base is provided by Entropy l-Diversity and is used in the following.

4   An Approach for Anonymization in Surveillance

After determining satisfying metrics it must be specified, which methods for anonymization are sufficient to achieve a specific level of anonymity.

4.1   Time

In existing work, the factor time has not been considered. However, time has an extensive impact on anonymization in surveillance. It can be used in three dimensions.

At first as a *temporal variance* Δz. If the date of the observation is published with reduced accuracy, the position can be published with a higher precision in return, while the anonymity is still at the same level.

Second as a latency λ, i. e., the time a surveillance system can wait until it provides an answer to a query. More future data can be used for anonymization, when allowing a latency.

At last, as the maximum frequency for requests ϕ. If it is too low, an attacker can trace an object just by sending requests.

4.2   Grid versus Graph

Two approaches exist for anonymization of position data. Either the observed area can be split into a grid, or a graph can be used. In case of the latter, nodes represent the objects and the (weighted) edges represent the distance between them. When using a grid, it is the objective to find the smallest set of neighboring fields that fulfills the anonymity requirements. When using graphs a clique problem must be solved, which may result in a bad performance. However, even if a grid approach is not optimal, it has performance advantages and it can also be chosen in what direction the selected region is extended on the grid, which makes it more difficult to find an object in a raster field.

4.3   Finding a suitable algorithm

When following the grid-based approach, an algorithm can either work top-down or bottom-up. Grutser and Grundwald propose in [GG03] a hierarchical top-down algorithm that is based on a Quad Tree Algorithm. In each step the segment, which contains the object, is picked and is split in four squares of the same size. The algorithm stops, if the number of objects in a segment is $< k$. The position is then replaced by the segment that was split. No matter whether top-down or bottom-up, when using a hierarchical algorithm, the accuracy is drastically reduced with each step, and the way of anonymization is thus designating.

A compromise between speed (grid-based method) and accuracy is the approach from Bamba and Lui [BL07]. Furthermore, it is the only approach that considers l-Diversity and k-Anonymity. The area that is released instead of a position must contain $k − 1$ other objects and must span over l regions. The algorithm is also based on a grid, but in each step only one segment of the grid is added to the released region (north, east, west, south). The algorithm offers the option to separate k-Anonymity, which is related to the objects and l-Diversity, which is related to the segments of the released region. Hence, the attribute region is not allocated to positions, instead it is related to segments of the grid. This results in many advantages:

- If k-Anonymity and l-Diversity are both related to objects, k is high on the one side and l is low on the other side. This effect is prevented.

- When observing a single object, l-Diversity ensures that the region is only related to the observed object. No prediction for other objects can be made by considering the borders.

- As A-anonymity and l-Diversity are decoupled, both parameters can be changed independently and according to the scenario. Both metrics can be weighted differently.

- The sensitivity of regions does not depend on the number of people that are in it.

- The approach can be extended to consider multiple levels of sensitivity for different regions.

The named separation can only be performed, because a grid-based approach has been chosen. A trade-off between performance and accuracy can be achieved by setting the density of the grid and choosing the algorithm for extension of the region. A top-down approach is faster, if the size of the final segment is close to the size of the observed area. Such a region only contains a minimum of information and is not useful in practice. Hence, a bottom-up approach should be chosen.

As shown above, time is an important factor. Thus, an algorithm should be extended with another dimension. The grid then consists of cubes instead of squares. It must also be considered that time has only an influence on k-Anonymity and not on l-Diversity. This leads to three QoS parameters that should be used. The maximal temporal variance Δz_{max}, the maximal latency λ_{max} and the maximal frequency for requests ϕ_{max}.

4.4 Faked positions

Positions of non existing objects can be used to anonymize data. Kideo et al. [KYS05] and Xiao et al. [XMX08] propose approaches. In Kido's approach, the user creates several dummies. In the field of surveillance, the surveillance system must perform this task. Both approaches are based on coincidence. Hence they do not consider the semantic information related to the observer area. This makes it easy to detect faked positions, if one object is observed for a longer time. In addition, the usage of an observation itself can be put into question, if the system contains wrong information.

4.5 Location tracking

Gruteser and Lui [GL04] identified location tracking, i. e., tracking the path of a person, as a privacy concern. Their proposed solution does not go far beyond the principles of k-Anonymity and l-diversity. A limitation of the request frequency (bounding rate), as proposed, seems reasonable. In [BW09] Belle and Waldvogel take advantage of the crossing of paths to change IDs of objects. This and other approaches, e.g. [BS03], are limited by a low density. Hoh and Gruteser [HG05] weaken this limitation by releasing position data with a lower accuracy, if paths come closer (Path Confusion). An extension of this approach is Path Cloaking [HGXA07].

However, in surveillance the substitution of IDs is only an option, if an object is not observed for a longer period. A grid-based approach already implies a stronger crossing of paths. Thus, further anonymization is not required. It is important to

---

Algorithm 5.1 Position Privacy

Require: $\{ID, z\}, \{\delta_{max}, \Delta z_{max}, \lambda\}, \{k, l\}$
Ensure: $\{[x_1, x_2], [y_1, y_2], [z_1, z_2]\}$
  1: $z_2 \leftarrow$ random$(z - \Delta z_{max}, z + \min \Delta z_{max}, \lambda)$
  2: $x_2 \leftarrow$ xPosOf(ID, z_2)
  3: $y_2 \leftarrow$ yPosOf(ID, z_2)
  4: C $\leftarrow$ getCuboidOf(x_2, y_2, z_2)
  5: C $\leftarrow$ FUNCTION_FIND_K_CUBOID
     (C, z, $\{\delta_{max}, \Delta z_{max}, \lambda\}$, k)
  6: C $\leftarrow$ FUNCTION_FIND_L_CUBOID
     (C, δ_{max}, l)
  7: **return** C.XYZ

---

choose a bounding rate ϕ_{max}, which depends on the average moving speed of objects in the observed area. In general, it can be said that an object should be able to change regions or meet another object.

5 An algorithm for position data

As shown above, an algorithm that fulfills the requirements for anonymization of position data in surveillance should follow the approach from Bamba and Liu [BL07]. The existing approach must be extended with the temporal dimension and the parameters k and l are to be handled separately. The algorithm determines a k-anonymous and l-diverse space-time cuboid.

The Position Privacy Algorithm determines in lines 1 to 4 the initial cuboid C for the anonymization. To extend the cuboid in the temporal dimension, a starting point must be chosen randomly out of the valid time interval. The anonymization after k (line 5) and l (line 6) itself takes place in two separated functions.

At first, the cuboid is extended to contain at least k objects (Algorithm 5.2, line 1). This is done within the restrictions given by the variables δ_{max}, Δz_{max} and λ (line 2). In the lines 5 to 18, the increment of k for the extension of the cuboid is determined in the different directions and dimensions (if an extension is possible). In the last step the extension that leads to the highest increment of k is chosen (lines 19 to 23). This is repeated until the cuboid complies with the k value.

To achieve l-Diversity for the location, the cuboid must contain fields of the grid in a suitable diversity. The approach is similar to the k value. Time is not considered,

---

Algorithm 5.2 FUNCTION_FIND_K_CUBOID

Require: Ausgangsquader C, z, $\{\delta_{max}, \Delta z_{max}, \lambda\}$, k
Ensure: Ergebnisquader C
 1: **while** C.kValue < k **do**
 2:   **if** C.sizeX + gridElementSizeX $\leq \delta_{max}$ = **false**
      and C.sizeY + gridElementSizeY $\leq \delta_{max}$ = **false**
      and C.sizeZ + gridElementSizeZ $\leq \Delta z_{max}$ = **false then**
 3:     **return** PrivacyNotPossibleError
 4:   **end if**
 5:   **if** C.sizeX + gridElementSizeX $\leq \delta_{max}$ **then**
 6:     cuboidExtension(S) $\leftarrow$ C $\cup$ southern 3D row
 7:     cuboidExtension(N) $\leftarrow$ C $\cup$ northern 3D row
 8:   **end if**
 9:   **if** C.sizeY + gridElementSizeY $\leq \delta_{max}$ **then**
10:     cuboidExtension(E) $\leftarrow$ C $\cup$ eastern row
11:     cuboidExtension(W) $\leftarrow$ C $\cup$ western row
12:   **end if**
13:   **if** C.sizeZ + gridElementSizeZ $\leq \Delta z_{max}$ **then**
14:     **if** C.upperZ + gridElementSizeZ $\leq z + \lambda$ **then**
15:       cuboidExtension(F) $\leftarrow$ C $\cup$ 3D row in future
16:     **end if**
17:     cuboidExtension(P) $\leftarrow$ C $\cup$ 3D row in the past
18:   **end if**
19:   **for all** $d \in \{S, N, E, W, F, P\}$ **do**
20:     **if** C.kValue < cuboidExtension(d).kValue **then**
21:       C $\leftarrow$ cuboidExtension(d)
22:     **end if**
23:   **end for**
24: **end while**

---

as the room layout is static. Each field of the grid is assigned to the region ID of the region, which it covers for the most part.

6 Conclusion and future work

A lot of research has been done in the area of privacy and anonymization. Intelligent surveillance systems can imperil privacy. Hence, this work has analyzed the suitability of existing metrics and approaches for anonymization. Each observable

---

Algorithm 5.3 FUNCTION_FIND_L_CUBOID

Require: start cubiod C, δ_{max}, l
Ensure: result cuboid C
1: **while** C.LValue $<$ l **do**
2:    **if** C.sizeX + gridElementSizeX $\leq \delta_{max}$ = **false**
      and C.sizeY + gridElementSizeY $\leq \delta_{max}$ = **false then**
3:       **return** PrivacyNotPossibleError
4:    **end if**
5:    **if** C.sizeX + gridElementSizeX $\leq \delta_{max}$ **then**
6:       cuboidExtensionS ← C ∪ 3DZeile southern 3D row
7:       cuboidExtensionN ← C ∪ 3DZeile northern 3D row
8:    **end if**
9:    **if** C.sizeY + gridElementSizeY $\leq \delta_{max}$ **then**
10:      cuboidExtensionE ← C ∪ 3DZeile eastern 3D row
11:      cuboidExtensionW ← C ∪ 3DZeile western 3D row
12:   **end if**
13:   **for all** $d \in \{S, N, E, W\}$ **do**
14:      **if** C.LValue $<$ cuboidExtension(d).LValue **then**
15:         C ← cuboidExtension(d)
16:      **end if**
17:   **end for**
18: **end while**

---

attribute can result in privacy issues, but the position is the most important one. Thus an algorithm for anonymization of position data in intelligent surveillance has been proposed.

The anonymization of other attributes is currently being analyzed and an approach is being developed. Currently, the presented approach for position data is implemented in a demonstration system of the NEST architecture. In future, the system must then be tested under real time conditions.

Bibliography

[AL08]   Christer Andersson and Reine Lundin. On the fundamentals of anonymity metrics. In *The Future of Identity in the Information Society*, volume 262, page 325. Springer, 2008.

[BEVB09] Alexander Bauer, Thomas Emter, Hauke Vagts, and Jürgen Beyerer. Object oriented world model for surveillance systems. In Peter Elsner, editor, *Future Security: 4th Security Research Conference*, page 339. Fraunhofer Verlag, 2009.

[BL07]   Bhuvan Bamba and Ling Liu. Privacygrid: Supporting anonymous location queries in mobile environments. Technical report, GIT-CERCS, 2007.

[BS03]   Alastair Beresford and Frank Stajano. Location privacy in pervasive computing. *IEEE Pervasive Computing*, 2(1):46, January 2003.

[BW09]   Sebastian Kay Belle and Marcel Waldvogel. Pathforge:: Faithful anonymization of movement data. Technical Report KN-06-03-2009-DISY-01, University of Konstanz - DISY, 2009.

[BWJ05]   Claudio Bettini, X. Sean Wang, and Sushil Jajodia. Protecting privacy against location-based personal identification. In *Proceedings of the 2nd VLDB Workshop on Secure Data Management*, page 185. Springer-Verlag, 2005.

[CT91]   Thomas M. Cover and Joy A. Thomas. *Elements of Information Theory*. Wiley, New York, 1991.

[EGB08]   Thomas Emter, Ioana Gheta, and Jürgen Beyerer. Object oriented environment model for video surveillance systems. In Klaus Thoma, editor, *Future security: 3rd Security Research Conference*, pages 315–320. Fraunhofer IRB Verlag, September 2008.

[FNT04]   Douglas A. Fidaleo, Hoang-Anh Nguyen, and Mohan Trivedi. The networked sensor tapestry (nest): a privacy enhanced software architecture for interactive analysis of data in video-sensor networks. In *VSSN '04: Proceedings of the ACM 2nd international workshop on Video surveillance & sensor networks*, page 46, New York, NY, USA, 2004. ACM.

[GG03]   Marco Gruteser and Dirk Grunwald. Anonymous usage of location-based services through spatial and temporal cloaking. In *MobiSys '03: Proceedings of the 1st international conference on Mobile systems, applications and services*, page 31, New York, NY, USA, 2003. ACM.

[GL04]   Marco Gruteser and Xuan Liu. Protecting privacy in continuous location-tracking applications. *IEEE Security & Privacy*, 2:28, 2004.

[HG05]   Baik Hoh and M. Gruteser. Protecting location privacy through path confusion. In *Proceedings of the 1st International Conference on Security and Privacy for Emerging Areas in Communications Networks SecureComm 2005*, page 194, 2005.

[HGXA07]   Baik Hoh, Marco Gruteser, Hui Xiong, and Ansaf Alrabady. Preserving privacy in gps traces via uncertainty-aware path cloaking. In *CCS '07: Proceedings of the 14th ACM conference on Computer and communications security*, page 161, New York, NY, USA, 2007. ACM.

[KYS05]   Hidetoshi Kido, Yutaka Yanagisawa, and Tetsuji Satoh. An anonymous communication technique using dummies for location-based services. In *Proceedings of the International Conference on Pervasive Services ICPS '05*, page 88, 2005.
            B Lo, J. Sun, and S.A. Velastin. Fusing visual and audio information in a distributed intelligent surveillance system for public transport systems.

[MKGV07]   Ashwin Machanavajjhala, Daniel Kifer, Johannes Gehrke, and Muthuramakrishnan Venkitasubramaniam. L-diversity: Privacy beyond k-anonymity. *ACM Transactions on Knowledge Discovery from Data*, 1(1):3, 2007.

[MRV10]   Jürgen Moßgraber, Frank Reinert, and Hauke Vagts. An architecture for a task-oriented surveillance system – a service and event based approach. In *Proc. Fifth International Conference on Systems ICONS*, 11–16 April 2010.

[SMM+09]   Jeremy Schiff, Marci Meingast, Deirdre K. Mulligan, Shankar Sastry, and Ken Goldberg. Respectful cameras: Detecting visual markers in real-time to address privacy concerns. In *Protecting Privacy in Video Surveillance*, page 65. Springer, 2009.

[SPH$^+$05]   Andrew W. Senior, Sharath Pankanti, Arun Hampapur, Lisa M. G. Brown, Ying li Tian, Ahmet Ekin, Jonathan H. Connell, Chiao-Fe Shu, and Max Lu. Enabling video privacy through computer vision. *IEEE Security & Privacy*, 3(3):50, 2005.

[SS98]   Pierangela Samarati and Latanya Sweeney. Protecting privacy when disclosing information: k-anonymity and its enforcement through generalization and suppression. Technical report, Computer Science Laboratory, SRI International, 1998.

[SS08b]   Fleck Sven and Wolfgang Strasser. Smart camera based monitoring system and its application to assisted living. *Proceedings of the IEEE*, 96(10):1698, 2008.

[Swe02a]   Latanya Sweeney. Achieving k-anonymity privacy protection using generalization and suppression. *International Journal of Uncertainty, Fuzziness and Knowledge-Based Systems*, 10, 2002.

[VB09]   Hauke Vagts and Jürgen Beyerer. Security and privacy challenges in modern surveillance systems. In Peter Elsner, editor, *Future Security: 4th Security Research Conference*, page 94. Fraunhofer Verlag, October 2009.

[VV05]   M. Valera and S. A. Velastin. Intelligent distributed surveillance systems: a review. *IEEE Proceedings -Vision, Image and Signal Processing*, 152(2):192, 2005.

[WFWP09]   Raymond Chi-Wing Wong, Ada Wai-Chee Fu, Ke Wang, and Jian Pei. Anonymization-based attacks in privacy-preserving data publishing. *ACM Transactions on Database Systems*, 34(2):1, 2009.

[XMX08]   Zhen Xiao, Xiaofeng Meng, and Jianliang Xu. Quality aware privacy protection for location-based services. In *Advances in Databases: Concepts, Systems and Applications*, volume 4443 of *Lecture Notes in Computer Science*, page 434. Springer, 2008.

[ZKSY07]   Qing Zhang, Nick Koudas, Divesh Srivastava, and Ting Yu. Aggregate query answering on anonymized tables. In *Proceedings of the 23rd International Conference on Data Engineering*, page 116, Los Alamitos, CA, USA, 2007. IEEE Computer Society.

Natural Gaze Behavior During Human-Computer Interaction under Varying Mental Models

Thomas Bader

Vision and Fusion Laboratory
Institute for Anthropomatics
Karlsruhe Institute of Technology (KIT), Germany
thomas.bader@kit.edu

Technical Report IES-2010-09

Abstract: Natural gaze behavior during human-computer interaction provides valuable information about user's cognitive processes and intentions. Including it as an additional input modality therefore provides great potential to improve human-computer interaction. However, the relations between natural gaze behavior and underlying cognitive processes still is unexplored to a large extend. In this paper we identify and characterize major factors influencing natural gaze behavior during human-computer interaction with a focus on the role of user's mental model about the interactive system. In a user study we investigate how natural gaze behavior can be influenced by interaction design and point out implications for usage of gaze as additional modality in gaze-based interfaces.

1 Introduction

In general there are two ways to incorporate eye gaze as an input modality into multimodal human-computer interfaces. The first way is to force the user to consciously look at certain locations in order to trigger actions. An example for such approaches is eye typing, which has been studied for decades [MR02]. Eye gaze is used directly as pointing device and actions are mostly triggered by dwell times, which determine how long a certain object needs to be looked at until it is activated (e.g., a key on a virtual keyboard). The biggest advantage of such approaches is that they are easy and straightforward to implement and do not require analysis of complex gaze behavior. Especially for people with severe disabilities such input techniques often provide the only way for interacting with visual interfaces. However, for most people conscious and direct usage of gaze as input modality is very unnatural and hence requires training and/or induces cognitive workload [JK03].

The second way to use eye gaze as input modality is to interpret natural gaze behavior during human-computer interaction while using another modality as primary input modality. Promising examples for such interaction techniques are presented in [HMR03] and [ZMI99]. In both approaches natural gaze behavior is analyzed and the user is not forced to diverge from that natural behavior for interaction purposes. *iDict* [HMR03] analyzes the duration of fixations while the user reads a text in a foreign language and automatically provides a translation of the fixated word if a longer fixation is detected. In the approach "Manual And Gaze Input Cascaded (MAGIC) Pointing" [ZMI99] the mouse pointer is placed close to the currently fixated object in order to eliminate a large portion of the cursor movement. Both approaches do not use gaze directly as pointing or input device, but interpret gaze data in the context of the task (reading, pointing).

In general, the second approach has the advantage that valuable information contained in natural gaze behavior can be used for improving human-computer interaction. Additionally, the user has not to consciously diverge from natural gaze behavior, which would require training and would induce cognitive workload.

However, natural gaze behavior is highly complex and many different influencing factors have to be considered for appropriate interpretation. Especially the task and the experience of users have been shown to be key factors influencing natural gaze behavior [JWBF01, LM00].

In this paper we characterize different influences on natural gaze behavior during an object manipulation task, which was designed especially for that purpose. Additionally, we point out their implications for designing gaze-based multimodal interaction techniques.

2   User Study

2.1   Task and Apparatus

The task to be solved by participants is designed based upon a basic object manipulation task as it is common in many GUIs, where the visual representation of an object has to be moved from one location to another on a display. However, in order to being able to investigate effects of user's mental model on natural gaze behavior in a controlled way, we designed the mapping between input and system reaction in an unusual way not expected by the users. This ensures that all users have the same level of knowledge about the system at the beginning of the experiment and can be considered as novice users. Additionally, we are able to monitor changes in natural gaze behavior with increasing knowledge about the system.

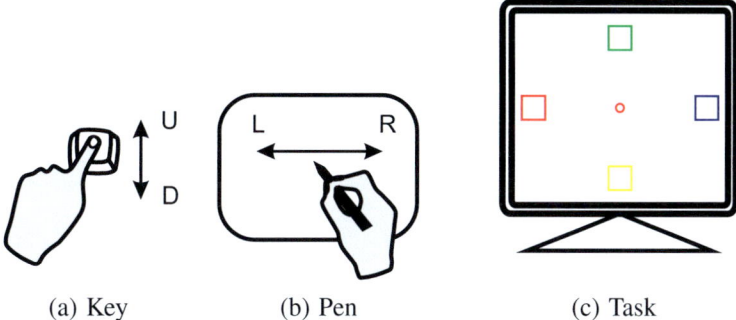

(a) Key   (b) Pen   (c) Task

Figure 2.1: Input devices and task.

As input devices we use one single key of a keyboard (Figure 2.1(a)) and a pen tablet, while only horizontal movements of the pen on the tablet are interpreted by the system (Figure 2.1(b)). The task is illustrated in Figure 2.1(c). A colored point that initially is displayed at the center of the display has to be moved to one of the four squares, which has the same color.

For manipulating the object position we implemented two different interaction techniques. The mapping between inputs and system state transitions (position of the point) is graphically illustrated for the first technique in Figure 2.2(a). For example, a horizontal movement of the pen to the right (R) causes a movement of the point to the upper right if the key is not pressed (U) and to the lower right if the key is pressed (D). For the second technique the object is expanded as shown in Figure 2.2(b) left as soon as the pen touches the tablet. Then the mapping is the same as for the first technique, while the object starts to move from the respective position in expanded state.

In preliminary experiments with Technique1 we observed that experience of users seems to have significant influence on proactivity of gaze behavior. Novice users, for example, mainly directed visual attention towards the initial object position at the beginning of the task. In contrast, expert users predominantly anticipated future object positions. With Technique2 we want to investigate whether it is possible to induce more proactive gaze behavior, especially for novice users, by avoiding visual feedback in proximity to the initial object position right before the first object movement.

The size of the display is 33,7 × 27 cm with a resolution of 1280 × 1024 pixels. Eye-gaze of the users was captured during task execution by a Tobii 1750 tracking device.

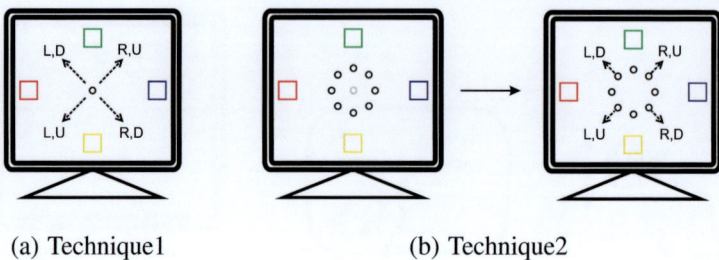

(a) Technique1   (b) Technique2

Figure 2.2: Mapping of input to system actions for different interaction techniques.

2.2 Participants

Since we want to investigate effects of mental model building on natural gaze behavior we chose a between-subjects design to avoid any prior knowledge of participants about the task or interaction techniques. We had two groups with 10 participants each. Participants were between 21 and 32 years old and did not know anything about the experiment, except that their gaze is measured.

2.3 Procedure

The experiment was organized in two phases $A1$ and $A2$ with 40 runs each. Every run consists of moving an object from its initial position at the center of the screen to the respective target area.

Between the two phases users were asked to fill in a questionnaire in order to capture their mental model. However, in this paper we focus on analysis of objective data only and analysis of subjective data obtained from the questionnaire will be reported in future papers.

In order to allow for a more detailed analysis of the temporal development of objective measures in subsequent sections the two phases are further divided into $A1/1$, $A1/2$, $A2/1$ and $A2/2$ with 20 runs each.

3 Results

Most interesting from the interaction design perspective are gaze movements that occur before any object movement. In the following we denote such gaze data as

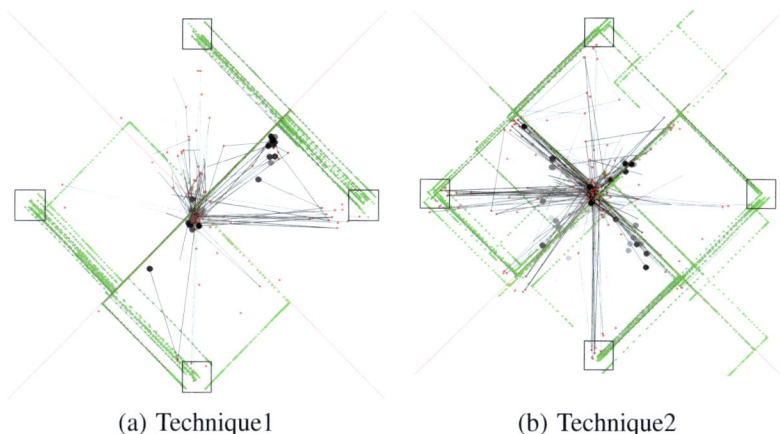

(a) Technique1   (b) Technique2

Figure 3.1: Data captured for different interaction techniques during phase $A1$ from one user for each technique.

pre-object gaze data and *pre-object fixations*, respectively. Such data allows for estimating user's intentions previous to any input made by the user. Therefore in this work we mainly focus on the analysis of such data.

In Figure 3.1 a plot of object- and gaze-data during the first 40 runs is shown for each of the two interaction techniques for one user. Green dots represent object positions, small red dots connected by gray lines are pre-object fixations and larger dots, colored from gray to black, indicate the last pre-object fixation for each run. The red diagonal lines indicate possible movement directions of the object from its initial position and were not shown to the users during the experiments.

For the first interaction technique two things can easily be seen from Figure 3.1. First, the preferred policy for solving the task seems to be first moving the object along the diagonal line reaching from the lower left to the upper right (D_1, see Figure 3.2(b) for definition). This corresponds to an input sequence where the key is not pressed (U) during the first phase. Second, fixations are mainly located at three different positions on the screen. While the last fixation before the first object movement is either located at the initial position of the object or along the preferred diagonal axis D_1, other fixations also can be observed towards the target area.

Both observations in average can be confirmed for all participants. In Figure 3.2(a) the distribution of tasks, which were solved by moving the object first along the

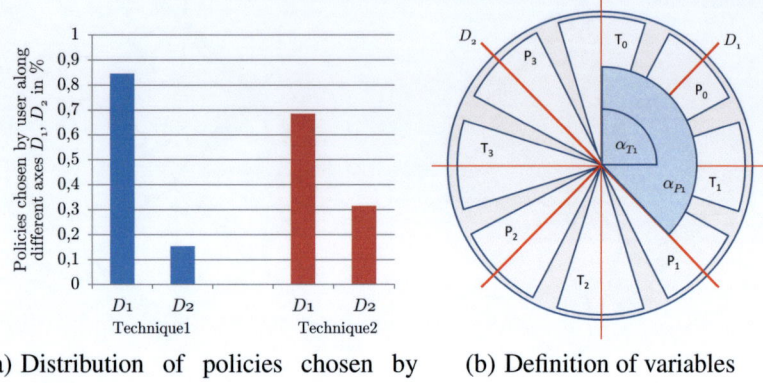

(a) Distribution of policies chosen by   (b) Definition of variables
users

Figure 3.2: Evaluation of user input.

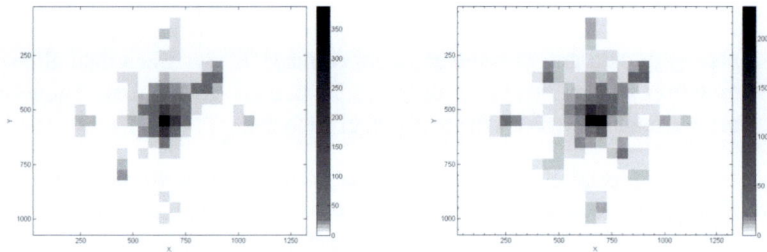

(a) Pre-object fixations for technique1   (b) Pre-object fixations for technique2

Figure 3.3: Distribution of pre-object fixations.

different axes D_1 and D_2, is shown for both interaction techniques. A clear majority of the users first moved the object along D_1 for both interaction techniques. However, the policies with first movement direction along axis D_2 was used more often for Technique2 (31.5 %) compared to Technique1 (15.38 %) .

This difference in interaction behavior also shows an effect on pre-object gaze behavior. Figure 3.3 shows the distribution of positions of all pre-object fixations for all users and tasks for the two interaction techniques. Note that the color scale at the lower end is not linear in order to improve the visibility of the plot. Both plots show that most pre-object fixation are centered around the initial position of the object. However, also a significant amount of fixations can be observed at different locations on the screen, which are related to the task. Except from the initial object position for Technique1 fixations are mainly distributed along axis D_1 or are located at the target areas. The plot for Technique2 in Figure 3.3(b) shows also fixations along axis D_2 and in general more proactive fixations. For further task related characterization of fixations we use two features:

- *Distance d from initial object position*
- *Direction α of vector between fixation and object position*

Along d fixations are classified in *proactive fixations* ($d > r_p$) and *reactive fixations* ($d \leq r_p$). While reactive fixations indicate attention allocation towards the current state of the object, proactive fixations are induced by mental planing activity for solving the task or anticipation of future system states. In order to distinguish between proactive fixations which are directed towards one of the target areas $T_0, ..., T_3$ and those directed towards a certain policy $P_0, ..., P_3$ we evaluate α for every proactive fixation regarding the underlying target for attention allocation A as follows:

$$A = \begin{cases} T_i & \text{if } |\alpha_{T_i} - \alpha| < \alpha_{max} \\ P_i & \text{if } |\alpha_{P_i} - \alpha| < \alpha_{max} \end{cases},$$

where α_{T_i} and α_{P_i} denote directions of vectors between the initial object position and the corresponding target T_i or first movement direction of policy P_i (see Figure 3.2(b)).

The thresholds $r_p = 100$ and $\alpha_{max} = 20°$ are chosen based on the analysis of gaze data captured during the experiments.

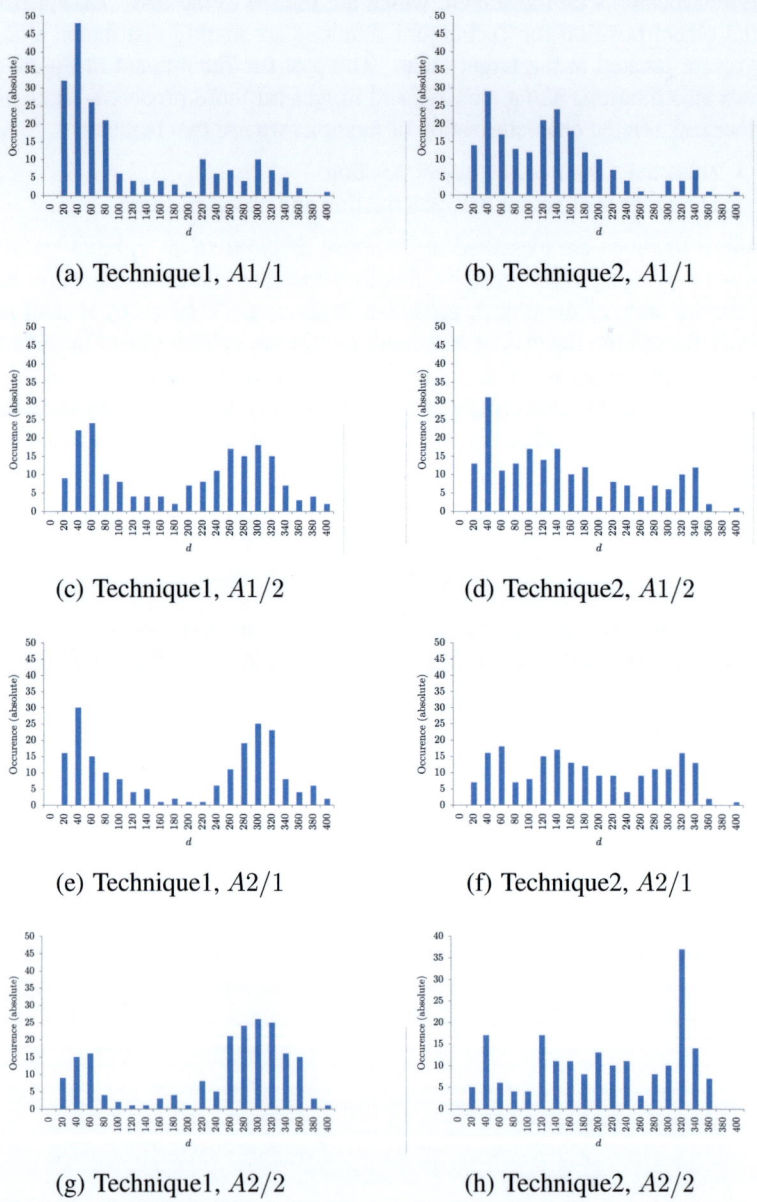

(a) Technique1, $A1/1$

(b) Technique2, $A1/1$

(c) Technique1, $A1/2$

(d) Technique2, $A1/2$

(e) Technique1, $A2/1$

(f) Technique2, $A2/1$

(g) Technique1, $A2/2$

(h) Technique2, $A2/2$

Figure 3.4: Development of distribution of d over time for both interaction techniques.

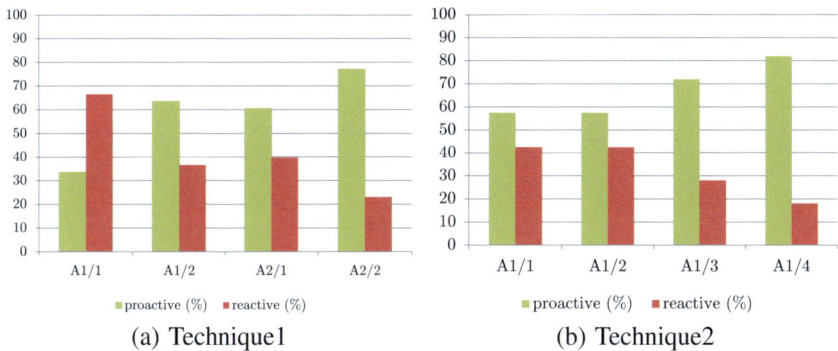

(a) Technique1   (b) Technique2

Figure 3.5: Development of ratio between proactive and reactive fixations with increasing knowledge about the system

In Figure 3.4 the distributions of d for the last pre-object fixation are shown for the different phases of the experiment. The plots show both, significant influence of growing experience on the location of the last pre-object fixation and significant differences between the two interaction techniques. For Technique1 initially most of the fixations are located closely around the object position and hence are classified as reactive fixations. For phase $A1/1$ (first 20 runs) with Technique1 66.5% of all last pre-object fixations are reactive and 33.5% are proactive. In contrast, during phase $A1/1$ with Technique2 57.5% of the fixations are proactive and 42.5% reactive. The development of the ratio of proactive and reactive fixations over all phases of the experiment is shown in Figure 3.5. On average the ratio for Technique1 is 58.625/41.375 (proactive/reactive) and 67.25/32.75 for Technique2.

As already mentioned above we further analyze pre-object proactive fixations regarding the underlying target of visual attention. Figure 3.6 shows the distribution of A over all possible targets $T_0, ..., T_3, P_0, ..., P_3$ for all last pre-object fixations. The different areas represent the categories as defined above by r_p and α_{max} and are colored according to the occurrence of fixations within the corresponding area on the screen.

For both techniques the number of last pre-object fixations that occur on the object are reduced from phase $A1$ to phase $A2$ of the experiment almost to the half. For Technique2 approximately 10% less fixations are made on the object for both of the two phases compared to Technique1. In all plots among all policies $P_0, ..., P_3$ a clear majority of fixations can be found along policy P_0. While for Technique1 proactive fixations are mainly distributed along axis D_1 (policies P_0 and P_2), for

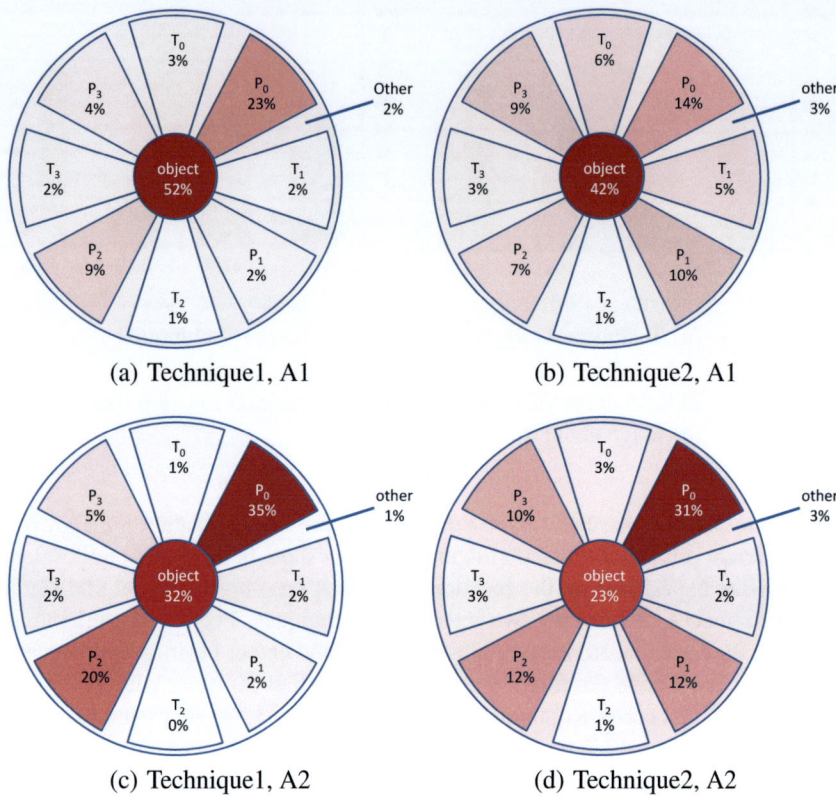

(a) Technique1, A1   (b) Technique2, A1

(c) Technique1, A2   (d) Technique2, A2

Figure 3.6: Distribution of target of visual attention of last fixation before first object movement for all users and tasks

Technique2 an almost equal distribution over policies P_1, P_2 and P_3 can be observed. This corresponds to findings illustrated in Figure 3.2(a), where similar differences in policies chosen by the users for solving the task are depicted.

4 Discussion

The results in the previous section show that both independent variables we used in our experiment, namely the interaction technique and the experience of users, have significant influence on natural gaze behavior during human-computer interaction.

For both interaction techniques increasing experience of the user with the system resulted in a highly increased number of proactive fixations with increasing orientation towards policies at the expense of decreasing orientation towards target areas. This development can be explained from an information theoretical perspective. The more knowledge the user has about the dynamics of the system the less new information can be acquired by reactive fixations on the initial object position and by observing the first object movement, respectively. If future expected object positions can be accurately predicted by acquired knowledge based on inputs, it is more efficient to directly draw visual attention towards expected future object states, e.g., in order to support accurate positioning of the object at the intended target location. The decreasing orientation of visual attention towards target areas can be explained by the same effect. Increasing knowledge of the location of certain target areas decreases the value of directing visual attention towards the target area.

When comparing gaze data for the different interaction techniques a significantly increased number of proactive fixations and a slight increase in fixations directed towards the target areas can be observed for Technique2. Additionally, while for Technique1 the policies along axis D_1 are predominantly chosen by the users and proactive fixations are mainly distributed along this axis, with Technique2 the policies along axis D_2 are chosen significantly more often and fixations along $P_1, ..., P_3$ are almost equally distributed. Obviously, the different ways how visual feedback is organized for the different interaction techniques not only influences natural gaze behavior, but also human decision processes and task solution strategies.

For both interaction techniques and independent from experience of users by far most of the proactive fixations are made along P_0. Participants' gaze behavior seems to be more proactive when moving the object from the left to the right than into the opposite direction. Possible explanations for that bias could be found by further examination of influence of writing direction, handedness or other cultural and individual factors.

For designing interaction based on natural gaze behavior the observations above have different implications. Natural gaze behavior is influenced by many different factors. These factors can either be used for adapting human-computer interaction or they prevent the development of consistent interaction techniques due to their dependency from uncontrollable and varying environmental conditions (e.g., experience of users, different cultural background).

In this user study we identified 4 classes of major factors influencing natural gaze behavior during object manipulation and characterized their influence in proactivity and direction of visual attention:

1. task / goal
2. policy / strategy
3. experience of users / state of mental model
4. visual feedback / interaction technique

We further identified further phenomenons, which probably could be explained by individual differences among users and/or cultural factors (e.g., increased proactivity for P_0).

The first two factors can be used for estimating user's intention from gaze data. However, their visibility in gaze data in the form of proactive fixations towards a certain task related location on the display depends to a large extend on the third factor, namely the state of user's mental model. This fact in principal can be used for estimating user's experience and adaption of interaction. However, if the main goal is to design a consistent gaze-based interaction technique for novice and experienced users the goal would be to minimize the influence of experience on natural gaze behavior. According to the results of our study one option would be to use the fourth factor and to design interaction techniques that reduce this influence as demonstrated with Technique2. However, as we showed in the results section there still remain variances in natural gaze behavior, which probably can be explained by individual differences among users or cultural factors. These factors have also to be considered when interpreting natural gaze behavior and designing appropriate system reactions.

5   Conclusion

By the experiment described in this paper we were able to identify different factors influencing natural gaze behavior during an object manipulation task and to characterize their influence on proactivity and direction of fixation towards different task-related targets. Additionally, we demonstrated that the influence of individual factors can be changed by interaction design and adjusted visual feedback, respectively.

The results reported in this paper show the variety of information contained in natural gaze behavior. By analyzing natural gaze behavior during human-computer interaction information like user's intention or experience can be inferred which can be used for designing proactive or adaptive interfaces.

In future work we plan to further validate the identified dependencies with more complex tasks and to design and evaluate gaze-based multimodal interaction techniques with a focus on multimodal combination of gesture and gaze for interaction in multi-display environments.

Bibliography

[HMR03]   Aulikki Hyrskykari, Päivi Majaranta, and Kari-Jouko Räihä. Proactive response to eye movements. In M. Rauterberg, editor, *Human Computer Interaction INTERACT 2003*, pages 129–136. IOS Press, September 2003.

[JK03]   Robert Jacob and Keith Karn. *Eye Tracking in Human-Computer Interaction and Usability Research: Ready to Deliver the Promises*, pages 573–605. Elsevier Science, 2003.

[JWBF01] Roland S. Johansson, Göran Westling, Anders Bäckström, and J. Randall Flanagan. Eye-hand coordination in object manipulation. *The Journal of Neuroscience*, 21(17):6917–6932, 2001.

[LM00]   Michael F. Land and Peter McLeod. From eye movements to actions: how batsmen hit the ball. *Nature Neuroscience*, 3:1340–1345, 2000.

[MR02]   Päivi Majaranta and Kari-Jouko Räihä. Twenty years of eye typing: systems and design issues. In *ETRA '02: Proceedings of the 2002 symposium on Eye tracking research & applications*, pages 15–22, New York, NY, USA, 2002. ACM.

[ZMI99]   Shumin Zhai, Carlos Morimoto, and Steven Ihde. Manual and gaze input cascaded (magic) pointing. In *CHI99*, pages 246–253. ACM Press, 1999.

Bibliography

An Illumination Device for the Acquisition of Image Series under Variable Illumination Directions

Robin Gruna

Vision and Fusion Laboratory
Institute for Anthropomatics
Karlsruhe Institute of Technology (KIT), Germany
robin.gruna@ies.uka.de

Technical Report IES-2010-10

Abstract: Analyzing scenes under variable illumination has been an important and widely studied research area in the field of computer vision. In this technical report, we present an illumination device for capturing image series of small objects under variable illumination directions. Due to using a digital projector as programmable light source and a parabolic reflector to reflect the emitted illumination patterns, the device dispenses with the need of moving parts. Furthermore, we demonstrate the utility of illumination series for unsupervised surface defect detection by applying statistical anomaly detection to the obtained reflectance data.

1 Introduction

Imaging and analyzing objects under different illumination directions has long been an active research area in both computer vision and computer graphics. While computer graphics aim to synthesize realistic images from appearance models, computer vision is concerned with the problem of deducing properties of a scene based on its appearance. Therefore, many algorithms from both disciplines rely on an accurate analysis of how light reflects off surfaces and how the appearance of a scene depends on different illumination conditions.

In this technical report, we present an acquisition device to image objects under variable illumination directions. The device utilizes a parabolic mirror to direct illumination patterns, emitted by a digital projector, onto an object to be investigated (see Figure 1.1). At the same time, the appearance of the object is captured with a camera with fixed viewpoint. The illumination device has the following features:

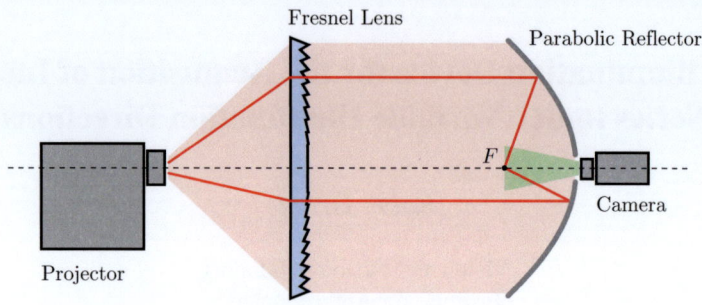

Figure 1.1: Device for variably illuminating an object from different directions. A digital LCD projector, a Fresnel lens, a parabolic reflector with a center hole and a digital camera are aligned along their optical axes. By placing the optical center of the projector at the focal point of the Fresnel lens, all emitted light rays intersect at the focal point F of the reflector.

- *No moving parts:* Since the device dispenses with the need to position parts mechanically, image acquisition with different illumination conditions is less time-consuming and becomes more accurate and repeatable.

- *Directional and spectral modulation:* The device is able to emulate illumination conditions provided by distant, arbitrary extended light sources. Hence, the illumination direction can be varied over nearly the whole hemisphere. In addition, the spectral appearance of an object can be sampled coarsely by projecting colored illumination patterns or using a color camera for image capturing.

- *Unattended data acquisition:* Since a digital light projector is used as programmable light source, images of a test object under various illumination conditions can be acquired and evaluated automatically. This renders the device particularly suitable for the application and evaluation of data-driven image analysis methods.

The remainder of this report is organized as follows: In the next section, we give an extensive literature review to show the relevance of variable illumination conditions across many research areas. Next, the setup of our illumination device is described in detail and how it is used for illumination series acquisition (Section 3). In Section 4, we employ unsupervised anomaly detection to evaluate image series with variable illumination. Finally, we discuss planned extensions of the illumination device and conclude in Section 5.

2   Related Work and Background

Analyzing scenes under variable illumination has been an important and widely studied research area in the field of computer graphics and vision. At the same time, significant effort has been put into the development of variable illumination devices. In the following, we give an overview of related work on illumination research and of various illumination devices from the literature.

Object and Face Recognition   Murase and Nayar [MN94] addressed the problem of determining the illumination for which certain objects are most distinguishable in appearance from each other. To achieve this, for each illumination direction the objects are represented as parametrized manifolds in Eigenspace. By determining the shortest distance between the object manifolds, the optimal illumination direction is the one that maximizes this distance. To acquire images under variable illumination, they developed an acquisition device which uses a motorized turntable and light bulbs that are uniformly distributed in a plane around the turntable.

In a theoretical work, Belhumeur and Kriegmann [BK98] raised the question of "what is the set of images of an object under all possible lighting conditions". They showed that the set of images of an object under arbitrary illumination forms a convex cone in the space of all possible images. Restricted to objects with convex Lambertian surface, the illumination cone can be determined from three properly chosen images. Ramamoorthi [Ram02] and Basri et al. [BJ03] extend this work by proving that the set of images of a convex Lambertian object, obtained under variable lighting conditions, lies very close to a low-dimensional linear subspace. These results indicate that regardless of the complexity of the illumination, linear subspace methods can be used for object recognition under lighting variability.

Reflectometry   Reflectometry is concerned with measuring how light is reflected at the surface of real-world materials. Reflectance acquisition and modeling is essential for rendering realistic images in computer graphics. Surface reflectance at a single point can be described by the 4D *bidirectional reflection distribution function (BRDF)*, which gives the ratio of radiance, the amount of light reflected by the surface in every direction, to irradiance, the amount of light falling on the surface in every direction. The incoming and outgoing directions are both defined with respect to the local surface normal at the considered point. Over the past years, much efforts have been made to enhance the measurement of BRDFs using elaborated illumination systems.

The most common approach to measure BRDFs is by a gonioreflectometer, which mechanically positions a light source and a photoelectric sensor at various locations on a hemisphere above a flat material sample. To speed-up the measurement process, various acquisition devices with few moving elements were proposed (see [WLL+08] for an extended review) that employ cameras to measure radiance and digital projectors as programmable light sources. Ward [War92] employed a half-silvered hemispherical mirror and a camera with a fish-eye lens to capture the entire hemisphere of reflected light directions simultaneously. Dana and Wang [DW04a] introduced a device which is able to measure *spatially-varying BRDFs (SVBRDFs)*, i.e., a set of surface points with mutually independent BRDFs, without the need of complex mechanical apparatus. The device uses an off-axis parabolic mirror to capture a large range of viewing direction and to provide illumination directions over the hemisphere. The incident illumination direction can be controlled by planar motions of the light source and material sample. An optical setup for BRDF measurement without any moving parts was presented by Gosh et al. [GAHO07], who use two curved, rotationally symmetric mirrors and a digital projector as light source. By projecting light as a sequence of basis functions, BRDFs can be measured with few images.

Appearance Acquisition and Representation   Appearance acquisition addresses the problem of modelling the relationship between a given real-word scene and the light that illuminates it with the aim to predict the scene's appearance in novel illumination conditions (or viewpoints). Therefore, many acquisition procedures utilize special illumination devices for capturing images under different illumination conditions. For modelling the appearance of a scene, basically two approaches can be distinguished, namely local and global scene descriptions [Fuc08].

Local descriptions model the appearance of a scene by a set of surfaces that scatter and reflect light according to their known material properties. Since local appearance descriptions are specified in a local coordinate frame on the scene surface, they describe the light scattering effects that occur immediately at the surface. A simple and prominent local appearance descriptor is the BRDF, which is appropriate for modelling objects and scenes consisting of the same pure material. To describe the inhomogeneous reflectance of real-word surfaces rather than the reflectance at a singe point, the BRDF representation can extended with dependence on surface position by two spatial dimensions to the 6D *spatially-varying BRDF*

(SVBRDF). Due to the complexity of SVBRDFs, sampling the angular domain of view and light directions as well as the spatial domain densely becomes very time-consuming, even with elaborated acquisition devices. Much research has been devoted on data-driven modeling of SVBRDFs, that is, features like redundancy and symmetry are exploited in the reflectance data space to simplify the measurement process. Recently, Dong et al. [DWT$^+$10] proposed an approach to SVBRDF modeling that bases on the idea that the reflectance over a given material sample forms a low-dimensional manifold.

In global appearance modeling, the light transport in the whole scene is considered, i.e., the relationship between the incident light field and the exitant light field that results from the interaction of light with the scene. This relationship can be described by the *reflectance field*, which was introduced by Debevec et al. [DHT$^+$00] as a 8D function for global scene description. Reflectance fields are parameterized in arbitrary world coordinates, e.g., in camera coordinates, and therefore make abstraction from the geometry of the scene. By restricting the incident light fields to a distant directional illumination and reducing the exitant light field to a single viewpoint, a 4D slice of the 8D reflectance field can be considered. For sampling such a 4D slice, Debecev et al. used a mechanical illumination device called Light Stage to lit an object by a directional light source and to capture images from a fixed viewpoint. Since reflectance fields represent the scene appearance in a global manner they are able capture non-local illumination effects such as self-shadowing, interreflections, translucency, refraction and subsurface-scattering. As a consequence, the 4D response of the reflectance field at a given scene point across all lighting and viewing directions is not a physically valid BRDF since it violates Helmholtz reciprocity and energy conservation.

A closely related concept to a 6D slide of the reflectance filed is the *Bidirectional Texturing Function (BTF)*, introduced by Dana et al. [DvGNK99]. Similar to the SVBRDF, the BTF is a 6D function that depends on position, lighting and viewing directions, but includes non-local illumination effects caused by the surface geometry. Therefore, the BTF is considered as a spatially dependent set of so-called *apparent BRDFs* [WHON97], that can be thought of as BRDFs modulated by a visibility function defined by the neighboring geometric mesostructure [KMBK03]. As with the reflectance field, the BTF makes abstraction of the scene geometry but at a smaller measurement scale. Commonly, BTFs are measured by robotic gantries which are able to capture images of a given surface patch for every illumination and viewing direction. An acquisition device for BTF capturing without any mechanical parts was introduced by Han et al. [HP03]. They utilized a kaleidoscope and a beam splitter to align the view of a camera and a projector. Illumination and capturing a surface patch through the kaleidoscope then results in an kaleidoscopic image that shows the illuminated surface from multiple viewpoints.

Photometric Stereo   Photometric stereo is a well-established technique for shape recovery using shading information from images captured under different illumination directions. In its early formulations, e.g., by Woodham [Woo89], Lambertian surface reflectance and prior knowledge of the illumination setting were assumed.

Recently, much research has been done to weaken these constrains in order to use photometric stereo for real-world scenes with partly-known or unknown reflectance properties. For instance, it has been shown that the reflectance of many real-world surfaces can be approximated by the sum of specular and diffuse lobes [BP03][MZKB05]. By evaluating color or identifying specular pixels, the diffuse component can be extracted and used for surface shape estimation.

An example-based approach to photometric stereo has been proposed by Hertzmann et al. [HS03], where the surface reflectance, illumination direction and shape may all be unknown. By exploiting the fact that points with the same surface orientation must have similar appearance under variable illumination, the shape of a test object can be reconstructed when imaged together with a reference object with known shape and similar material. Alldrin et al. [AZK08] and Goldman et al. [GCHS10] presented a method for simultaneously recovering shape and spatially-varying reflectance of a scene from photometric stereo images. While differing in their approach to appearance modelling, both techniques utilize an optimization procedure to fit model parameters and to estimate scene properties from these.

Acquisition and Evaluation of Illumination Series   In the field of image processing often the term *illumination series* is used to refer to a set of images taken with fixed viewing parameters but varied illumination conditions. Much research has been reported on the acquisition and evaluation of illumination series in the field of automated visual inspection in order to enhance image processing. As opposed to photometric stereo, often explicit shape reconstruction is not the main objective here.

Puente [Leo97] proposed an image fusion algorithm to compute images with maximal contrast from an illumination series. To this end, an energy functional is introduced and minimized which specifies the desired requirements on the image fusion result. For image series acquisition, an illumination system was set up consisting of a parabolic reflector which is illuminated by a circular array of LEDs. By turning on LEDs at different locations, a test object at the focal point of the reflector can be illuminated from different directions. Heizmann used an identical illumination device for the analysis of forensic striation marks [Hei04].

Lindner [Lin09] proposed several methods for surface segmentation using varying illumination directions and demonstrated the superiority of illumination series over a single image. For this purpose, different reflection features are extracted for each pixel and used for unsupervised clustering. With this approach, a wide variety of textures on structured surfaces could have been segmented. In [Gra10], Grassi used illumination series to detect and classify varnish defects on wood surfaces. By constructing invariant features, good detection and classification ratios could have been achieved.

In order to segment images into material types, [WGSD09] used illumination series acquired with a dome providing lighting from many directions. A hemispherical harmonics model is fit to the measured reflectance values and the model coefficients are used to train a multi-class Support Vector Machine. To account for geometric dependencies on the measured reflectance, photometric stereo is applied to estimate the surface normal at each pixel and to transform the measurements to the local surface reference frame.

Koppal et al. [KN06] considered illumination series acquired by a smoothly moving distant light source. By this, continuous appearance profiles are generated and used for clustering scene points to their surface normals. In order to minimize the dependency of the profiles on material properties, a feature extraction technique and clustering metric is proposed that bases on the class of linearly separable BRDFs which were introduced by Narasimhan et al. [NRN03].

In the field of illumination planning and optimal light source placements, Lensch et al. [LLSS03] determined illumination directions by minimizing the uncertainty in the estimated parameters of a BRDF model. By this, reflectance measurement is performed more effectively and less measurements suffice to model the reflectance properties of an object.

Jehle et al. [JSJ10] learned optimal illumination directions for material classification by using an embedded feature selection method for a random forest classifier. For illumination series acquisition, an illumination device very similar to the one presented in this report is used. However, our device, developed independently, differs in the wax coating of the parabolic mirror to obtain a homogeneous illumination of the test object.

3   Acquisition of Illumination Series

3.1   Illumination Device

The proposed illumination device is shown in Figure 1.1. The optical components are a digital LCD projector, a Fresnel lens, a parabolic reflector featuring a center hole and a digital camera. All components are aligned along their optical axes.

The projector serves as programmable light source, which allows to control the relative radiance along the emitted light rays independently. If a pinhole model is assumed for the projector, each projector pixel can be thought of as the source of a single ray of light that emanates from the optical center of the projector. By placing the projector at the focal point of the Fresnel lens, the light rays are collimated by the lens and converge at the focal point F of the parabolic reflector. Therefore, the illumination direction of light rays incident to the focal point can be controlled by projecting spatially resolved illumination patterns.

To image objects under different illumination directions, a test object is placed at the focal point of the parabolic reflector and the reflected radiance is captured by a camera attached to the center hole of the reflector. Although the proposed illumination device allows to project arbitrary complex illumination patterns, in this report we consider a simple binary illumination pattern depicted in Figure 3.1. The illumination pattern consists of a single circular spot of white pixels with all other pixels being black. Due to the spatial extend of the illumination spot, this illumination pattern leads to a ray-bundle rather than to a single ray. However, each individual light ray of the bundle follows the laws of reflection and refraction and hence a cone-shaped illumination is incident to F.

By establishing a Cartesian coordinate system with its origin at the focal point F of the parabolic reflector and its Z-axis aligned with the optical axis and pointing into the direction of the camera, we are able to parametrize the illumination pattern as well as the resulting illumination direction incident to F, see Figure 3.1. The position of the illumination spot is considered in the X-Y-plane and can alternatively be represented by its radial coordinate r and angular coordinate φ in polar coordinates. The resulting illumination is then described by the illumination vector $L(\varphi, \theta)$ that points in the direction of the cone-shaped illumination. The angular coordinates of $L(\varphi, \theta)$ are derived as follows: the azimuthal coordinate φ equates the angular coordinate of the illumination pattern and the polar coordinate θ is given by

$$\theta := \arctan \frac{4fr}{4f^2 - r^2},$$

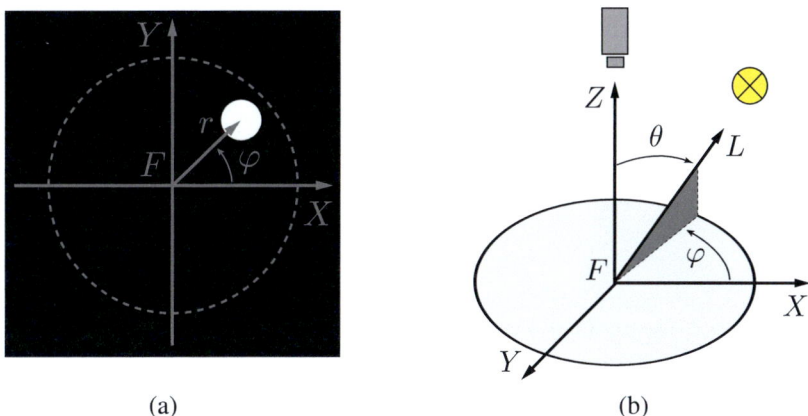

(a)   (b)

Figure 3.1: (a) Illumination pattern used in our experiments. The circular illumination spot is parametrized using polar coordinates r and φ. The pole of the coordinate system is aligned with the focal point F of the parabolic reflector. (b) Projecting the illumination pattern from Figure (a) with the illumination device (Figure 1.1) approximates a distant illumination whose direction is described by the
azimuthal angle φ and polar angle θ with origin F. The relationship between the
illumination pattern and the illumination direction is given through Equation (3.1).

where f denotes the focal length of the parabolic reflector.

Note that given highly accurate optical components and a perfectly calibrated
setup, all emitted light rays by the projector would intersect at a small point at
the focus F of the parabolic reflector. Clearly this is not practical to illuminate
even small test objects. By moving the test object slightly before or behind the focal point would result in a spatial extension of the directed illumination, however,
as consequence, the position of the illumination will also vary.

To account for this problem, we use a parabolic reflector which is not perfectly
specular, having a matte surface appearance. Hence, the specular reflection at the
reflector surface becomes partly diffuse and the incident ray bundles from the projector are reflected in a small solid angle toward the focal point F. This results in
a broadening of the area for which the direction of the incident illumination can
be varied. To enhance this effect, we use wax based transparent dulling spray to
coat the surface of the reflector in order to further increase the diffuse component
of the reflection, see Figure 3.2. However, care must be taken to keep the propor-
tion between diffuse and specular reflection right, since a diffuse coating causes

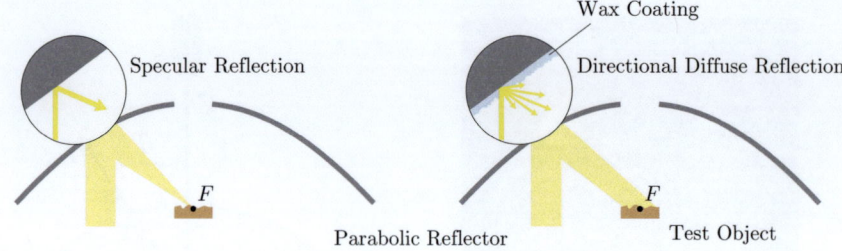

Figure 3.2: Projected ray bundle reflected at the surface of the parabolic reflector. A thin wax layer is used to roughen the specular surface of the reflector in order to obtain a diffuse directed reflection and to broaden the illuminated area size at F.

undesirable interreflections and the directional property of the illumination may get lost. By applying the dulling spray sparsely, we yield a circular area of radius $\approx 15\,mm$ around F for which we can control the direction of the incident illumination. In a similar approach in [PHD06], heated acrylic is inflated to roughen the texture of a hemispherical mirror.

3.2   Illumination Series Acquisition

The illumination device introduced in Section 3.1 is used to capture images of small test objects under varying illumination. To accomplish this, the illumination pattern shown in Figure 3.1 is used with fixed size r and polar parametrization $\phi \in [0, 2\pi)$ and $\theta \in [0, \pi)$. Since the spatial extend of the objects to be illuminated is small ($\approx 15\,mm$) compared to the diameter of the parabolic reflector (600 mm), we make the approximation that the projection of the illumination pattern emulates a distant, collimated point light source. This means, for each scene point the illumination originates from the same direction with the same intensity. Therefore, an image can be formalized as mapping (per color-channel)

$$g : \Omega \times \Psi \to \mathbb{R}_0^+$$

where $\Omega \subset \mathbb{Z}^2$ is the domain of pixel positions and $\Psi = [0, 2\pi) \times [0, \pi)$ the space of illumination parameters. Debevec et al. [DHT+00] refer to g as the *reflectance field* of a scene, which describes the optical response of a scene illuminated by a distant light source. Although the digital projector is able to project light of different colors, we do not consider the spectral modulation of the illumination in this report. By varying the illumination direction and capturing images $g(\mathbf{x}, \boldsymbol{\omega}_i)$,

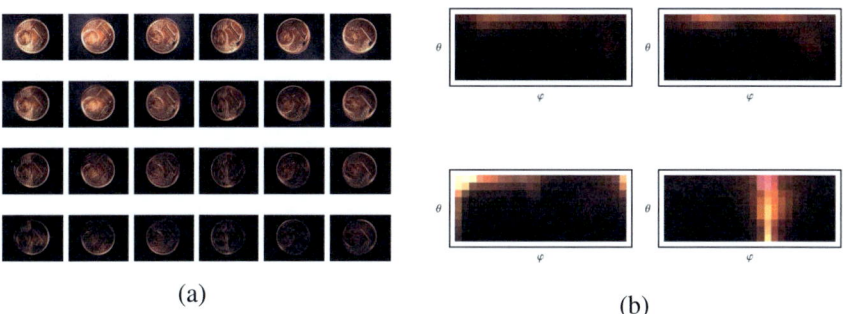

(a)

(b)

Figure 3.3: (a) Illumination series of a test object for various illumination directions. (b) Reflectance functions at different pixel locations. The upper two reflectance functions depict the illumination-depend appearance of two surface points with similar surface geometry. The lower reflectance functions correspond to a surface edge (left) and shadowed surface point (right), respectively.

we obtain an illumination series

$$I := \{g(\mathbf{x}, \boldsymbol{\omega}_i), \, i = 0, \ldots, n - 1\}$$

where $\mathbf{x} \in \Omega$ denotes the pixel location and $\omega \in \Psi$ describes the illumination direction incident on the test object within a hemisphere (see Figure 3.3(a) for an example). The illumination series I can be considered as samples of the mapping g with respect to the parameter space Ψ.

By considering a fixed pixel locations $\mathbf{x}_0$ in Ω, the *reflectance function*

$$r_{\mathbf{x}_0}(\boldsymbol{\omega}_i) := g(\mathbf{x}_0, \boldsymbol{\omega}_i), \quad i = 0, \ldots, n - 1$$

can be defined, describing the illumination-dependent appearance at individual pixels, see Figure 3.3(b). Note that the reflectance function is image-based and that it includes non-local and geometry-induced illumination effects like the foreshortening term, interreflections and self-shadowing. Therefore, the term "reflectance" should be understood with care since $r_{\mathbf{x}_0}(\boldsymbol{\omega}_i)$ is not a physically plausible BRDF slice of the corresponding surface element. Instead, $r_{\mathbf{x}_0}(\boldsymbol{\omega}_i)$ can be considered as a 2D slice of the *apparent* BRDF (see Section 2), which includes non-local illumination effects.

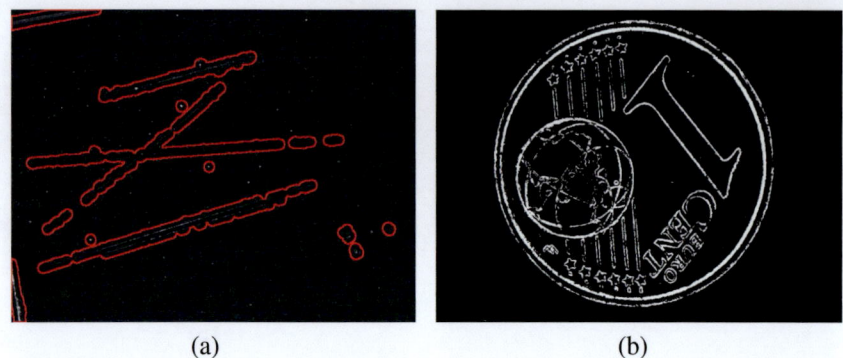

(a)   (b)

Figure 4.1: RX anomaly detection applied to illumination series. (a) Inspection of a wooden test surface. Surface scratches are marked as abnormal pixels and hence become visible and detectable by succeeding image processing operations. (b) Anomaly detection in the illumination series of a coin. By thresholding the detector output, the RX detector operates as edge detector.

4   Anomaly Detection in Reflectance Data

In the following, we present a first approach to unsupervised defect detection using illumination series. In automated visual inspection, collecting labeled training data is often expensive or difficult, since possible defects are not known a priori. However, in many cases it can be assumed that defects are rare and occur with low probability compared to the nominal inspection state. This is especially true for their appearance under variable illumination directions and hence for the reflectance function of defective surface regions.

In order to detect defects by their illumination-dependent appearance in an unsupervised manner, we apply the anomaly detector developed by Reed and Yu (*RX detector* [RY90]) to illumination series. The RX detector bases on a Gaussian background model and is widely used in hyperspectral image analysis, enabling one to detect regions of interest without prior knowledge whose signatures are spectrally distinct form their surroundings. Applied to an illumination series, the RX detector implements a filter specified by

$$\delta_{\mathrm{RDX}}(\mathbf{x}) = (r_{\mathbf{x}}(\boldsymbol{\omega}_i) - \mu)^T \mathbf{C}^{-1}(r_{\mathbf{x}}(\boldsymbol{\omega}_i) - \mu),$$

where $\mu \in \mathbb{R}^n$ is the sample mean and $\mathbf{C} \in \mathbb{R}^{n \times n}$ the sample covariance matrix of the reflectance functions in the image series. Therefore, the detector output

$\delta_{RDX}(\mathbf{x})$ is the Mahalanobis distance between a tested pixel and the mean reflectance function. Large distances correspond to low probabilities of occurrence, and hence, by displaying the detector output as grayscale image, more anomalous pixels appear brighter.

In a first experiment, an illumination series of $n = 144$ grayscale images of a wooden surface with various surface defects was recorded. In Figure 4.1(a), the output of the RX-detector $\delta_{RDX}(\mathbf{x})$ applied to the whole illumination series is shown. As it can be seen, surface defects like scratches and nicks are displayed as anomalous pixels. In a subsequent step, a threshold can be applied to the detector output to segment anomalous surface regions. In doing so, the threshold value controls the false-alarm rate for the detection process. In Figure 4.1(b), the RX detector is applied to the illumination series of a coin and the detector output is thresholded. As it can be seen, the RX detector operates as edge detector identifying regions that correspond to geometric edges.

5 Conclusions and Future Work

We have presented an illumination device to acquire images of small test objects under variable illumination directions from nearly the full hemisphere. Since the device has no moving parts, illumination series can be acquired unattended once a test object as been setup. Furthermore, illumination conditions can be varied adaptively depending on the outcome of preceding image processing operations.

One of the major issue when building and evaluating the device was to ensure a spatially homogeneous irradiance on the test object. Due to the low quality of the used optical components and the adjustment by hand, the illumination slightly varies spatially across the scene, dependent on the projected direction. To reduce this effect, we roughened the surface of the reflector with a thin wax layer to broaden the illuminated area. Another way to solve the problem of inhomogeneous illumination is to use prospective shading correction techniques as employed by Jehle et al. [JSJ10].

In an exemplary application, we show how a classic anomaly detection method can be applied to illumination series for defect detection and pixel exact edge detection. Surely, with the processing of illumination series instead of single images, the question arises how illumination series can be acquired in a planned manner, using different sources of information.

Currently, the proposed illumination device acquires color images with a trichromatic camera. By extending the device with a camera with a liquid-crystal tunable filter (LCTF), dense multispectral reflectance measurements can be obtained.

Such measurements can be used to investigate the interaction between spectral and geometric material properties, which is still an open research issue in reflectometry [WLL+08] [NRH+92] and may eventually be exploited for improved material-based image analysis.

Moreover, we plan to extend the device to capture 6D reflectance fields [DHT+00]. Today, light field cameras can be bought for reasonable prices and hence have become attractive for academic research. By acquiring a partial light field of a test object, not only the appearance under angularly-varying illumination directions but also from different viewpoints can be investigated. As a consequence, depth information from the test object can be obtained.

Bibliography

[AZK08]   N. Alldrin, T. Zickler, and D. Kriegman. Photometric stereo with non-parametric and spatially-varying reflectance. In *Computer Vision and Pattern Recognition, 2008. CVPR 2008. IEEE Conference on*, pages 1–8. IEEE, 2008.

[BJ03]   Ronen Basri and David W. Jacobs. Lambertian reflectance and linear subspaces. *IEEE Transactions on Pattern Analysis and Machine Intelligence*, 25(2):218–233, 2003.

[BK98]   Peter N. Belhumeur and David J. Kriegman. What is the set of images of an object under all possible illumination conditions? *Int. J. Comput. Vision*, 28(3):245–260, 1998.

[BP03]   S. Barsky and M. Petrou. The 4-source photometric stereo technique for three-dimensional surfaces in the presence of highlights and shadows. *IEEE Transactions on Pattern Analysis and Machine Intelligence*, pages 1239–1252, 2003.

[DHT+00]   P. Debevec, T. Hawkins, C. Tchou, H. P Duiker, W. Sarokin, and M. Sagar. Acquiring the reflectance field of a human face. In *Proceedings of the 27th annual conference on Computer graphics and interactive techniques*, pages 145–156, 2000.

[DvGNK99]   Kristin J. Dana, Bram van Ginneken, Shree K. Nayar, and Jan J. Koenderink. Reflectance and texture of real-world surfaces. *ACM Trans. Graph.*, 18(1):1–34, 1999.

[DW04a]   Kristin J. Dana and Jing Wang. Device for convenient measurement of spatially-varying bidirectional reflectance. *Journal of the Optical Society of America A*, 21(1):1–12, January 2004.

[DWT+10]   Yue Dong, Jiaping Wang, Xin Tong, John Snyder, Yanxiang Lan, Moshe Ben-Ezra, and Baining Guo. Manifold bootstrapping for SVBRDF capture. *ACM Trans. Graph.*, 29(4):1–10, 2010.

[Fuc08]   Martin Fuchs. *Advanced Methods for Relightable Scene Representations in Image Space*. PhD thesis, Universität des Saarlandes, 2008.

[GAHO07]   A. Ghosh, S. Achutha, W. Heidrich, and M. O'Toole. BRDF acquisition with basis illumination. In *Computer Vision, 2007. ICCV 2007. IEEE 11th International Conference on*, pages 1–8, 2007.

[GCHS10]   D.B. Goldman, B. Curless, A. Hertzmann, and S.M. Seitz. Shape and Spatially-Varying BRDFs from photometric stereo. *Pattern Analysis and Machine Intelligence, IEEE Transactions on*, 32(6):1060–1071, 2010.

[Gra10]   Ana Pérez Grassi. *Variable illumination and invariant features for detecting and classifying varnish defects.* KIT Scientific Publishing, Karlsruhe, 2010.

[Hei04]   Michael Heizmann. *Auswertung von forensischen Riefenspuren mittels automatischer Sichtprüfung.* KIT Scientific Publishing, June 2004.

[HP03]   Jefferson Y. Han and Ken Perlin. Measuring bidirectional texture reflectance with a kaleidoscope. *ACM Trans. Graph.*, 22(3):741–748, 2003.

[HS03]   Aaron Hertzmann and Steven M. Seitz. Shape and materials by example: A photometric stereo approach. *Computer Vision and Pattern Recognition, IEEE Computer Society Conference on*, 1:533, 2003.

[JSJ10]   M. Jehle, C. Sommer, and B. Jähne. Learning of optimal illumination for material classification. *Pattern Recognition*, pages 563–572, 2010.

[KMBK03]   M.L. Koudelka, S. Magda, P.N. Belhumeur, and D.J. Kriegman. Acquisition, compression, and synthesis of bidirectional texture functions. In *Proc. 3rd Int. Workshop on Texture Analysis and Synthesis*, pages 59–64. Citeseer, 2003.

[KN06]   S.J. Koppal and S.G. Narasimhan. Clustering appearance for scene analysis. In *Computer Vision and Pattern Recognition, 2006 IEEE Computer Society Conference on*, volume 2, pages 1323–1330, 2006.

[Leo97]   Fernando Puente Leon. Enhanced imaging by fusion of illumination series. In *Proceedings of SPIE*, pages 297–308, Munich, Germany, 1997.

[Lin09]   Christoph Lindner. *Segmentierung von Oberflächen mittels variabler Beleuchtung.* Shaker, 1., aufl. edition, October 2009.

[LLSS03]   H. Lensch, J. Lang, A.M. Sá, and H.P. Seidel. Planned sampling of spatially varying BRDFs. In *Computer Graphics Forum*, volume 22, pages 473–482. Wiley Online Library, 2003.

[MN94]   Hiroshi Murase and Shree K. Nayar. Illumination planning for object recognition using parametric eigenspaces. *IEEE Trans. Pattern Anal. Mach. Intell.*, 16(12):1219–1227, 1994.

[MZKB05]   S.P. Mallick, T.E. Zickler, D.J. Kriegman, and P.N. Belhumeur. Beyond lambert: reconstructing specular surfaces using color. In *Computer Vision and Pattern Recognition, 2005. CVPR 2005. IEEE Computer Society Conference on*, volume 2, pages 619–626 vol. 2, 2005.

[NRH+92]   FE Nicodemus, JC Richmond, JJ Hsia, IW Ginsberg, and T. Limperis. Geometrical considerations and nomenclature for reflectance. In *Radiometry*, pages 94–145. Jones and Bartlett Publishers, Inc., 1992.

[NRN03]   S.G. Narasimhan, Visvanathan Ramesh, and S.K. Nayar. A class of photometric invariants: separating material from shape and illumination. In *Computer Vision, 2003. Proceedings. Ninth IEEE International Conference on*, pages 1387–1394 vol.2, 2003.

[PHD06]   Pieter Peers, Tim Hawkins, and Paul Debevec. A reflective light stage. Technical report, ICT-TR-04.2006, 2006.

[Ram02]   Ravi Ramamoorthi. Analytic PCA construction for theoretical analysis of lighting variability in images of a lambertian object. *IEEE Trans. Pattern Anal. Mach. Intell.*, 24:1322–1333, October 2002.

[RY90]   I.S. Reed and X. Yu. Adaptive multiple-band CFAR detection of an optical pattern with unknown spectral distribution. *Acoustics, Speech and Signal Processing, IEEE Transactions on*, 38(10):1760–1770, 1990.

[War92]   Gregory J. Ward. Measuring and modeling anisotropic reflection. *SIGGRAPH Comput. Graph.*, 26(2):265–272, 1992.

[WGSD09]   O. Wang, P. Gunawardane, S. Scher, and J. Davis. Material classification using BRDF slices. *Computer Vision and Pattern Recognition, IEEE Computer Society Conference on*, 0:2805–2811, 2009.

[WHON97]   T.T. Wong, P.A. Heng, S.H. Or, and W.Y. Ng. Image-based rendering with controllable illumination. In *Proceedings of the Eurographics Workshop on Rendering Techniques*, volume 97, pages 13–22. Citeseer, 1997.

[WLL+08]   T. Weyrich, J. Lawrence, H. Lensch, S. Rusinkiewicz, and T. Zickler. Principles of appearance acquisition and representation. In *International Conference on Computer Graphics and Interactive Techniques*. ACM New York, NY, USA, 2008.

[Woo89]   Robert J. Woodham. Photometric method for determining surface orientation from multiple images. In *Shape from shading*, pages 513–531. MIT Press, 1989.

A First Approach to Typewritten Character Segmentation using Graph Cuts

Martin Grafmüller

Vision and Fusion Laboratory
Institute for Anthropomatics
Karlsruhe Institute of Technology (KIT), Germany
grafmueller@kit.edu

Technical Report IES-2010-11

Abstract: One important step for character recognition is character segmentation, since this mainly influences the quality of the characters and thus the classification result. There are several difficulties in character segmentation, e.g. if characters in a line of text are too close together then the segmentation algorithm may merge these characters, on the other hand characters may fall apart if a character is not connected with respect to the segmentation direction. To deal with such kinds of wrong segmentation, a graph based approach is introduced in this technical report. First experiments show that the approach is promising, but still has some shortcomings.

1 Introduction

Character segmentation is still an ongoing research topic, since it essentially affects classification. The character segmentation methods are commonly based on projection analysis, connected component processing, or segmentation based on recognition [Lu95, CL96, SSR10]. The challenging task is to correctly segment touching, overlapping, or fragmented characters. If one of these difficulties causes wrongly segmented characters, correct classification is very difficult and costly. On the other hand most character segmentation methods are based on binarized images. Unfortunately, binarization can even enforce the appearance of touching or fragmented characters. Hence, many segmentation errors can be omitted if the segmentation method is based on gray scale images.

1.1   Related Work

A character segmentation method that works on gray scale images is introduced in [LeB97]. It is based on the ratio of vertical gray level projection and the sum of vertical gradients. The author points out, that the procedure works good even on touching characters under severe conditions. A similar method is proposed in [LL95]. This method is based on projection profiles in combination with topographic features for presegmentation. For the segmentation itself, they use multistage graph search to determine the nonlinear segmentation path. The authors show that the method performs better than methods based on binarized images. A method for character segmentation of license plates is introduced in [ZZ03]. This method combines projection profile analysis with the Hough transform. According to the authors this has the advantage that no rotational correction is needed and it is robust to illumination changes. In [NYK$^+$05] another character segmentation approach for license plates is introduced. However, this method is based on binarized images on which the degradation—fragmented, overlapped, or connected characters—of the characters is adaptively detected. With the detection result, the degradations of the characters are corrected by applying corresponding morphological operations. The characters are finally segmented based on the vertical histogram combined with the costs of the segmentation lines. A character segmentation method of license plates based on binarized images is as well introduced in [PYX08]. Firstly, the skew angle in horizontal and in vertical direction is estimated with a least squares approach. For segmentation they use a projection method, which was improved to remove noisy regions in between the characters additionally. In [Yan00] the author proposes a segmentation method especially for dot matrix characters. The author investigates three methods for pitch estimation. The methods are based on autocorrelation, Fourier analysis, and peak-valley analysis, respectively. The peak-valley analysis shows the most promising result, but it fails in the case of skewed text lines or italic fonts. A segmentation method that deals with touching italic typewritten fonts is introduced in [LNCS04]. Based on the determination of the slant angle and a contour analysis, they locate segmentation points. Furthermore, the authors use dynamic programming to find the best cut path, which is associated with the segmentation points. For the final decision whether a cut path is correct, they apply a neural network to the segmented regions. The output of the neural network is a confidence value on which the decision for the best segmentation path is based. Unfortunately, their comparison to other methods is not very significant, since these methods do not consider the slant angle of the text at all. Hence, it is clear that the results of the other methods do not look very promising. Another method that works on typewritten gray scale characters is proposed in [TCJY07]. They have their main focus on smeared characters. Based on the connected component analysis on the binarized images, they determine whether any of the characters are smeared. If so, they apply a shortest path algorithm on the gray scale images to locate the best segmentation path. They also point out the big influence of the binarization step, which can result in touching or fragmented characters. The results are promising, but the shortcoming is the detection of smeared characters and the decision whether or not two characters are still connected. In [Suw05] the author introduces a graph-based segmentation approach for handwritten connected numerals. The numerals were smoothed and afterwards thinned on which the graph representation is based. They investigate to determine whether two numerals are touched at multiple points or not. If the case of multiple touches of two numerals is detected, the shortest path through the graph between the obtained connecting points is determined. The segmentation is achieved by dividing the edges and vertices along the shortest path into two disconnected subgraphs. However, this method is only applied to binary images with two touching characters.

1.2   Contribution

The method proposed in this technical report is on segmenting typewritten characters from gray scale images containing one line of text only. It is assumed that the characters' height is the height of the text line image, i.e. the characters are touching top and bottom of the image. Similar to the method mentioned before, it is also based on graphs. However, not the character is represented by the graph, but the image containing one line of typewritten characters. The graph must represent the text line in a way that the cut of minimum cost through the graph is the segmentation cut through the image in front of or in between two characters. The result of the minimum cost cut through a graph from the source to the sink terminal is equivalent to the result obtained by maximum flow algorithms, see [JFZ63]. The graph cut method can be efficiently used to solve discrete energy functionals with binary variables that are graph representable. For some conditions even the global minimum cut can be found, i.e. the global minimum of the energy functional [BVZ01, KZ04]. In the case of a one dimensional energy functional—the argument is a function of one binary variable—the result is the same as can be obtained by dynamic programming. However, the graph cut approach can also be efficiently applied if the energy functional is multi-dimensional. Due to this advantages graph cut techniques have been successfully applied to many image processing tasks like image segmentation, multi-camera scene reconstruction, image restoration, and stereo vision [BVZ01, BK04, BFL06, KZ04]. Another approach is the synthesis of image and video textures, which was introduced in [KSE$^+$03].

1.3 Outline

The fundamentals of the energy functionals that can be minimized using the graph cut technique are discussed in the next section. Furthermore, the general conditions for a valid energy functional are mentioned and adapted to the character segmentation task. In Section 3, it is explained how the graph is built, which represents the energy functional. Some experiments are described in Section 4 and the pros and cons of the method are pointed out. In the last section the report is concluded and some remarks for future work are given.

2 Energy Formulation

In this section the energy formulation for typewritten character segmentation is introduced. For this reason, it is referred to the fundamentals of energy functionals that can be minimized by minimizing the costs of a cut through a graph. The single energy terms that are important for the proposed method are discussed explicitly. For the following introduction let the gray scale image with the characters be

$$G \quad : \quad \mathcal{P} := \{1,\ldots,M\} \times \{1,\ldots,N\} \quad \to \quad \{0,\ldots,255\} \ ,$$

where M and N indicate the number of rows and columns of the image, respectively. The indices of the pixels are expressed as ordered pair $\mathbf{p} = (m,n) \in \mathcal{P}$.

2.1 General Formulation

The typewritten character segmentation is based on the minimization of an energy functional that has in general the form

$$E\left(\mathbf{l}\right) := \sum_{\mathbf{p}\in\mathcal{P}} D_{\mathbf{p}}\left(l_{\mathbf{p}}\right) + \sum_{(\mathbf{p},\mathbf{q})\in\mathcal{N}} V_{\mathbf{pq}}\left(l_{\mathbf{p}},l_{\mathbf{q}}\right) \ . \tag{2.1}$$

This functional is well known from other applications in image processing, e.g.image segmentation, image restoration, or stereo vision [BK04]. In equation (2.1), $D_{\mathbf{p}}\left(l_{\mathbf{p}}\right)$ denotes the position penalty, which is dependent on the label $l_{\mathbf{p}} \in \mathcal{L}$. The labeling assigns one label $l_{\mathbf{p}}$ of the label set $\mathcal{L}$ to every pixel $\mathbf{p} \in \mathcal{P}$ of the image. Since in this approach character segmentation is considered to be a binary problem the label set is defined by $\mathcal{L} := \{0,1\}$. With the second term in equation (2.1) the labeling of discontinuous label assignments can be penalized, i.e.the cost for the labeling $l_\mathbf{p}$ of pixel $\mathbf{p}$ if pixel $\mathbf{q}$ is labeled $l_\mathbf{q}$. The set $\mathcal{N} \subseteq \mathcal{P} \times \mathcal{P}$ describes the neighborhood relation between the pixels. All the pixels $\mathbf{q}$ for which $(\mathbf{p}, \mathbf{q}) \in \mathcal{N}$ are called the neighbors of $\mathbf{p}$, i.e.$\mathcal{N}_\mathbf{p} := \{\mathbf{q} \in \mathcal{P} | (\mathbf{p}, \mathbf{q}) \in \mathcal{N}\}$ is the neighborhood of the pixel $\mathbf{p}$.

According to [KZ04, BFL06] the binary labeling problem can be solved in polynomial time and the global optimum solution can be determined. However, the only constraint is that the energy functional must be regular, which ensures that it is representable by a graph. That is, the minimum cost cut of this graph is equal to the minimum of the energy functional. For the regularity of a function the following constraints apply:

- A function with only one binary variable is always regular.

- A function with two binary variables is regular if

$$V_{\mathbf{pq}}(0,0) + V_{\mathbf{pq}}(1,1) \le V_{\mathbf{pq}}(0,1) + V_{\mathbf{pq}}(1,0), \quad \forall \, \mathbf{p}, \mathbf{q} \in \mathcal{P} \,.$$

- The sum of two regular functions is regular too.

If the regularity is not fulfilled or a multi-label problem has to be optimized, minimization of the energy functional becomes NP-hard. More information on this can be found in [KZ04, BFL06].

2.2 Energy Model for Character Segmentation

The first idea of using graph cuts for character segmentation, is based on [KSE+03]. However, they use graph cuts to find an optimal cut to merge two image patches. For character segmentation it can be used to find a segmentation path through an image—the image contains only characters—in such a way that the image is split in between two characters. However, it turned out that this approach has several drawbacks. Since the image is cut into two images, where both contain characters, the method has to be applied multiple times. This raises the question when to stop the iteration. The task is even getting worse, since the number of characters in both images is unknown. Hence, the method that is proposed in this report does not cut the image at an arbitrary position, but cuts the image in front of—depending on the size of the background region in front of the first character—or right after the leftmost character. In that case, too, the algorithm has to be applied multiple times, but it can be stopped if the image is smaller than the width of the narrowest character.

First of all, the position penalty function is defined in a way that the graph is cut right after the first character. To guarantee that the image is cut on the left hand side of the line of text, the position penalty for label $l_{\mathbf{p}} = 0$ is chosen to be

$$
D_{\mathbf{p}}(l_{\mathbf{p}} = 0) := \begin{cases} \frac{c_{\mathrm{d}}}{(M-2)}(n-1) , & 0 < n \leq \frac{M}{2} \\[2ex] \frac{c_{\mathrm{d}}}{3M}(n+M) , & \frac{M}{2} < n \leq 2M \\[2ex] c_{\mathrm{d}} , & 2M < n \leq N \end{cases}
$$

with

$$
\mathbf{p} = (m, n) , \quad m = 1, \ldots, M , \quad n = 1, \ldots, N .
$$

In this equation, the constant c_{d} is a weighting factor with respect to the neighborhood interaction term in (2.1). The position penalty for the label $l_{\mathbf{p}} = 1$ is given by

$$
D_{\mathbf{p}}(l_{\mathbf{p}} = 1) := c_{\mathrm{d}} - D_{\mathbf{p}}(l_{\mathbf{p}} = 0) .
$$

These position penalties are the basis for assigning the leftmost character to the object ($l_{\mathbf{p}} = 0$) and the rest to the background ($l_{\mathbf{p}} = 1$). With this position penalty, the maximal width that can be assigned to the object is $2M$. This is chosen, since a character is mostly higher than wide, i.e.it is sure that $2M$ is larger than the width of one character. The illustration of the position penalty function is given in Figure 3.1 on the bottom. If the remaining text line image is shorter than $2M$, then the position penalty is changed in a way that the minimum cut is assumed to be in the middle of the image.

With the definition above, it is known where the image is approximately cut, but it is not sure whether the cut is between two or in front of the first character. This raises the need of the second term of the energy functional (2.1). This is used to ensure that the cut goes through a region that belongs to the background. Note, since the neighborhood is symmetric for the discontinuity penalty holds that

$$
V_{\mathbf{pq}}(l_{\mathbf{p}}, l_{\mathbf{q}}) = V_{\mathbf{qp}}(l_{\mathbf{p}}, l_{\mathbf{q}}) .
$$

The penalty is defined by

$$
V_{\mathbf{pq}}(l_{\mathbf{p}}, l_{\mathbf{q}}) := f_{\mathrm{s}}(W(\mathbf{p}, \mathbf{q}) \cdot \delta(l_{\mathbf{p}}, l_{\mathbf{q}})) ,
$$

where $W(\mathbf{p}, \mathbf{q})$ indicates the weight between pixel $\mathbf{p}$ and $\mathbf{q}$ of the image and function $\delta(\cdot, \cdot)$ is equal to zero if $l_{\mathbf{p}} = l_{\mathbf{q}}$ and one otherwise. The function $f_{\mathrm{s}}(\cdot)$ denotes a scaling function, to adjust the range and the influence of the discontinuity penalty on the energy functional. To minimize the influence of illumination changes, it is chosen to normalize the discontinuity penalty to mean zero and subsequently it is scaled to the interval $[0, c_s]$. The upper bound of the interval c_s is chosen subject to the desired influence of the discontinuity penalty with respect to the position penalty. For example, if c_s is too low, than the segmentation is mostly influenced by the position penalty. Whereas the discontinuity penalty is dominant, if c_s is too high.

Using the previous energy functions, the energy functional given in (2.1) is consistent with the *Ising* model. The *Ising* model is a special case of the *Potts* model, which covers the general case of more than two labels. The models are discontinuity preserving functions and often used in image processing. The *Ising* model ensures that the global minimum of the binary energy functional (2.1) can be found by the graph cut method [BK04], i.e. the energy functional is regular.

Since with this method at most one character can be cut off the text line, it is repeated as long as the image width is still wider than the narrowest expected character. In the case that spaces are between or in front of a character in the image, it may happen that the image is cut in front of the first character, i.e. this image does not contain a character, but only background. However, such images can be identified by either considering the image mean or the width of the image.

3 Graph Representation

For the calculation of the minimum cut through a graph, the energy functional (2.1) must be representable by a graph. In Section 2.2, it has already been mentioned that the energy functional is regular and thus representable by a graph. The graph $\mathcal{G} := (\mathcal{V}, \mathcal{E})$ is fully characterized by the vertices $\mathcal{V}$ and the edges $\mathcal{E}$ connecting the vertices. The set of vertices

$$\mathcal{V} := \{v_{\mathbf{p}} | \mathbf{p} \in \mathcal{P}\} \cup \{s, t\}$$

contains one vertex $v_{\mathbf{p}}$ corresponding to every pixel $\mathbf{p} \in \mathcal{P}$ of the image and two additional terminal vertices. The terminal vertices represent the labels 0 (source terminal s) and 1 (sink terminal t), i.e. object and background, respectively. The total number of vertices of the graph is

$$|\mathcal{V}| = |\mathcal{P}| + 2 = M \cdot N + 2 \, .$$

The vertices are connected via edges, where the edge from vertex $v_{\mathbf{p}}$ to vertex $v_{\mathbf{q}}$ is denoted by $e_{\mathbf{pq}}$. The edges of the graph can be distinguished into three classes. The s-links e_{sp} and t-links e_{pt} are edges connected with the object and background terminal, respectively, and the n-links are connections between neighboring pixels. The set of edges

$$\mathcal{E} := \left\{ \bigcup_{\mathbf{p} \in \mathcal{P}} \{e_{\mathbf{sp}}, e_{\mathbf{pt}}\} \right\} \cup \left\{ \bigcup_{(\mathbf{p},\mathbf{q}) \in \mathcal{N}} \{e_{\mathbf{pq}}\} \right\},$$

is the union of the sets of all pixels connected to the terminal links and the set of all edges between neighboring pixels. The set $\mathcal{N}$ contains the eight adjacent pixels of the pixel $\mathbf{p}$. Since the energy functional has already been introduced, it has only to be defined how the graph and the energy functional (2.1) come together. Depending on the class of edge, the corresponding edge weights are given by

$$
\begin{array}{llll}
s\text{-links}: & w_{sp} := D_{\mathbf{p}}\,(l_{\mathbf{p}} = 0) & & \mathbf{p} \in \mathcal{P}\,, \\
t\text{-links}: & w_{\mathbf{pt}} := D_{\mathbf{p}}\,(l_{\mathbf{p}} = 1) & & \mathbf{p} \in \mathcal{P}\,, \\
n\text{-links}: & w_{\mathbf{pq}} := f_{\mathrm{s}}\,(W(\mathbf{p},\mathbf{q}) \cdot \delta(l_{\mathbf{p}}, l_{\mathbf{q}})) & & (\mathbf{p},\mathbf{q}) \in \mathcal{N}\,.
\end{array}
$$

$W(\mathbf{p}, \mathbf{q})$ represents the inverted mean value of two horizontal or diagonal adjacent pixels. The inverted mean value of two pixels is chosen, since this value is low if both pixels belong to the background. It is medium, if one pixel belongs to a character and one to the background. For two pixels that belong to a character this value is high. Hence, a cut is preferred in the background region, since there the weights are lower. For vertical adjacent pixels the weight is set to twice the mean value of the two gray values. This favors that the background region is vertically cut.

As already mentioned the cost of the minimum cut through the graph is equivalent to the minimum of the energy functional defined in equation 2.1. The cut severs the graph into to disjoint graphs, where one is connected to the source s and one to sink t. After the cut, the sets of vertices connected to source and sink are denoted by $\mathcal{S}$ and $\mathcal{T}$, respectively. With respect to the labels this means that label $l_{\mathbf{p}} = 0$ is assigned to vertex $v_{\mathbf{p}} \in \mathcal{S}$ and label $l_{\mathbf{q}} = 1$ to vertex $v_{\mathbf{q}} \in \mathcal{T}$. The minimum cut costs are given by the sum of the weights of the edges that are cut. This can formally be expressed as

$$C_{\mathcal{ST}} := \sum_{\substack{\mathbf{p} \in \mathcal{S}, \\ \mathbf{q} \in \mathcal{T}, \\ e_{\mathbf{pq}} \in \mathcal{E}}} w_{\mathbf{pq}}\,.$$

An example is given in Figure 3.1, where the graph is indicated in the image on top. The two terminal vertices are connected to every pixel according to the position penalty function, which is given in the plot on the bottom. Note, in spite of the connections of the terminal vertices shown in Figure 3.1 to the pixels at the border of the image only, all pixels are connected to both terminals, i.e.the position penalty plotted in Figure 3.1 is applied to each row of the image and is valid for the label $l_{\mathbf{p}} = 0$. The connections represented by the discontinuity penalty are based on the gray values of the image. Furthermore, the first minimum cost path is emphasized in black. For segmenting all characters the first segmented part is removed and the source terminal is connected to the new image.

Graph with the minimum cut indicated in black.

Position penalty $D_{\mathbf{p}}(l_{\mathbf{p}} = 0)|_m$ for each row m of the image.

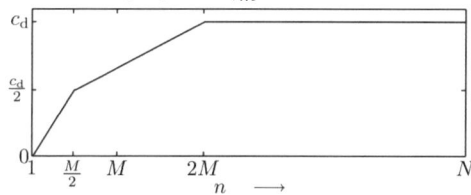

Figure 3.1: Example of the graph and the position penalty function.

Now the graph is fully defined, in which the minimum cut can be exactly determined in polynomial time. In the next section the rather theoretical consideration up to now is supplemented by some experiments.

4   Experiments

In addition to the fundamentals of character segmentation using graph cuts that have been introduced so far, some experiments are given in this section. Based on these experiments the results of the proposed method are discussed in detail.

For the experiments some conditions have to be mentioned. Since it is assumed that the characters are of a width not larger than twice the characters' height, the position penalty introduced in Section 2.2 is restricted to this, i.e.it is essential that $N > 2M$. Hence, the position penalty is slightly changed, if this not applies. In fact it is chosen that the most probable segmentation cut is approximately in the middle of the image. Since we assume that no character is wider than half of its height this is used as the stopping criterion ($N \leq \frac{M}{2}$) of the iteration. The constant of the position penalty is set to $c_d = 255$, since this is the interval in which the values of an 8 bit gray scale image lie. For most examples the constant in the discontinuity penalty is chosen $c_s = 40 \cdot c_d$, i.e.this penalty is weighted 40 times higher than the position penalty. There is only one example where it is chosen differently, which is especially mentioned.

4.1   Results

In Figure 4.1 the same text line is given as in Figure 3.1. The image in this figure also shows the segmentation cuts in black. These cuts are determined by iteratively applying the method proposed in this report. As we can see, the segmentation cuts are mostly vertical, since the weights of the discontinuity penalty in vertical direction are two times higher. Even though the typewritten characters are written in italic characters, the segmentation cuts are correct in this example.

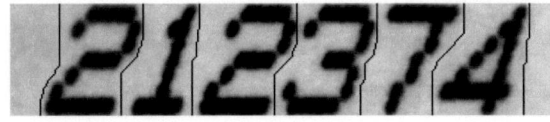

Figure 4.1: Text line of typewritten italic characters. The segmentation cuts are indicated in black.

The example in Figure 4.2 shows a text line with typewritten dot matrix characters. The segmentation cuts are also indicated in black, which show that all characters are segmented correctly. Usually this kind of font is very difficult to segment, since dots of the characters may not be touching, e.g.the dots of the digit "4" in this image. One thing that can be noticed in the figure, the region after the character—only background—is segmented as well. However, in most cases these regions can be rejected not to be a character by considering the mean gray value of this region or its width.

Figure 4.2: Text line of typewritten dot matrix characters.

The text line in the image in Figure 4.3 is a little curved and the characters are badly printed. The characters are segmented correctly though. Another difficulty is that the character distance is very small, e.g.the digit "6" six and the following two digits "9" are very close together, thus segmentation of these characters is very hard.

Figure 4.3: Segmentation of badly printed characters.

In Figure 4.4 a text line is given, which contains touching and badly printed characters. Some are not even readable for humans. However, the segmentation result looks promising. The example shows that with this method even touching characters can be segmented correctly. The only shortcoming noticed with this example is, that the method is very sensitive to the scaling constant c_s of the discontinuity penalty. For the correct segmentation of all characters of this text line it is set to $c_s = 20 \cdot c_d$.

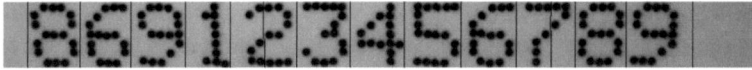

Figure 4.4: Segmentation of badly printed and touching characters.

As already mentioned, the segmentation of dot matrix characters can be very difficult due to non-touching dots. In Figure 4.5 another example of a text line containing dot matrix characters is given. For most characters the segmentation is correct, but the digits "2" and "7" in this image are split. In consideration of this shortcoming it is assumed that the segmentation result can be further improved, if the discontinuity penalty is especially adapted to dot matrix fonts, i.e.more information about the neighborhood of a pixel must be considered.

Figure 4.5: Wrongly segmented dot matrix characters.

A third text line with dot matrix characters is given in Figure 4.6. The dots of the characters in this image are mostly touching. But in some cases dots are not touching, which leads two times to a wrong segmentation of the digit "9". Since this kind of mistake is without any further expense hard to detect, it will also have an effect on classification. Both digits "9" would probably be classified as "3".

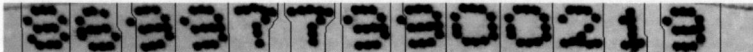

Figure 4.6: Text line with wrongly segmented dot matrix characters.

4.2 Discussion

Based on the previous experiments some pros and cons of the proposed procedure are discussed. Since this is just the first approach using graph cuts for character segmentation, there are still a lot of shortcomings. Nevertheless, the experiments done so far on badly printed or merged characters and on dot matrix fonts, show promising results. The position penalty introduced in Section 2.2 makes sure that the characters are segmented from left to right. Due to this restriction it seems to be the better approach than to allow a segmentation cut anywhere in the image. However, we assume that the method can be further improved, if the position penalty is adaptive to the characters' width and not fixed to twice the characters' height. The experiments also have shown that the method is sensitive to the illumination conditions, although the discontinuity penalty is normalized with respect to the image mean. Furthermore, in some cases the scaling constant c_s can influence the segmentation result dramatically. These are two shortcomings that come along with the discontinuity penalty and shows that this is an important topic for further research. Part of future investigations must also be more experiments to show the robustness and the reliability and an evaluation in comparison to methods mentioned in Section 1.

5 Conclusion

A typewritten character segmentation method has been introduced, which is based on graph cuts. For the graph representation of the images the commonly used energy functional has been adapted to the character segmentation task. The functional consists of two components. The first one is adapted such that the characters are segmented out of the image from left to right. The second component penalizes discontinuities and brighter regions to enforce the minimum cut between to characters. The method has to be iteratively applied, since only one cut can be obtained at a time. The experiments have shown that this first approach is promising, e.g.for the segmentation of merged or badly printed characters. However, there are still some shortcomings, which have to be rectified.

The main topic for future research is the selection of the discontinuity penalty. This regards the scaling as well as the influence of the neighborhood, since it is assumed that the improvement of both can definitely make the segmentation method more robust to noise and changing illumination conditions. Furthermore, the method has to be evaluated with respect to common methods.

Bibliography

[BFL06]   Yuri Boykov and Gareth Funka-Lea. Graph Cuts and Efficient N-D Image Segmentation. *Int. J. Comput. Vision*, 70(2):109–131, 2006.

[BK04]   Yuri Boykov and Vladimir Kolmogorov. An experimental comparison of min-cut/max-flow algorithms for energy minimization in vision. *IEEE Transactions on Pattern Analysis and Machine Intelligence*, 26(9):1124–1137, 2004.

[BVZ01]   Yuri Boykov, Olga Veksler, and Ramin Zabih. Fast approximate energy minimization via graph cuts. *IEEE Transactions on Pattern Analysis and Machine Intelligence*, 23(11):1222–1239, November 2001.

[CL96]   Richard G. Casey and Eric Lecolinet. A Survey of Methods and Strategies in Character Segmentation. *IEEE Transactions on Pattern Analysis and Machine Intelligence*, 18:690–706, 1996.

[JFZ63]   Lester R. Ford Jr., Delbert R. Fulkerson, and Arthur Ziffer. Flows in Networks. *Physics Today*, 16(7):54–56, 1963.

[KSE+03] Vivek Kwatra, Arno Schödl, Irfan Essa, Greg Turk, and Aaron Bobick. Graphcut textures: image and video synthesis using graph cuts. *ACM Trans. Graph.*, 22(3):277–286, 2003.

[KZ04]   Vladimir Kolmogorov and Ramin Zabih. What energy functions can be minimized via graph cuts? *IEEE Transactions on Pattern Analysis and Machine Intelligence*, 26(2):147–159, 2004.

[LeB97]   Frank LeBourgeois. Robust Multifont OCR System from Gray Level Images. *Int. Conf. on Document Analysis and Recognition*, 1:1–5, 1997.

[LL95]   Dong-June Lee and Seong-Whan Lee. A new methodology for gray-scale character segmentation and recognition. *International Conference on Document Analysis and Recognition*, 1:524–527, 1995.

[LNCS04] Yun Li, Satoshi Naoi, Mohamed Cheriet, and Ching Y. Suen. A segmentation method for touching italic characters. In *Proc. 17th Int. Conf. Pattern Recognition ICPR 2004*, volume 2, pages 594–597, 2004.

[Lu95]   Yi Lu. Machine printed character segmentation – An overview. *Pattern Recognition*, 28(1):67–80, 1995.

[NYK+05]   Shigueo Nomura, Keiji Yamanaka, Osamu Katai, Hiroshi Kawakami, and Takayuki Sh-
           iose. A novel adaptive morphological approach for degraded character image segmenta-
           tion. *Pattern Recognition*, 38(11):1961–1975, 2005.

[PYX08]   Mei-Sen Pan, Jun-Biao Yan, and Zheng-Hong Xiao. Vehicle license plate character
           segmentation. *International Journal of Automation and Computing*, 5:425–432, 2008.

[SSR10]   Tanzila Saba, Ghazali Sulong, and Amjad Rehman. A Survey on Methods and Strategies
           on Touched Characters Segmentation. *International Journal of Research and Reviews in
           Computer Science*, 1(2), 2010.

[Suw05]   Misako Suwa. Segmentation of Connected Handwritten Numerals by Graph Representa-
           tion. In *Proc. 8th Int. Conf. on Document Analysis and Recognition (ICDAR'05)*, pages
           750–754, Seoul, Korea, 2005.

[TCJY07]   Jia Tse, Dean Curtis, Christopher Jones, and Evangelos Yfantis. An OCR-independent
           character segmentation using shortest-path in grayscale document images. In *Proc. 6th
           Int. Conf. Machine Learning and Applications ICMLA 2007*, pages 142–147, 2007.

[Yan00]   Berrin A. Yanikoglu. Pitch-based segmentation and recognition of dot-matrix text.
           International Journal on Document Analysis and Recognition, 3:34–39, 2000.

[ZZ03]   Yungang Zhang and Changshui Zhang. A New Algorithm for Character Segmentation of
           License Plate. In *Proc. IEEE Intelligent Vehicles Symposium*, pages 106–109, 2003.

Data Association for Multi-Target-Tracking

Michael Grinberg

Vision and Fusion Laboratory
Institute for Anthropomatics
Karlsruhe Institute of Technology (KIT), Germany
michael.grinberg@kit.edu

Technical Report IES-2010-12

Abstract: This report describes problems of Multi-Target-Tracking and gives an introduction to the state-of-the-art methods of dynamic state estimation and data association in cluttered environments. A detailed derivation of the Probabilistic Data Association Filter and Joint Probabilistic Data Association Filter is given.

1 Introduction

Object detection and tracking is an important task in modern environment perception and surveillance systems. Its aim is continuous localization of people or objects in an environment by processing data of environment perception sensors such as sonars, radars, lidars, or video cameras. In general, the problem of object tracking can be divided into three subtasks: data association (re-identification), dynamic state estimation (filtering), and track management. The first subtask is responsible for the correct interpretation of the collected observations, i.e., assignment of sensor measurements to the tracked objects (tracks). The second subtask deals with estimation of the dynamic state of the objects (e.g., kinematics) from a sequence of noisy measurements. Finally, the third subtask is responsible for a consistent internal representation of the tracked objects, which includes initiation of new and deletion of obsolete tracks. The following sections give an introduction to the basic state-of-the-art methods for dynamic state estimation and data association in cluttered environments.

2 Dynamic State Estimation

Each measurement process contains sources of noise. Thus, obtained measurements may differ from the expected values. The aim of a dynamic state estimator is the determination of the real value of a not known system state from the obtained (noisy) measurements. This is done by the so-called filtering algorithms that aim at minimization of the noise effects. There exists a variety of such methods. Most of the modern tracking systems use statistical filters that are based on the Bayesian approach. They model system state and noise as random variables and estimate their statistics using certain assumptions about their nature.

Applications with real-time requirements often cannot consider the entire measurement history for achieving the best estimation result. Thus, they proceed recursively using only the last estimated system state and the current measurements. The underlying assumption is that all previous measurements are incorporated in the estimated state and are not required to be processed again in each time step (Markov property). The system evolution is thus modeled by means of a Markov process.

A system state $\mathbf{x}_k$ at discrete time point k is modeled as a realization of a random variable $\mathbf{X}$ in the state space $\mathcal{X}$. The system state between two discrete points in time k and $k + 1$ is assumed to behave according to a known system evolution function f (*system model*):

$$\mathbf{X}_{k+1} = f(\mathbf{X}_k, \mathbf{u}_k, \mathbf{W}_k),$$

where $\mathbf{u}_k$ represents the (known) system control parameters and $\mathbf{W}_k$ represents the stochastic component which cannot be modeled analytically (system noise).

The observations $\mathbf{z}_k$ are modeled as a realization of a random variable $\mathbf{Z}$ in the measurement space $\mathcal{Z}$. The measurement process is modeled by means of a *measurement model* $h(\mathbf{X}_k, \mathbf{V}_k)$:

$$\mathbf{Z}_k = h(\mathbf{X}_k, \mathbf{V}_k),$$

where $\mathbf{V}_k$ represents the stochastic component of the measurement process (measurement noise). Since the system state can not be observed directly, one speaks of the *Hidden Markov Model (HMM)*. The relation between system states and observations of a Hidden Markov Model for the case of discrete states is shown in Figure 2.1.

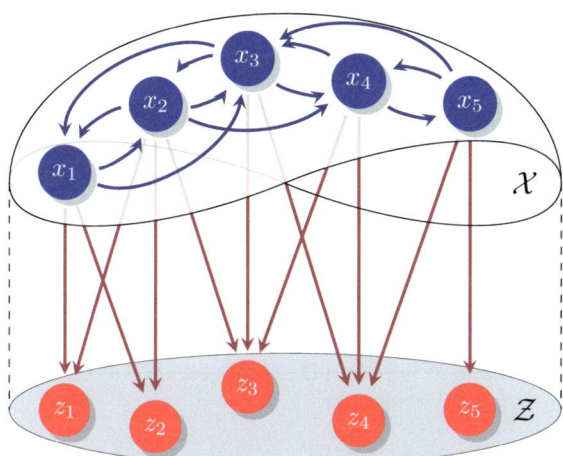

Figure 2.1: Relation between system states and observations in a Hidden Markov Model. Possible state transitions are represented by blue arrows, emission probabilities are indicated as purple arrows. Here, the subscripts of the states and observations are used not for indicating the time index k but serve for enumeration of the both sets.

The state estimation is done using the so-called Predictor-Corrector cycle, which consist of two steps:

Prediction of the probability density functions of the new system state and expected measurements based on the latest state estimate by using the system model and the measurement model.

Correction of the estimated system state and adaptation of the both models based on the actually obtained measurements. It is also called *Innovation*, *Update* or *Filtering*.

The basic principle of a recursive statistical filter is shown in Figure 2.2. The filter works recursively in a predictor-corrector cycle starting with an initial system state estimate $\hat{\mathbf{x}}_0$. Given a state estimation at time step $k - 1$ the filter propagates it in the time using the system model. In this way, an a-priori estimate of the current system state $\hat{\mathbf{x}}_k^-$ is obtained. Then, the measurement model is used for estimating the expected measurement $\hat{\mathbf{z}}_k$. After having obtained the actual measurement $\mathbf{z}_k$, a correction step is performed, in which both the current state and the uncertainties of the both models are updated based on the difference (residuals) between the predicted and actually obtained measurements.

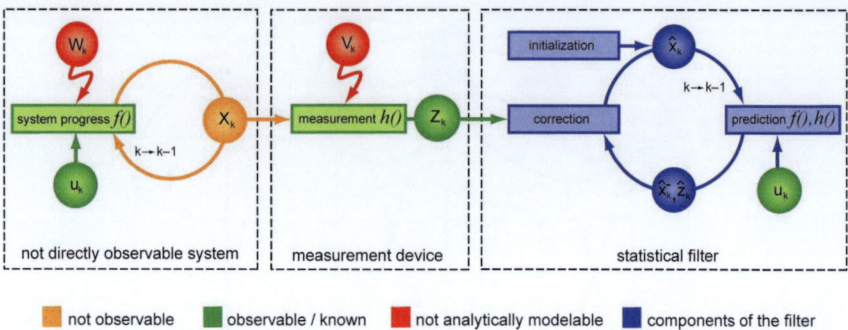

Figure 2.2: Illustration of the dependencies between the observed system and the filtering process of a statistical filter.

One of the simplest statistical dynamic state estimators is the *Kalman Filter* introduced by R. E. Kalman in 1960 [Kal60]. It assumes Gaussian distributions of both the state and the noise variables and provides equations for propagation of those distributions using linear system and measurement models. For the case of $\mathbf{W}_k$ and $\mathbf{V}_k$ being uncorrelated and having white Gaussian distribution with zero mean, the Kalman Filter is an optimal estimator in the sense of the least square errors and Bayesian filtering.

A Gaussian distribution can be represented by the two first moments (mean and covariance matrix) and is easily propagated through a linear system resulting in another Gaussian distribution. In case of non-linearities in at least one of the both models, this is not the case anymore. For coping with this problem two different approaches have been proposed. The first one aims at approximation of the non-linear function by using the Taylor series expansion around the mean of the Gaussian distribution (*Extended Kalman Filter (EKF)*, *Iterative Extended Kalman Filter (IEKF)*). The second approach aims at approximation of the distribution by means of a set of points that can be propagated through the non-linear functions and serve for determination of the new distribution parameters (*Unscented Kalman Filter (UKF)*, *Central Difference Kalman Filter (CDKF)* etc.). A generalization of this approach leads to the family of the *Sequential Monte Carlo Methods (SMCM)* also known as *Particle Filters (PF)*. An overview over different dynamic state estimators can be found in [BSL93, Bro98, Sim06]. Following subsections recapitulate the basics of the linear Kalman Filter, Extended Kalman Filter and Iterative Extended Kalman Filter since they build the basement for the data association methods presented in this paper.

2.1   Linear Kalman Filter

In the case of the linear Kalman Filter, system model and measurement model are given as linear equations

$$\mathbf{X}_{k+1} = \mathbf{F}\mathbf{X}_k + \mathbf{G}\mathbf{u}_k + \mathbf{W}_k \qquad \text{(state equation)} \qquad (2.1)$$

$$\mathbf{Z}_k = \mathbf{H}\mathbf{X}_k + \mathbf{V}_k \qquad \text{(measurement equation)}$$

with $\mathbf{F}$, $\mathbf{G}$ and $\mathbf{H}$ being the system matrix, the control matrix and the measurement matrix, respectively, and

$$\mathbf{X}_k \sim \mathcal{N}(\hat{\mathbf{x}}_k, \mathbf{P}_{\mathbf{X}_k \mathbf{X}_k}) \qquad (2.2)$$

with

$$\mathbf{P}_{\mathbf{X}_k \mathbf{X}_k} := \mathrm{Cov}(\mathbf{X}_k, \mathbf{X}_k) = \mathbb{E}\big[(\mathbf{X}_k - \hat{\mathbf{x}}_k)(\mathbf{X}_k - \hat{\mathbf{x}}_k)\big] .$$

The noise components $\mathbf{W}$ and $\mathbf{V}$ are assumed to be uncorrelated and to have white Gaussian distribution with zero mean and known covariance matrices $\mathbf{Q}_k$ and $\mathbf{R}_k$:

$$\mathbf{W}_k \sim \mathcal{N}(\mathbf{0}, \mathbf{Q}_k), \quad \mathbf{V}_k \sim \mathcal{N}(\mathbf{0}, \mathbf{R}_k),$$

$$\mathbf{P}_{\mathbf{W}_k \mathbf{W}_t} := \mathrm{Cov}(\mathbf{W}_k, \mathbf{W}_t) = \mathbb{E}\big[\mathbf{W}_k \mathbf{W}_t^T\big] = \begin{cases} \mathbf{Q}_k & \text{for } t = k \\ \mathbf{0} & \text{for } t \neq k, \end{cases}$$

$$\mathbf{P}_{\mathbf{V}_k \mathbf{V}_t} := \mathrm{Cov}(\mathbf{V}_k, \mathbf{V}_t) = \mathbb{E}\big[\mathbf{V}_k \mathbf{V}_t^T\big] = \begin{cases} \mathbf{R}_k & \text{for } t = k \\ \mathbf{0} & \text{for } t \neq k, \end{cases}$$

$$\mathbf{P}_{\mathbf{W}_k \mathbf{V}_t} := \mathrm{Cov}(\mathbf{W}_k, \mathbf{V}_t) = \mathbb{E}\big[\mathbf{W}_k \mathbf{V}_t^T\big] = \mathbf{0} \quad \text{for all } t \text{ and } k,$$

$$\mathbf{P}_{\mathbf{X}_k \mathbf{W}_t} := \mathrm{Cov}(\mathbf{X}_k, \mathbf{W}_t) = \mathbb{E}\big[\mathbf{X}_k \mathbf{W}_t^T\big] = \mathbf{0} \quad \text{for all } t \text{ and } k,$$

$$\mathbf{P}_{\mathbf{X}_k \mathbf{V}_t} := \mathrm{Cov}(\mathbf{X}_k, \mathbf{V}_t) = \mathbb{E}\big[\mathbf{X}_k \mathbf{V}_t^T\big] = \mathbf{0} \quad \text{for all } t \text{ and } k.$$

In the considered application there is no possibility to influence the observed system. Hence, the control parameter vector $\mathbf{u}$ will be omitted in the following.

As mentioned above, the Kalman Filter gives estimates of the two first moments $\hat{\mathbf{x}}_k$ and $\mathbf{P}_{\mathbf{X}_k \mathbf{X}_k}$ of the distribution of the true state $\mathbf{x}_k$. It is initialized at time step $k = 0$ with initial state estimate $\hat{\mathbf{x}}_0$ and covariance matrix $\mathbf{P}_{\mathbf{X}_0 \mathbf{X}_0}$. The recursive expression for the calculation of the a-priori estimates $\hat{\mathbf{x}}_k^-$ and $\mathbf{P}_{\mathbf{X}_k^- \mathbf{X}_k^-}$ at time step k from the a-posteriori estimates $\hat{\mathbf{x}}_{k-1}$ and $\mathbf{P}_{\mathbf{X}_{k-1} \mathbf{X}_{k-1}}$ at the previous time step $k - 1$ is derived by using the state equation (2.1) in the expectation value computation:

$$\hat{\mathbf{x}}_k^- = \mathbb{E}\big[\mathbf{X}_k | \mathbf{z}_{1:k-1}\big] = \mathbb{E}\big[\mathbf{F}\mathbf{X}_{k-1} + \mathbf{W}_{k-1} | \mathbf{z}_{1:k-1}\big] = \mathbf{F}\hat{\mathbf{x}}_{k-1}$$

and

$$\mathbf{P}_{\mathbf{X}_k^- \mathbf{X}_k^-} = \mathbb{E}\big[(\mathbf{X}_k - \hat{\mathbf{x}}_k^-)(\mathbf{X}_k - \hat{\mathbf{x}}_k^-)^T\big]$$
$$= \mathbb{E}\big[(\mathbf{F}\mathbf{X}_{k-1} + \mathbf{W}_{k-1} - \mathbf{F}\hat{\mathbf{x}}_{k-1})(\mathbf{F}\mathbf{X}_{k-1} + \mathbf{W}_{k-1} - \mathbf{F}\hat{\mathbf{x}}_{k-1})^T\big]$$
$$= \mathbf{F}\mathbf{P}_{\mathbf{X}_{k-1}\mathbf{X}_{k-1}}\mathbf{F}^T + \mathbf{Q}_k. \tag{2.3}$$

In equation (2.3), $\mathbf{Q}_k$ represents the unpredictable noise component. The uncertainty $\mathbf{P}_{\mathbf{X}_k^- \mathbf{X}_k^-}$ of the state grows in each time step by this expression. The counteraction is achieved by integrating new information about the system state that is contained in the new measurements. This is done in the correction step using innovation $\tilde{\mathbf{z}}_k = \mathbf{z}_k - \hat{\mathbf{z}}_k$:

$$\hat{\mathbf{x}}_k = \hat{\mathbf{x}}_k^- + \mathbf{K}_k(\tilde{\mathbf{z}}_k) = \hat{\mathbf{x}}_k^- + \mathbf{K}_k(\mathbf{z}_k - \hat{\mathbf{z}}_k) = \hat{\mathbf{x}}_k^- + \mathbf{K}_k(\mathbf{z}_k - \mathbf{H}\hat{\mathbf{x}}_k^-)$$
$$= (\mathbf{I} - \mathbf{K}_k\mathbf{H})\hat{\mathbf{x}}_k^- + \mathbf{K}_k\mathbf{z}_k,$$

and

$$\mathbf{P}_{\mathbf{X}_k \mathbf{X}_k} = \mathbb{E}\big[(\mathbf{X}_k - \hat{\mathbf{x}}_k)(\mathbf{X}_k - \hat{\mathbf{x}}_k)\big] = \mathbf{P}_{\mathbf{X}_k^- \mathbf{X}_k^-} + \mathbf{K}_k\mathbf{H}\mathbf{P}_{\mathbf{X}_k^- \mathbf{X}_k^-}$$

with Kalman gain $\mathbf{K}_k = \mathbf{P}_{\mathbf{X}_k^- \mathbf{X}_k^-}\mathbf{H}^T\mathbf{P}_{\tilde{\mathbf{Z}}_k \tilde{\mathbf{Z}}_k}^{-1}$ and innovation covariance

$$\mathbf{P}_{\tilde{\mathbf{Z}}_k \tilde{\mathbf{Z}}_k} = \mathbb{E}\big[\tilde{\mathbf{Z}}_k \tilde{\mathbf{Z}}_k^T\big] = \mathbb{E}\big[\big((\mathbf{Z}_k - \hat{\mathbf{z}}_k) - 0\big)\big((\mathbf{Z}_k - \hat{\mathbf{z}}_k) - 0\big)^T\big] (= \mathbf{P}_{\mathbf{Z}_k \mathbf{Z}_k})$$
$$= \mathbb{E}\big[(\mathbf{H}(\mathbf{X}_k - \hat{\mathbf{x}}_k) + \mathbf{V}_k)(\mathbf{H}(\mathbf{X}_k - \hat{\mathbf{x}}_k) + \mathbf{V}_k)^T\big]$$
$$= \mathbf{H}\mathbf{P}_{\mathbf{X}_k \mathbf{X}_k}\mathbf{H}^T + \mathbf{R}_k.$$

2.2   Extended Kalman Filter

In the case of non-linearities in the system and measurement models, the state and measurement equation are given by

$$\mathbf{X}_{k+1} = f(\mathbf{X}_k, \mathbf{W}_k)$$
$$\mathbf{Z}_k = h(\mathbf{X}_k, \mathbf{V}_k).$$

In the most of the cases, additive noise model is assumed so that

$$\mathbf{X}_{k+1} = f(\mathbf{X}_k) + \mathbf{W}_k$$
$$\mathbf{Z}_k = h(\mathbf{X}_k) + \mathbf{V}_k.$$

The Extended Kalman Filter approximates the non-linear functions f and h using Taylor series expansion around the current mean estimate. Truncation of the Taylor series after the first element leads to a linear function, which can be used for propagation of the Gaussian distribution as in the linear case. The a-priori estimate for the system state and expected measurement can be obtained directly using both nonlinear functions. When propagating state covariance and computing Kalman gain, Jacobians $\mathbf{F}_{k-1}$ and $\mathbf{H}_k$ are used:

Prediction: $\quad \hat{\mathbf{x}}_k^- = f(\hat{\mathbf{x}}_k), \quad \mathbf{P}_{\mathbf{X}_k^- \mathbf{X}_k^-} = \mathbf{F}_{k-1} \mathbf{P}_{\mathbf{X}_{k-1} \mathbf{X}_{k-1}} \mathbf{F}_{k-1}^T + \mathbf{Q}_k$

Correction: $\quad \hat{\mathbf{x}}_k = \hat{\mathbf{x}}_k^- + \mathbf{K}_k(\mathbf{z}_k - h(\hat{\mathbf{x}}_k^-)), \quad \mathbf{P}_{\mathbf{X}_k \mathbf{X}_k} = (\mathbf{I} - \mathbf{K}_k \mathbf{H}_k) \mathbf{P}_{\mathbf{X}_k^- \mathbf{X}_k^-}$

with

$$\mathbf{K}_k = \mathbf{P}_{\mathbf{X}_k^- \mathbf{X}_k^-} \mathbf{H}_k^T \mathbf{P}_{\tilde{\mathbf{Z}}_k \tilde{\mathbf{Z}}_k}^{-1}$$

$$\mathbf{P}_{\tilde{\mathbf{Z}}_k \tilde{\mathbf{Z}}_k} = \mathbf{H}_k \mathbf{P}_{\mathbf{X}_k^- \mathbf{X}_k^-} \mathbf{H}_k^T + \mathbf{R}_k$$

and the Jacobians

$$\mathbf{F}_{k-1} = \left. \frac{\mathrm{d}f}{\mathrm{d}\mathbf{x}} \right|_{\hat{\mathbf{x}}_{k-1}} \quad \text{and} \quad \mathbf{H}_k = \left. \frac{\mathrm{d}h}{\mathrm{d}\mathbf{x}} \right|_{\hat{\mathbf{x}}_k^-} .$$

2.3 Iterative Extended Kalman Filter

The Extended Kalman Filter linearizes the measurement function around the a-priori state estimate $\hat{\mathbf{x}}_k^-$ although a better state estimate is given after the integration of the current measurement. Linearization around the a-posteriori state estimate $\hat{\mathbf{x}}_k$ may improve the estimation. This potential is exploited in the iterative version of the EKF, the Iterative Extended Kalman Filter (IEKF). IEKF iteratively repeats the correction step with the recalculated linearization of the measurement model until a termination constraint is fulfilled. For ensuring non-recurrent integration of the measurement $\mathbf{z}_k$ during the iterations, a correction term $\mathbf{H}_k^{(i)}(\hat{\mathbf{x}}_k^- - \hat{\mathbf{x}}_k^{(i)})$ is used in each iteration i:

$$\hat{\mathbf{x}}_k^{(i+1)} = \hat{\mathbf{x}}_k^- + \mathbf{K}_k^{(i)}(\mathbf{z}_k - h(\hat{\mathbf{x}}_k^{(i)}) - \mathbf{H}_k^{(i)}(\hat{\mathbf{x}}_k^- - \hat{\mathbf{x}}_k^{(i)}))$$

$$\mathbf{K}_k^{(i)} = \mathbf{P}_{\mathbf{X}_k^- \mathbf{X}_k^-} (\mathbf{H}_k^{(i)})^T (\mathbf{P}_{\tilde{\mathbf{Z}}_k \tilde{\mathbf{Z}}_k}^{(i)})^{-1}$$

with

$$\mathbf{H}_k^{(i)} = \left. \frac{\mathrm{d}h}{\mathrm{d}\mathbf{x}} \right|_{\hat{\mathbf{x}}_k^{(i)}}$$

and start value $\hat{\mathbf{x}}_k^{(0)} = \hat{\mathbf{x}}_k^-$.

3   Data association

In order to correctly perform the update step, statistical state estimators such as the Kalman Filter assume a correct assignment of measurements to tracks. A correct assignment means that in each time step each track is associated with a single measurement that has been originated from the corresponding object. The problem of assigning measurements to the existing tracks is called the data association problem. Data association is not always a trivial process. Given multiple active tracks and multiple detections, there are often several assignment possibilities being more or less probable. Figure 3.1 illustrates the data association ambiguity in case of three objects and four measurements.

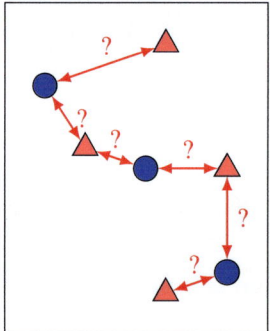

Figure 3.1: Illustration of a possible data association ambiguity in case of three tracks and four measurements. The three expected measurements are visualized by blue circles, the actually obtained – by red triangles.

Further uncertainties are introduced through the fact that a measurement may be evoked not only by a real object but may emerge due to concentration of noise in the data (clutter) or may be missing due to weaknesses of the sensors or of the subsequent data processing algorithms. And, finally, in some systems an object may evoke multiple measurements and several objects may give a joint measurement. This makes unambiguous assignments difficult or even impossible. In case of extended targets this is even worse since object observability represents another uncertainty source. Partial and full occlusions result in incomplete and missing detections and make data association even more challenging.

There exists a number of algorithms for solving the data association problem in multi-target applications. Hereby, a differentiation between the so-called *single scan algorithms* (also referred to as *Single Hypotheses Tracking (SHT)*) and *multiscan algorithms* (also referred to as *Multi-Hypotheses Tracking (MHT)*) is done.

While single scan algorithms consider only data of the current frame (scan), multiscan algorithms simultaneously evaluate multiple hypotheses maintaining them throughout several frames in anticipation that the new data will allow to resolve emerging conflicts [Rei79, CH96]. In practice, single scan algorithms are often preferred due to their simplicity and low computational cost. In the following, algorithms assuming that the number of tracks is known and a detection corresponds to a single track and vice versa will be presented.

3.1 Nearest Neighbor Algorithms

One of the simplest data association algorithms is the *Nearest Neighbor algorithm (NN)*. It is a typical single scan algorithm since it considers only measurements belonging to the current data frame (scan). NN algorithm considers only one data association hypothesis, assigning for each track the closest measurement. As shown in Figure 3.2 (a), in multi-target tracking scenarios, the NN algorithm is not optimal since it might assign a single measurement to multiple tracks despite the presence of other measurements. There exists an iterative version of the NN algorithm which prohibits multiple selections. It sequentially choses track-measurement pairs with the closest distance and excludes them from further consideration. This algorithm is suboptimal too, since it minimizes the track-to-measurement distances sequentially and thus may miss the global minimum as shown in Figure 3.2 (b). This problem can be solved by the *Global Nearest Neighbor algorithm (GNN)* which seeks for the globally optimal solution with respect to track-to-measurement distances (Figure 3.2 (c)).

3.2 Probabilistic Data Association (PDA)

Nearest Neighbor algorithms make a hard decision by minimizing distances between the predicted and real measurements. This decision might be optimal with respect to the distances in the current frame, however it may be still suboptimal with respect to the whole measurement sequence. Especially in applications where missing detections or obtaining clutter-based detections is possible, the Global Nearest Neighbor algorithm may lead to severe tracking errors. This problem was studied thoroughly in the radar tracking literature and led to development of statistical methods based on the idea of the probabilistic data association.

The main idea of such methods is weighting of different association hypotheses according to their probabilities thus minimizing the association error. Similarly to NN and GNN, PDA-based methods consider at each point in time only currently incoming measurements, i.e., they are single scan algorithms. However,

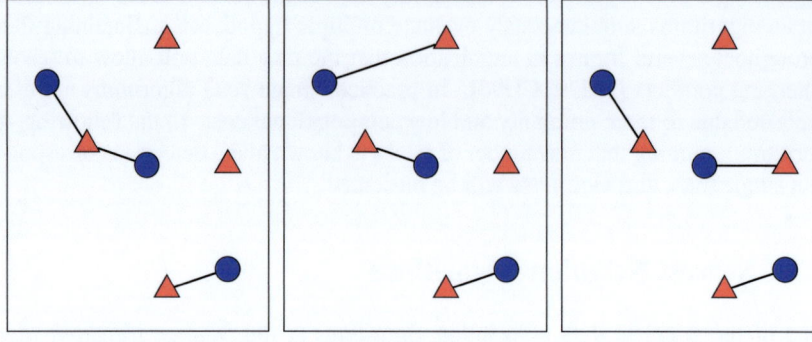

(a) Association by means of the simple Nearest Neighbor algorithm

(b) Association by means of the iterative NN algorithm

(c) Association by means of the Global Nearest Neighbor algorithm

Figure 3.2: Illustration of Nearest Neighbor data association.

when updating a track, instead of choosing a single measurement with highest association probability they evaluate multiple association hypotheses and use all neighboring measurements weighting them according to the probabilities of the corresponding hypotheses (*All-Neighbours Data Association*). Due to this *soft decision* approach, PDA-based methods suffer less from data association errors and are thus better suitable for applications with clutter-based and missing detections. Although PDA-based methods work with multiple association hypotheses they are also referred to as single hypotheses tracking algorithms since the hypotheses are combined to a single hypothesis prior to innovation. The remainder of this section addresses basics of the *Probabilistic Data Association algorithm (PDA)* proposed by Bar-Shalom et. al. [BST75, BS78].

The PDA considers each track separately. Let the considered track be denoted by $\mathbf{x}$ with $\mathbf{X}_k \sim \mathcal{N}(\hat{\mathbf{x}}_k, \mathbf{P}_{\mathbf{X}_k\mathbf{X}_k})$ as in (2.2). Under Gaussian distribution assumption, the a-priori probability density of the predicted measurement position is given by

$$f_{\mathbf{z}_k^{\mathbf{x}}} = f(\mathbf{z}_k^{\mathbf{x}}|\mathcal{Z}_{1:(k-1)}^{\mathbf{x}}) = \mathcal{N}(\mathbf{z}_k; \hat{\mathbf{z}}_k^{\mathbf{x}}, \mathbf{P}_{\mathbf{Z}_k\mathbf{Z}_k}^{\mathbf{x}}),$$

with

$$\hat{\mathbf{z}}_k^{\mathbf{x}} = \mathbf{H}\hat{\mathbf{x}}_k^- \quad \text{and} \quad \mathbf{P}_{\mathbf{Z}_k\mathbf{Z}_k}^{\mathbf{x}} = \mathbf{H}\mathbf{P}_{\mathbf{X}_k^-\mathbf{X}_k^-}\mathbf{H}^T + \mathbf{R}.$$

For preventing associations with too far lying and thus too improbable measurements a selection region referred to as the *gating region* or *validation gate* $\Gamma_k^{\mathbf{x}}$ is defined around $\hat{\mathbf{z}}_k$ with volume $V_k^{\mathbf{x}}$. Associations are only performed with measurements falling inside the gating region. The probability of the correct measurement

$\mathbf{z}_k$ to lie inside the gating region is given by

$$P_G^{\mathbf{x}_k} = P(\mathbf{z}_k \in \Gamma_k^{\mathbf{x}}) = \int\limits_{V_k^{\mathbf{x}}} f_{\mathbf{Z}_k^{\mathbf{x}}} \, d\mathbf{z}_k \, . \tag{3.1}$$

The a-priori probability density function that accounts for gating is thus defined as:

$$p(\mathbf{z}_k^{\mathbf{x}} | \mathcal{Z}_{1:(k-1)}) := \begin{cases} \frac{1}{P_G} f_{\mathbf{Z}_k^{\mathbf{x}}} & \text{for} \quad \mathbf{z}_k^{\mathbf{x}} \in \Gamma_k^{\mathbf{x}} \\ 0 & \text{for} \quad \mathbf{z}_k^{\mathbf{x}} \notin \Gamma_k^{\mathbf{x}} \end{cases} .$$

Often, validation gates are defined as hyper-ellipsoidal regions around $\hat{\mathbf{z}}_k^{\mathbf{x}}$ such that $P_G^{\mathbf{x}_k} = P_G$ is a constant. This is done by choosing

$$\Gamma_k^{\mathbf{x}}(\gamma) = \{ \mathbf{z} : (\mathbf{z} - \hat{\mathbf{z}}_k^{\mathbf{x}})^T (\mathbf{P}_{\mathbf{Z}_k \mathbf{Z}_k}^{\mathbf{x}})^{-1} (\mathbf{z} - \hat{\mathbf{z}}_k^{\mathbf{x}}) \le \gamma \} \tag{3.2}$$

with a constant parameter γ. As the measurements are normally distributed, it holds that

$$(\mathbf{Z} - \hat{\mathbf{z}}_k^{\mathbf{x}})^T (\mathbf{P}_{\mathbf{Z}_k \mathbf{Z}_k}^{\mathbf{x}})^{-1} (\mathbf{Z} - \hat{\mathbf{z}}_k^{\mathbf{x}}) \sim \chi_{n_{\mathbf{z}}}^2 \quad \Rightarrow \quad P_G = P(\mathbf{z}_k \in \Gamma_k^{\mathbf{x}}(\gamma)) = \chi_{n_{\mathbf{z}}}^2(\gamma) \, ,$$

with $n_{\mathbf{z}}$ being the dimension of the measurement $\mathbf{z}$. Defining a constant P_G leads to certain γ, which can be obtained from the quantile tables of the $n_{\mathbf{z}}$-dimensional chi-square distribution ($\gamma = \chi_{n_{\mathbf{z}}, P_G}^2$). This allows for determination of $\Gamma_k^{\mathbf{x}} = \Gamma_k^{\mathbf{x}}(\gamma)$ as well as $V_k^{\mathbf{x}} = V_k^{\mathbf{x}}(\gamma)$ which is given as

$$V_k^{\mathbf{x}}(\gamma) = c_{n_{\mathbf{z}}} \gamma^{\frac{n_{\mathbf{z}}}{2}} \left| \mathbf{P}_{\mathbf{Z}_k \mathbf{Z}_k}^{\mathbf{x}} \right|^{\frac{1}{2}} \, ,$$

where $c_{n_{\mathbf{z}}}$ is the volume of the $n_{\mathbf{z}}$-dimensional unity sphere ($c_1 = 2, c_2 = \pi, c_3 = \frac{4}{3}\pi, c_4 = \frac{1}{2}\pi^2, \cdots$).

The set of $m_k^{\mathbf{x}}$ measurements falling into the gating region of a track $\mathbf{x}$ at time step k is denoted by $\mathcal{Z}_k^{\mathbf{x}}$: $\mathcal{Z}_k^{\mathbf{x}} = \{ \mathbf{z}_{k,1}, \ldots, \mathbf{z}_{k,m_k^{\mathbf{x}}} \} \in \Gamma_k^{\mathbf{x}}$. For better readability, the superscript $\mathbf{x}$ in $m_k^{\mathbf{x}}$ will be omitted in the following. For each measurement $\mathbf{z}_{k,j} \in \mathcal{Z}_k^{\mathbf{x}}$ a hypothesis is formed, where this measurement is assumed being correct while all other $m_k - 1$ measurements in the gate are assumed to be caused by clutter. This hypothesis is denoted as $\theta_k^{\mathbf{x} \to \mathbf{z}_j}$ with $j \in \{1 \ldots m_k\}$. $\theta_k^{\mathbf{x} \to \mathbf{z}_0}$ denotes the hypothesis of none of the m_k measurements in gate being correct, i.e., that all of them stem from clutter or are false alarms.

In the innovation step of the Bayesian state estimator, estimates produced by each hypothesis are weighted with the weighting factors $\beta_k^{\mathbf{x} \to \mathbf{z}_j}$ (with $j \in \{0 \ldots m_k\}$)

that are defined as

$$\beta_k^{\mathbf{x} \to \mathbf{z}_j} = P(\theta_k^{\mathbf{x} \to \mathbf{z}_j} | \mathcal{Z}_{1:k}^{\mathbf{x}})$$

with $\mathcal{Z}_{1:k}^{\mathbf{x}} = \{\mathcal{Z}_1^{\mathbf{x}}, \dots, \mathcal{Z}_k^{\mathbf{x}}\}$ and $\sum_{j=0}^{m_k} \beta_k^{\mathbf{x} \to \mathbf{z}_j} = 1$. The weighting factors are calculated using Bayes' theorem:

$$\begin{aligned}
\beta_k^{\mathbf{x} \to \mathbf{z}_j} &= P(\theta_k^{\mathbf{x} \to \mathbf{z}_j} | \mathcal{Z}_{1:k}^{\mathbf{x}}) = P(\theta_k^{\mathbf{x} \to \mathbf{z}_j} | \mathcal{Z}_k^{\mathbf{x}}, m_k, \mathcal{Z}_{1:(k-1)}^{\mathbf{x}}) \\
&= \frac{1}{c_k} p(\mathcal{Z}_k^{\mathbf{x}} | \theta_k^{\mathbf{x} \to \mathbf{z}_j}, m_k, \mathcal{Z}_{1:(k-1)}^{\mathbf{x}}) P(\theta_k^{\mathbf{x} \to \mathbf{z}_j} | m_k, \mathcal{Z}_{1:(k-1)}^{\mathbf{x}})
\end{aligned}$$

with c_k being the normalization factor. Assuming a Gaussian measurement distribution, the likelihood of the true measurement $\mathbf{z}_{k,j}$ $(j \neq 0)$ is given by

$$\begin{aligned}
p(\mathbf{z}_{k,j} | \theta_k^{\mathbf{x} \to \mathbf{z}_j}, m_k, \mathcal{Z}_{1:(k-1)}^{\mathbf{x}}) &= \tfrac{1}{P_G} f_{\mathbf{z}_k^{\mathbf{x}}} = \tfrac{1}{P_G} \mathcal{N}(\mathbf{z}_{k,j}; \hat{\mathbf{z}}_k^{\mathbf{x}}, \mathbf{P}_{\mathbf{Z}_k \mathbf{Z}_k}^{\mathbf{x}}) \\
&= \tfrac{1}{P_G} \mathcal{N}(\mathbf{z}_{k,j} - \hat{\mathbf{z}}_k^{\mathbf{x}}; 0, \mathbf{P}_{\mathbf{Z}_k \mathbf{Z}_k}^{\mathbf{x}}) = \tfrac{1}{P_G} \mathcal{N}(\tilde{\mathbf{z}}_{k,j}^{\mathbf{x}}; 0, \mathbf{P}_{\mathbf{Z}_k \mathbf{Z}_k}^{\mathbf{x}}) \\
&= \tfrac{1}{P_G} \cdot |2\pi \cdot \mathbf{P}_{\mathbf{Z}_k \mathbf{Z}_k}^{\mathbf{x}}|^{-\frac{1}{2}} \cdot e^{-\frac{1}{2}(\tilde{\mathbf{z}}_{k,j}^{\mathbf{x}})^T (\mathbf{P}_{\mathbf{Z}_k \mathbf{Z}_k}^{\mathbf{x}})^{-1} \tilde{\mathbf{z}}_{k,j}^{\mathbf{x}}}
\end{aligned}$$

with innovation $\tilde{\mathbf{z}}_{k,j}^{\mathbf{x}} = \mathbf{z}_{k,j} - \hat{\mathbf{z}}_k^{\mathbf{x}}$.

Clutter measurements are assumed to be independent from the correct measurement. Their position is assumed to be independent and identically distributed over the whole gating region with uniform distribution on $\Gamma_k^{\mathbf{x}}$. Under these assumptions,

$$p(\mathbf{z}_{k,i} | \theta_k^{\mathbf{x} \to \mathbf{z}_j}, m_k, \mathcal{Z}_{1:(k-1)}^{\mathbf{x}}) = \frac{1}{V_k} \quad j \neq i.$$

The likelihood of the entire measurement set $\mathcal{Z}_k^{\mathbf{x}}$ falling into the gating region of the track $\mathbf{x}$ at time step k given that either all of them are false alarms $(\theta_k^{\mathbf{x} \to \mathbf{z}_0})$ or the measurement j is the correct measurement and all other measurements are false alarms $(\theta_k^{\mathbf{x} \to \mathbf{z}_j}, j = 1 \dots m_k)$ is given by

$$p(\mathcal{Z}_k^{\mathbf{x}} | \theta_k^{\mathbf{x} \to \mathbf{z}_0}, m_k, \mathcal{Z}_{1:(k-1)}^{\mathbf{x}}) = \prod_{i=1}^{m_k} p(\mathbf{z}_{k,i} | \theta_k^{\mathbf{x} \to \mathbf{z}_0}, m_k, \mathcal{Z}_{1:(k-1)}^{\mathbf{x}}) = \frac{1}{V_k^{m_k}},$$

$$\begin{aligned}
p(\mathcal{Z}_k^{\mathbf{x}} | \theta_k^{\mathbf{x} \to \mathbf{z}_j}, m_k, \mathcal{Z}_{1:(k-1)}^{\mathbf{x}}) &= \prod_{i=1}^{m_k} p(\mathbf{z}_{k,i} | \theta_k^{\mathbf{x} \to \mathbf{z}_j}, m_k, \mathcal{Z}_{1:(k-1)}^{\mathbf{x}}) \\
&= \frac{1}{V_k^{m_k-1}} \frac{1}{P_G} \mathcal{N}(\tilde{\mathbf{z}}_{k,j}^{\mathbf{x}}; 0, \mathbf{P}_{\mathbf{Z}_k \mathbf{Z}_k}^{\mathbf{x}}), \quad j = 1, \cdots, m_k.
\end{aligned}$$

The probability mass function of the hypothesis $\theta_k^{\mathbf{x}\to\mathbf{z}_j}$ conditioned on m_k and $\mathcal{Z}_{1:(k-1)}^{\mathbf{x}}$ is given by

$$
\begin{aligned}
P(\theta_k^{\mathbf{x}\to\mathbf{z}_j}|m_k, \mathcal{Z}_{1:(k-1)}^{\mathbf{x}}) &= P(\theta_k^{\mathbf{x}\to\mathbf{z}_j}|m_k) \\
&= \frac{P(m_k|\theta_k^{\mathbf{x}\to\mathbf{z}_j})P(\theta_k^{\mathbf{x}\to\mathbf{z}_j})}{\sum_{j=0}^{m_k} P(m_k|\theta_k^{\mathbf{x}\to\mathbf{z}_j})P(\theta_k^{\mathbf{x}\to\mathbf{z}_j})},
\end{aligned}
\tag{3.3}
$$

where $P(\theta_k^{\mathbf{x}\to\mathbf{z}_j})$ (with $j = 1...m_k$) denotes the a-priori probability that the measurement $\mathbf{z}_j$ originated from track $\mathbf{x}$, $P(\theta_k^{\mathbf{x}\to\mathbf{z}_0})$ denotes the a-priori probability that none of the measurements in the gate has been evoked by track $\mathbf{x}$ and $P(m_k|\theta_k^{\mathbf{x}\to\mathbf{z}_0})$ and $P(m_k|\theta_k^{\mathbf{x}\to\mathbf{z}_j})$ denote the probabilities for receiving m_k measurements given that either none or one of them stems from track $\mathbf{x}$.

$P(\theta_k^{\mathbf{x}\to\mathbf{z}_0})$ is obviously given by

$$
P(\theta_k^{\mathbf{x}\to\mathbf{z}_0}) = 1 - P_D P_G,
\tag{3.4}
$$

where P_D is the probability that the track evokes a measurement (detection probability), and P_G is the probability of the measurement to fall into the gating region as defined in (3.1).

Under the assumption that each of the m_k measurements in the gate has equal probability of being evoked by track $\mathbf{x}$, the a-priori association probability $P(\theta_k^{\mathbf{x}\to\mathbf{z}_j})$ for $j = 1...m_k$ is given by

$$
P(\theta_k^{\mathbf{x}\to\mathbf{z}_j}) = \frac{1}{m_k} P_D P_G \quad \forall j = 1,...,m_k.
$$

The probability of the number of measurements being m_k given one of the association hypotheses $\theta_k^{\mathbf{x}\to\mathbf{z}_0}$ or $\theta_k^{\mathbf{x}\to\mathbf{z}_j}$ is equivalent to the probability of the number of false measurements being m_k or $m_k - 1$ correspondingly:

$$
\begin{aligned}
P(m_k|\theta_k^{\mathbf{x}\to\mathbf{z}_0}) &= \mu_F(m_k), \\
P(m_k|\theta_k^{\mathbf{x}\to\mathbf{z}_j}) &= \mu_F(m_k - 1)
\end{aligned}
\tag{3.5}
$$

with $\mu_F(m)$ being the probability mass function for the number of clutter-based measurements. $\mu_F(m)$ can be modeled in different ways. The number of the clutter-based measurements can be assumed either to have Poisson distribution (*parametric model*) or to be equally distributed over the set $\{0, \cdots, N - 1\}$ with N being the maximal number of clutter-based measurements (*non-parametric model*).

Parametric model: Poisson distribution

$$\mu_F(m) = e^{-\hat{m}_k}\frac{\hat{m}_k^m}{m!} = e^{-\lambda V_k}\frac{(\lambda V_k)^m}{m!}, \qquad m \in \mathcal{N}_0,$$

with λ being the mean clutter density and $\hat{m}_k := \lambda V_k$ being the expected number of clutter measurements in the gating region. If λ is a-priori not known, $\hat{m}_k$ can be estimated by using $\hat{m}_k = m_k - P_D P_G$.

Non-parametric model: Uniform distribution

$$\mu_F(m) = \frac{1}{N}, \qquad m = 0, 1, \ldots, N-1,$$

where N can be chosen as a great enough arbitrary number since it will be canceled in $P(\theta_k^{\mathbf{x}\to\mathbf{z}_j}|m_k, \mathcal{Z}_{1:(k-1)}^{\mathbf{x}})$.

Using (3.4) - (3.5) in (3.3) leads to

$$P(\theta_k^{\mathbf{x}\to\mathbf{z}_j}|m_k, \mathcal{Z}_{1:(k-1)}^{\mathbf{x}}) = \begin{cases} \frac{\mu_F(m_k)(1-P_D P_G)}{\mu_F(m_k)(1-P_D P_G)+m_k\cdot\mu_F(m_k-1)\frac{P_D P_G}{m_k}} & j=0 \\ \frac{\mu_F(m_k-1)\frac{P_D P_G}{m_k}}{\mu_F(m_k)(1-P_D P_G)+m_k\cdot\mu_F(m_k-1)\frac{P_D P_G}{m_k}} & j=1,\ldots,m_k \end{cases}$$

and thus to

$$P(\theta_k^{\mathbf{x}\to\mathbf{z}_j}|m_k, \mathcal{Z}_{1:(k-1)}^{\mathbf{x}}) = \begin{cases} \frac{(1-P_D P_G)\lambda V_k}{P_D P_G m_k+(1-P_D P_G)\lambda V_k} & j=0 \\ \frac{P_D P_G}{P_D P_G m_k+(1-P_D P_G)\lambda V_k} & j=1,\ldots,m_k \end{cases}$$

for the *parametric model* and to

$$P(\theta_k^{\mathbf{x}\to\mathbf{z}_j}|m_k, \mathcal{Z}_{1:(k-1)}^{\mathbf{x}}) = \begin{cases} (1-P_D P_G) & j=0 \\ \frac{1}{m_k}P_D P_G & j=1,\ldots,m_k \end{cases}$$

for the *non-parametric model*.

This leads to the following weighting factors $\beta_k^{x\to z_j}$:

$$\beta_k^{x\to z_j} = \begin{cases} \frac{b}{b+\sum_{i=1}^{m_k} e_i} & j=0 \\ \frac{e_j}{b+\sum_{i=1}^{m_k} e_i} & j=1,\ldots,m_k \end{cases}$$

with

$$e_j = e^{-\frac{1}{2}(\tilde{\mathbf{z}}_{k,j}^{\mathbf{x}})^T (\mathbf{P}_{\tilde{\mathbf{z}}_k \mathbf{z}_k}^{\mathbf{x}})^{-1} \tilde{\mathbf{z}}_{k,j}^{\mathbf{x}}}$$

and

$$b = \lambda |2\pi \mathbf{P}_{\tilde{\mathbf{Z}}_k \mathbf{Z}_k}^{\mathbf{x}}|^{\frac{1}{2}} \frac{(1-P_D P_G)}{P_D} = \begin{cases} \left(\frac{2\pi}{\gamma}\right)^{\frac{n_z}{2}} \lambda V_k c_{n_z} \frac{(1-P_D P_G)}{P_D} , & \text{parametric model} \\[2ex] \left(\frac{2\pi}{\gamma}\right)^{\frac{n_z}{2}} m_k c_{n_z} \frac{(1-P_D P_G)}{P_D} , & \text{non-parametric model.} \end{cases}$$

For each hypothesis, the corresponding state estimate is given by

$$\hat{\mathbf{x}}_k^{\mathbf{z}_j} = \mathbb{E}[\mathbf{X}_k | \theta_k^{\mathbf{x} \to \mathbf{z}_j}, \mathcal{Z}_{1:k}^{\mathbf{x}}] = \begin{cases} \hat{\mathbf{x}}_k^- & j = 0 \\ \hat{\mathbf{x}}_k^- + \mathbf{K}_k(\mathbf{z}_{k,j} - \hat{\mathbf{z}}_k^{\mathbf{x}}) & j = 1, \ldots, m_k . \end{cases}$$

When considering all hypotheses, this leads to the following composite state estimate for the track $\mathbf{x}$:

$$\hat{\mathbf{x}}_k = \mathbb{E}[\mathbf{X}_k | \mathcal{Z}_{1:k}^{\mathbf{x}}] = \sum_{j=0}^{m_k} \mathbb{E}[\mathbf{X}_k | \theta_k^{\mathbf{x} \to \mathbf{z}_j}, \mathcal{Z}_{1:k}^{\mathbf{x}}] \cdot P(\theta_k^{\mathbf{x} \to \mathbf{z}_j} | \mathcal{Z}_{1:k}^{\mathbf{x}})$$

$$= \sum_{j=0}^{m_k} \hat{\mathbf{x}}_k^{\mathbf{z}_j} \beta_k^{\mathbf{x} \to \mathbf{z}_j} = \sum_{j=0}^{m_k} \beta_k^{\mathbf{x} \to \mathbf{z}_j} \hat{\mathbf{x}}_k^- + \mathbf{K}_k \sum_{j=1}^{m_k} \beta_k^{\mathbf{x} \to \mathbf{z}_j} (\mathbf{z}_{k,j} - \hat{\mathbf{z}}_k^{\mathbf{x}})$$

$$= \hat{\mathbf{x}}_k^- + \mathbf{K}_k \sum_{j=1}^{m_k} \beta_k^{\mathbf{x} \to \mathbf{z}_j} \tilde{\mathbf{z}}_{k,j}^{\mathbf{x}} \tag{3.6}$$

with composite innovation $\tilde{\mathbf{z}}_{k,\text{Comp}}^{\mathbf{x}} := \sum_{j=1}^{m_k} \beta_k^{\mathbf{x} \to \mathbf{z}_j} \tilde{\mathbf{z}}_{k,j}^{\mathbf{x}}$.

Although the equation (3.6) seems to be linear, this is not the case as the weighting factors $\beta_k^{\mathbf{x} \to \mathbf{z}_j}$ depend on $\tilde{\mathbf{z}}_{k,j}^{\mathbf{x}}$.

The covariance matrix $\mathbf{P}_{\mathbf{X}_k \mathbf{X}_k}$ is calculated according to

$$\mathbf{P}_{\mathbf{X}_k \mathbf{X}_k} = \beta_k^{\mathbf{x} \to \mathbf{z}_0} \mathbf{P}_{\mathbf{X}_k^- \mathbf{X}_k^-} + (1 - \beta_k^{\mathbf{x} \to \mathbf{z}_0}) \mathbf{P}_{\mathbf{X}_k \mathbf{X}_k}^c + \tilde{\mathbf{P}}_k$$

with

$$\mathbf{P}_{\mathbf{X}_k \mathbf{X}_k}^c = (\mathbf{I} - \mathbf{K}_k \mathbf{H}_k) \mathbf{P}_{\mathbf{X}_k^- \mathbf{X}_k^-}$$

and

$$\tilde{\mathbf{P}}_k = \mathbf{K}_k \left(\sum_{j=1}^{m_k} \beta_k^{\mathbf{x} \to \mathbf{z}_j} \tilde{\mathbf{z}}_{k,j}^{\mathbf{x}} (\tilde{\mathbf{z}}_{k,j}^{\mathbf{x}})^T - \tilde{\mathbf{z}}_{k,\text{Comp}}^{\mathbf{x}} (\tilde{\mathbf{z}}_{k,\text{Comp}}^{\mathbf{x}})^T \right) \mathbf{K}_k^T .$$

Hereby, the predicted covariance matrix $\mathbf{P_{X_k X_k}}$ is weighted with the factor $\beta_k^{\mathbf{x} \to \mathbf{z}_0}$, which is related to the case of none of the obtained measurement being correct. $\mathbf{P}_{\mathbf{X}_k \mathbf{X}_k}^c$ is the covariance matrix calculated under the assumption that the innovation is performed with the correct measurement, i.e., without association error. It is weighted with the factor $(1 - \beta_k^{\mathbf{x} \to \mathbf{z}_0})$. Since it is not known which of the m_k measurements is the correct one, the state covariance is increased by means of the matrix $\tilde{\mathbf{P}}_k$ which incorporates the measurement association errors.

3.3 Joint Probabilistic Data Association (JPDA)

In the PDA, each track is considered separately. This justifies the assumption that either all or all but one measurements falling into the gating region of a track are due to clutter. In the presence of multiple closely spaced targets this assumption may be invalid since true measurements of one target may fall into the gating region of another target causing permanent non-random interference. This issue is accounted for in the extension of the PDA called *Joint Probabilistic Data Association (JPDA)* proposed by Bar Shalom et al. [FBSS83]. Instead of considering each track separately, JPDA considers association configurations, the so-called *joint events*. A joint event $\Theta_k(T)$ is defined as an conjunction of associations $\theta_k^{\mathbf{x}_{t_j} \to \mathbf{z}_j}$ between measurements $\mathbf{z}_j$ and possible causes $\mathbf{x}_{t_j}$ that can be given by either an existing track ($t_j \neq 0$) or clutter ($t_j = 0$):

$$\Theta_k(T) = \bigcap_{j=1}^{m_k} \theta_k^{\mathbf{x}_{t_j} \to \mathbf{z}_j}, \quad T = (t_1, ..., t_{m_k}), \quad t_j \in \{0, \dots, n_k\},$$

with n_k being number of currently tracked targets. T are ordered sets of m_k (possibly repeating) track numbers including 0, which represents the clutter source.

For reduction of complexity, tracks are partitioned into independent clusters and joint events are built for each cluster separately. A cluster is defined as a set of tracks which share no measurements with tracks that do not belong to the cluster.

For easier clutter handling, clutter measurements are considered to be identically distributed over the whole cluster volume V independently of the gating regions of the tracks. This implies that each measurement should be able to be associated with each track in the cluster and hence $P_G = 1$. However, this would also imply usage of too far lying measurements for update of a track. In order to avoid this, a binary *validation matrix* Ω_k is defined:

$$\Omega_k = [\omega_{ji}]_k, \quad j = 1, \cdots, m_k; \quad i = 0, 1, \cdots, n_k$$

with

$$\omega_{ji} = \begin{cases} 0 & \text{if} \quad \mathbf{z}_j \notin \Gamma^{\mathbf{x}_i}(\gamma) \\ 1 & \text{if} \quad \mathbf{z}_j \in \Gamma^{\mathbf{x}_i}(\gamma), \end{cases}$$

and gating regions $\Gamma^{\mathbf{x}_i}(\gamma)$ as defined in (3.2). The first column ($i = 0$) of Ω_k stands for association with no track, i.e., indicates that a measurement j stems from clutter. As mentioned above, this can be applicable to each measurement in cluster, hence $\forall j : \omega_{j0} = 1$.

Each joint event $\Theta_k(T)$ can be represented through a binary matrix $\hat{\Omega}(\Theta_k(T))$ with

$$\hat{\Omega}(\Theta_k(T)) = [\hat{\omega}_{ji}(\Theta_k(T))], \quad j = 1, \cdots, m_k; \quad i = 0, 1, \cdots, n_k$$

and

$$\hat{\omega}_{ji}(\Theta_k(T)) = \begin{cases} 1 & \text{if} \quad \theta_k^{\mathbf{x}_i \to \mathbf{z}_j} \subset \Theta_k(T) \\ 0 & \text{else}. \end{cases}$$

In JPDA, a joint event $\Theta_k(T)$ is considered to be "feasible" under following conditions:

- A measurement may have only one origin:

$$\sum_{i=0}^{n_k} \hat{\omega}_{ji}(\Theta_k(T)) = 1, \quad j = 1, \cdots, m_k$$

- A track may evoke at most one measurement:

$$\sum_{j=1}^{m_k} \hat{\omega}_{ji}(\Theta_k(T)) \leq 1, \quad i = 1, \cdots, n_k.$$

A matrix $\hat{\Omega}$ defining a feasible event $\Theta_k(T)$ can be built from the validation matrix Ω_k by picking out elements in a way such that each row and each column contains at most one "1". The only exception is made for the first column which may contain multiple non-zero entries since more than one measurement may be due to clutter. The set of all feasible joint events in the following is denoted by Ξ_k with

$$\sum_{\{\Theta_k(T) \in \Xi_k\}} P(\Theta_k(T)) = 1.$$

For better readability, in the following three auxiliary entities $\vartheta_i(\Theta_k(T))$, $\tau_j(\Theta_k(T))$ and $\phi(\Theta_k(T))$ are defined for a joint event $\Theta_k(T)$:

$$\vartheta_i(\Theta_k(T)) := \sum_{j=1}^{m_k} \hat{\omega}_{ji}(\Theta_k(T)), \quad i = 1, \cdots, n_k$$

$$\tau_j(\Theta_k(T)) := \sum_{i=1}^{n_k} \hat{\omega}_{ji}(\Theta_k(T)), \quad j = 1, \cdots, m_k$$

$$\phi(\Theta_k(T)) := \sum_{j=1}^{m_k} (1 - \tau_j(\Theta_k(t)))$$

$\vartheta_i(\Theta_k(T))$ indicates whether in $\Theta_k(T)$ the ith track has been assigned a measurement. $\tau_j(\Theta_k(T))$ indicates whether the jth measurement has been assigned to a track. Finally, $\phi(\Theta_k(T))$ specifies the number of the clutter based measurements in $\Theta_k(T)$.

The weighting factors $\beta_k^{\mathbf{x}_i \to \mathbf{z}_j}$ $(i = 1, \cdots, n_k; \quad j = 0, \cdots, m_k)$ can be calculated as follows:

$$\beta_k^{\mathbf{x}_i \to \mathbf{z}_j} := P(\theta_k^{\mathbf{x}_i \to \mathbf{z}_j} | \mathcal{Z}_{1:k}) = \sum_{\Theta_k(T) \in \Xi_k} P(\Theta_k(T) | \mathcal{Z}_{1:k}) \, \hat{\omega}_{ji}(\Theta_k(T)).$$

The a-posteriori probability of a joint event $\Theta_k(T)$ conditioned on all received measurements including the current measurement set can be calculated using the Bayes' rule:

$$P(\Theta_k(T) | \mathcal{Z}_{1:k}) = P(\Theta_k(T) | \mathcal{Z}_k, m_k, \mathcal{Z}_{1:(k-1)}) \qquad (3.7)$$
$$= \tfrac{1}{c_k} p(\mathcal{Z}_k | \Theta_k(T), m_k, \mathcal{Z}_{1:(k-1)}) P(\Theta_k(T) | m_k, \mathcal{Z}_{1:(k-1)})$$

with c_k being the normalization constant.

Similar to the calculations in the PDA, the likelihood of a measurement $\mathbf{z}_{k,j}$ given that it stems from a track $\mathbf{x}_{t_j}$ with $t_j \neq 0$ or from clutter ($t_j = 0$) is given by

$$p(\mathbf{z}_{k,j} | \theta_k^{\mathbf{x}_{t_j} \to \mathbf{z}_j}, \mathcal{Z}_{1:(k-1)}) = \begin{cases} \mathcal{N}(\mathbf{z}_{k,j}; \hat{\mathbf{z}}_k^{\mathbf{x}_{t_j}}, \mathbf{P}_{\mathbf{z}_k \mathbf{z}_k}^{x_{t_j}}) & \text{for } t_j \neq 0, \\ \frac{1}{V} & \text{for } t_j = 0. \end{cases}$$

Under the previously mentioned independence assumption of the clutter-based measurements and the true measurements, this leads to the following expression for the likelihood of the current measurement set $\mathcal{Z}_k$ conditioned on a joint event

$\Theta_k(T)$ and number of measurements being m_k:

$$p(\mathcal{Z}_k|\Theta_k(T), m_k, \mathcal{Z}_{1:(k-1)}) = \prod_{j=1}^{m_k} p(\mathbf{z}_{k,j}|\theta_k^{\mathbf{x}_{t_j} \to \mathbf{z}_j}, \mathcal{Z}_{1:(k-1)})$$

$$= \frac{1}{V^{\phi(\Theta_k(T))}} \prod_{j=1}^{m_k} \left(\mathcal{N}(\mathbf{z}_{k,j}; \hat{\mathbf{z}}_k^{x_{t_j}}, \mathbf{P}_{\mathbf{z}_k \mathbf{z}_k}^{x_{t_j}}) \right)^{\tau_j(\Theta_k(T))}$$

where $\phi(\Theta_k(T))$ is the number of the clutter-based measurements in the joint event $\Theta_k(T)$ and $\tau_j(\Theta_k(T))$ serves for picking out the likelihoods of the measurements, that in $\Theta_k(T)$ have been declared as being non-clutter.

The a-priori probability $P(\Theta_k(T)|m_k, \mathcal{Z}_{1:(k-1)})$ of a joint event $\Theta_k(T) \in \Xi_k$ in (3.7), conditioned on the number of received measurements is equivalent to the probability of assigning the tracks according to $\vartheta_i(\Theta_k(T))$ and getting additionally $\phi(\Theta_k(T))$ clutter-based measurements:

$$P(\Theta_k(T)|m_k, \mathcal{Z}_{1:(k-1)})$$
$$= P\big(\Theta_k(T), \vartheta(\Theta_k(T))_1, \ldots, \vartheta_{n_k}(\Theta_k(T)), \phi(\Theta_k(T))|\mathcal{Z}_{1:(k-1)}\big)$$
$$= P\big(\Theta_k(T) \,|\, \vartheta(\Theta_k(T))_1, \ldots, \vartheta_{n_k}(\Theta_k(T)), \phi(\Theta_k(T))\big)$$
$$\cdot P\big(\vartheta_1(\Theta_k(T)), \ldots, \vartheta_{n_k}(\Theta_k(T)), \phi(\Theta_k(T))|\mathcal{Z}_{1:(k-1)}\big).$$

An expression for the computation of the first factor follows from combinatorics with an assumption that each of the joint events $\Theta_k(T)$ has equal a-priori probability. It is given as a reciprocal of the number of all events that assign measurements to the tracks as defined by $\vartheta_i(\Theta_k(T))$ for $i = 1, \ldots, n_k$ and have $\phi(\Theta_k(T))$ clutter measurements:

$$P(\Theta_k(T)|\vartheta_1(\Theta_k(T)), \ldots, \vartheta_{n_k}(\Theta_k(T)), \phi(\Theta_k(T))) = \left(\frac{m_k!}{\phi(\Theta_k(T))!} \right)^{-1}$$
$$= \frac{\phi(\Theta_k(T))!}{m_k!}$$

The second factor is given by

$$P(\vartheta_1(\Theta_k(T)), \ldots, \vartheta_{n_k}(\Theta_k(T)), \phi(\Theta_k(T))|\mathcal{Z}_{1:(k-1)})$$
$$= \prod_{i=1}^{n_k} \left((P_D^{\mathbf{x}_i})^{\vartheta_i(\Theta_k(T))} \cdot (1 - P_D^{\mathbf{x}_i})^{1-\vartheta_i(\Theta_k(T))} \right) \cdot \mu_F(\phi(\Theta_k(T)))$$

with $P_D^{\mathbf{x}_i}$ being the probability for the track $\mathbf{x}_i$ to be detected and $\mu_F(\phi(\Theta_k(T)))$ being the probability mass function for the number of clutter-based measurements that can be modeled as described in Section 3.2 (see page 177).

This leads to

$$P(\Theta_k(T)|\mathcal{Z}_{1:k}) = \frac{\phi(\Theta_k(T))!}{c_k m_k!} \frac{\mu_F(\phi(\Theta_k(T)))}{V^{\phi(\Theta_k(T))}} \prod_{j=1}^{m_k} \left(\mathcal{N}(\mathbf{z}_{k,j}; \hat{\mathbf{z}}_k^{\mathbf{x}_{t_j}}, \mathbf{P}_{\mathbf{Z}_k\mathbf{Z}_k}^{x_{t_j}}) \right)^{\tau_j(\Theta_k(T))}$$

$$\cdot \prod_{i=1}^{n_k} \left((P_D^{\mathbf{x}_i})^{\vartheta_i(\Theta_k(T))} (1 - P_D^{\mathbf{x}_i})^{1-\vartheta_i(\Theta_k(T))} \right)$$

and hence to

$$P(\Theta_k(T)|\mathcal{Z}_{1:k}) = \lambda^{\phi(\Theta_k(T))} \frac{e^{-\lambda V}}{c_k \cdot m_k!} \prod_{j=1}^{m_k} \left(\mathcal{N}(\mathbf{z}_{k,j}; \hat{\mathbf{z}}_k^{\mathbf{x}_{t_j}}, \mathbf{P}_{\mathbf{Z}_k\mathbf{Z}_k}^{x_{t_j}}) \right)^{\tau_j(\Theta_k(T))}$$

$$\cdot \prod_{i=1}^{n_k} \left((P_D^{\mathbf{x}_i})^{\vartheta_i(\Theta_k(T))} (1 - P_D^{\mathbf{x}_i})^{1-\vartheta_i(\Theta_k(T))} \right)$$

for the *parametric model* of clutter distribution and to

$$P(\Theta_k(T)|\mathcal{Z}_{1:k}) = \frac{1}{\tilde{c}_k} \frac{\phi(\Theta_k(T))!}{V^{\phi(\Theta_k(T))}} \prod_{j=1}^{m_k} \left(\mathcal{N}(\mathbf{z}_{k,j}; \hat{\mathbf{z}}_k^{\mathbf{x}_{t_j}}, \mathbf{P}_{\mathbf{Z}_k\mathbf{Z}_k}^{x_{t_j}}) \right)^{\tau_j(\Theta_k(T))}$$

$$\cdot \prod_{i=1}^{n_k} \left((P_D^{\mathbf{x}_i})^{\vartheta_i(\Theta_k(T))} (1 - P_D^{\mathbf{x}_i})^{1-\vartheta_i(\Theta_k(T))} \right)$$

for the *nonparametric model* of clutter distribution.

4   Conclusion and Outlook

This report has presented basics of the state-of-the-art methods for tracking of multiple objects in cluttered environments. An overview and a detailed description of the basic state-of-the-art approaches for data association and dynamic state estimation has been given. However, all described data association approaches consider existence of the tracked targets as given. Track initiation and maintenance has to be done outside of scope of the tracking algorithms. In practice, target existence is often subject to uncertainties due to great amount of clutter and missing detections. An elegant way of modeling those uncertainties has been proposed by Mušicki et al. The *Integrated PDA (IPDA)* and *Joint Integrated PDA (JIPDA)* algorithms proposed in [MES94, ME02] are extensions of the PDA and JPDA algorithms respectively. Additionally to the expressions for data association probabilities they provide expressions for computation of the track existence probabilities that are directly accounted for (integrated) when computing the association probabilities.

Track existence is modeled as a Markov process with the constant state transition probabilities between the states "track exists" and "track does not exist". The observability aspect can be also accounted for by using three states ("track exists and is observable", "track exists but is not observable" and "track does not exist").

Estimation of the track existence probability offers a solid basis for track initiations and terminations and allows for better handling of clutter and missing detections. However, in some applications such as vision-based object tracking, corrupted measurements due to split, merged and incomplete detections bear an additional source for problems. Here, the above-mentioned approaches have to be extended in order to be able to cope with the introduced effects. Low-level information, which can be obtained by robust re-identification and tracking of dedicated feature points in the image, offers great potential for solving such problems. An approach that utilizes such information and allows for handling of incomplete, split and merged detections has been proposed in [GOB09]. It is called Feature-Based Probabilistic Data Association and Tracking Algorithm (FBPDA).

Bibliography

[Bro98]   Eli Brookner. *Tracking and Kalman filtering made easy*. John Wiley & Sons, New York, 1998.

[BS78]   Yaakov Bar-Shalom. Tracking Methods in a Multitarget Environment. In *IEEE Transactions on Automatic Control*, volume 23, pages 618–626, 1978.

[BSL93]   Yaakov Bar-Shalom and Xiao-Rong Li. *Estimation and Tracking: Principles, techniques, and software*. Artech House, Boston, London, 1993.

[BST75]   Yaakov Bar-Shalom and Edison Tse. Tracking in a Cluttered Environment with Probability Data Association. *Automatica*, 11:451–460, 1975.

[CH96]   Ingemar J. Cox and Sunita L. Hingorani. An efficient implementation of Reid's multiple hypothesis tracking algorithm and its evaluation for the purpose of visual tracking. In *IEEE Transactions on Pattern Analysis and Machine Intelligence*, volume 18, pages 138–150, 1996.

[FBSS83]   T. E. Fortmann, Y. Bar-Shalom, and M. Scheffe. Sonar Tracking of Multiple Targets Using Joint Probabilistic Data Association. *IEEE Journal of Oceanic Engineering*, 8(3):173–183, 1983.

[GOB09]   Michael Grinberg, Florian Ohr, and Jürgen Beyerer. Feature-Based Probabilistic Data Association (FBPDA) for Visual Multi-Target Detection and Tracking under Occlusions and Split and Merge Effects. In *Proceedings of the 12th International IEEE Conference on Intelligent Transportation Systems*, pages 291–298, 2009.

[Kal60]   R. E. Kalman. A new approach to linear filtering and prediction problems. *Journal of Basic Engineering*, 82(1):35–45, 1960.

[ME02]   Darko Mušicki and Rob Evans. Joint Integrated Probabilistic Data Association - JIPDA. In *Proceedings of the 5th International Conference on Information Fusion*, pages 1120–1125, 2002.

[MES94]   Darko Mušicki, Rob Evans, and S. Stankovic. Integrated Probabilistic Data Association. In *IEEE Transactions on Automatic Control*, volume 39, 1994.

[Rei79]   Donald B. Reid. An Algorithm for Tracking Multiple Targets. In *IEEE Transactions on Automatic Control*, volume AC-24, pages 843–854, 1979.

[Sim06]   Dan Simon. *Optimal state estimation: Kalman, H∞, and nonlinear approaches*. Wiley-Interscience, Hoboken, NJ, 2006.

Information Management in World Modeling

Andrey Belkin

Vision and Fusion Laboratory
Institute for Anthropomatics
Karlsruhe Institute of Technology (KIT), Germany
belkin@ies.uka.de

Technical Report IES-2010-13

Abstract: Modern autonomous systems are performing complex tasks in a real-world environment. This requires a comprehensive overview on the environment, for which the mere storage and retrieval of acquired information is not sufficient. Sophisticated cognitive processing like situation recognition or proactive planning can be realized on the basis of consistent and efficient world modeling. Since autonomous systems have to cope with uncertain and incomplete information, probabilistic information management mechanisms are additionally required.

This contribution introduces new information management mechanisms for environment modeling. The proposed system uses a three pillar information architecture consisting of a prior knowledge, world model, and sensor data. The described Bayesian framework formalizes the information management, including information representaton by means of Degree-of-Belief (DoB) distributions with instantiation, deletion, and fusion mechanisms. In this contribution, a special focus is given to observation-to-instance mapping and decision mechanisms for creating a new instance or updating already existing instances in the model.

1 Introduction

Modern autonomous systems are performing more and more complex tasks in a real-world environment. The rise of planning and cognition requirements demands more sophisticated information management systems, which are able to handle probabilistic descriptions, abstraction levels, multiple semantic relations as well as other complex problems. This contribution proposes an intelligent information management system applicable to a wide variety of types of autonomous systems.

The primary application of the system is a humanoid service robot, developed within the DFG SFB 588 "Humanoid robots" project [SFB].

The proposed information management system is designed in a three pillar structure consisting of a prior knowledge, world model, and sensor data, as described in Section 2. The world model is the central component of the system that describes current state of the environment and acts as an information hub to all other modules. Sensor data provides new information to the model. The prior knowledge pillar represents pre-defined information about the real world.

Besides the pillar architecture, the proposed system employs Progressive Mapping information architecture and semantic networks, as described in [Bel10, KBS$^+$10]. The Progressive Mapping allows for dynamic object updating with incoming information. All object attributes are modeled as probability distributions in a Degree-of-Belief (DoB) interpretation. This gives a possibility of developing of an information management and fusion system based on a Bayesian framework and data association mechanisms, as described in Section 3. Commonly used approaches for the modeling of information comprise semantic networks, predicate logic and formal languages [GRS03], ontologies, object-oriented and probabilistic approaches, e.g. [SM98, MA02, Bau09, GHB08, PBB08, HGLB10]. However, previously published approaches are domain specific and not transferable to other applications. Moreover, the existing world modeling systems provide no data association mechanisms, which are vital for updating object descriptions upon probabilistic observation-to-object assignments.

Data association is one of the main topics in tracking [HL01]. The exact Bayesian data association solution is in general incalculable. Thus, different approximations are employed, e.g. Joint Probabilistic Data Association Filter (JPDAF) [BSDH09] or Markov Chain Monte Carlo (MCMC) [Nea93]. One of the simplest methods for data association is the Nearest Neighbor Filter [RLBS96] that assigns each observation to the most probable object. The more complex procedure JPDAF performs a weighted update of all objects within some gating region according to association probabilities. JPDAF can be extended for instantiation and deletion mechanisms, handling existence probabilities of objects with Markov models [ME02]. A general Bayesian formalization of multi-target tracking with existency management was given in [VMB05, HM09].

At the end of this contribution, the application and the experimental set up of the modeling system is given in Section 4, followed by the Conclusion and Bibliography sections.

2   Three Pillar Architecture

The three pillar information management is designed to separate the domains of the information workflow into prior knowledge, world model, and sensor data (Fig. 2.1). In the following, objects, attributes and relations are considered as pieces of information. Each information piece is characterized by its uncertainty in form of a Degree-of-Belief (DoB) distribution [GHB08, HGLB10, KBS$^+$10, Bey99, BHSG08].

Prior Knowledge   World Model   Sensor Data

pre-defined   dynamic   raw

concepts   objects   data

prior knowledge complementing   request for information

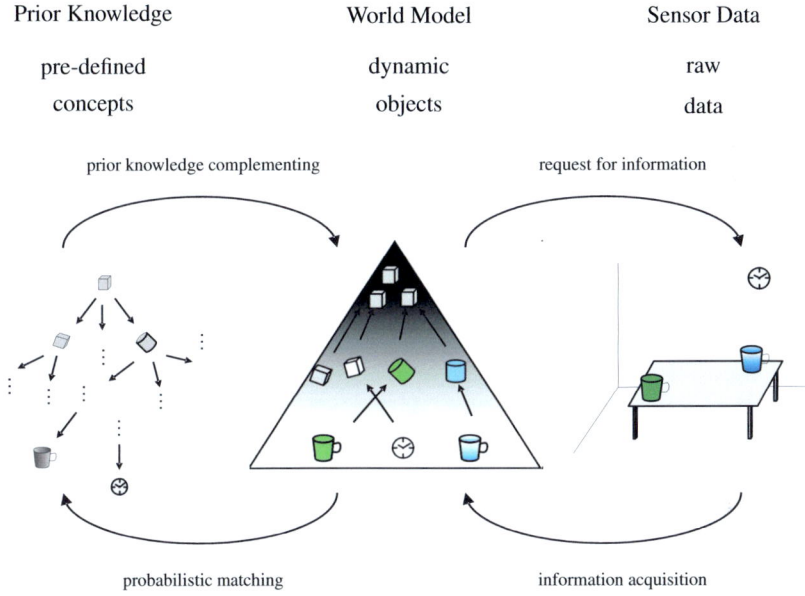

probabilistic matching   information acquisition

Figure 2.1: Three pillar information management structure.

World Model   The world model represents information the autonomous system has at hand about its current environment (short term memory). The information is represented in form of dynamic objects with attributes and relations by means of Progressive Mapping and semantic networks as described in [Bel10, KBS$^+$10]. Object attributes can be descriptive or non-descriptive. The only modeled non-descriptive attribute is the existence expressed in the probability that the corresponding environment element exists in the real world. Examples for descriptive attributes are type, position, or size. The attribute type is also represented by a DoB distribution thus it removes limitations of the classification approach.

As soon as new information comes from sensor modules, it is being compared to modeled objects in the world model. If no appropriate match was found, the so-called "blank object" is created representing existence of something. Starting with blank objects, the world model is updated in top-down and bottom-up ways.

The top-down update implies complementing of the world model by associating acquired information to existing objects [Bel10, KBS$^+$10]. In Fig. 2.1, this way is outlined by the arrow "information acquisition".

The bottom-up update implies referencing prior knowledge for complementing the world model. In Fig. 2.1, this is outlined by the arrow "prior knowledge complementation".

The information management consists of three steps:

- Creation of new objects upon new sensor data by means of Bayesian fusion, considering existence probability of the object. If the posterior probability is higher than a creation threshold, a new object is inserted in the world model [GHB08, KBS$^+$10, HGLB10].

- Information update upon new sensor data or prior knowledge complementation. The update is performed by means of Bayesian fusion using common prediction-correction strategy: The prediction step propagates the information from one time step to the next one using known evolution dynamic (e.g. distribution dispersions). In most cases, the entropy of the DoB distribution increases [Ber03]. The correction step fuses the prior information of the prediction step with the new information interpreted as a likelihood function. If no new information is provided from one time step to another, a function correlative to the Maximum Entropy distribution is used as the default likelihood function.

- Deletion of instances by reaching of some deletion threshold by the existence probability.

The exact description of creation, update and deletion steps is given in Section 3.

Parallel to management steps, additional checks are performed to ensure model correctness:

- **Validity checks** assure that the world model fulfills formal restrictions (for example, DoB distributions are valid);

- **Consistency checks** ensure that basic physical rules are satisfied, (e.g. objects are not hanging in the air or overlap with each other);

- **Relevance checks** assure that a correct abstraction level is chosen for the given task;

- **Actuality checks** ensure that the information is always up to date, (e.g. triggering exploration upon reaching re-confirmation threshold by existency probability).

Prior Knowledge   A second pillar (left in Fig. 2.1) is the prior knowledge (long term memory). It contains prior information of two types:

- Pre-defined concepts in a form of ontology (classes, attributes, specific objects, relations, and rules). The attributes and relations are represented by DoB distributions generated as a result of statistical analysis of the environment. These DoBs describe elements that might be encountered in the real world. The ontology can also contain information about specific environment elements known a priori (e.g. "person Andrey" or "white tea cup");

- Dynamically learned knowledge (e.g. specific environment elements observed during explorations).

Sensor data   The third information pillar (right in Fig. 2.1) represents sensor data.

Abstraction Levels   Different reactive and proactive tasks require different degrees of detail of information. Thus, the information in the world model has to be accessible on different abstraction levels (Fig. 2.2) [GHB08]. For example, a path planning task requires geometry information of the environment (e.g. topology, position and dimension of things). Other tasks, for example grasping, demand detailed information regarding form, grasp possibilities, footprints, etc [Bel10, KBS+10, GHBB10].

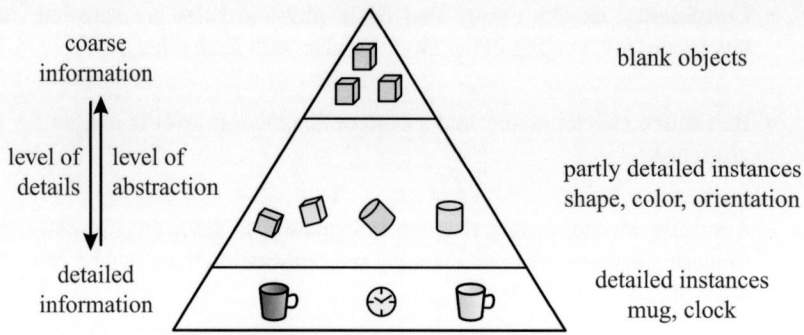

Figure 2.2: Abstraction pyramid.

3 Data Management

3.1 Probabilistic Description

Each information piece is given in form of a DoB distribution. The advantages of DoB distributions are described in [GHB08]. In the following the Bayesian framework is formalized as in [BGB+10b, BGB+10a].

An object i at time step k is presented as a DoB distribution $p(e_k^i, \underline{a}_k^i)$, where $e_k^i \in \{0, 1\}$ specifies whether the object exists ($e_k^i = 1$) or not exists ($e_k^i = 0$), and

$$\underline{a}_k^i := \left[t_k^i, \ \underline{a}_k^{i,1}, \ \ldots, \ \underline{a}_k^{i,n_a} \right]^{\mathrm{T}}$$

is a vector that is composed of the discrete type t_k^i of the instance i, and n_a (discrete or continuous) descriptive attributes $\underline{a}_k^{i,1}, \ldots, \underline{a}_k^{i,n_a}$. As in JPDAF, attributes of different objects are supposed to be independent.

In the case new sensor data does not match any object of the model, a new object is created. The decision is based on the posterior probability that a new existing environment element is detected at time step k, which has to exceed a creation threshold $p(e_k^i = 1) > \gamma_{\mathrm{i}}$.

On the other hand, an object is deleted from the world model, if the existence probability goes below the deletion threshold $p(e_k^i = 1) < \gamma_{\mathrm{e}}$, with $\gamma_{\mathrm{e}} < \gamma_{\mathrm{i}}$. The relation between γ_{e} and γ_{i} is necessary for ensuring a hysteresis, i.e., created instance should not be immediately deleted (Fig. 3.1).

An additional threshold γ_{r} with $\gamma_{\mathrm{e}} < \gamma_{\mathrm{r}} < \gamma_{\mathrm{i}}$ is employed to explicitly trigger the re-confirmation of the existence, before the deletion decision is taken.

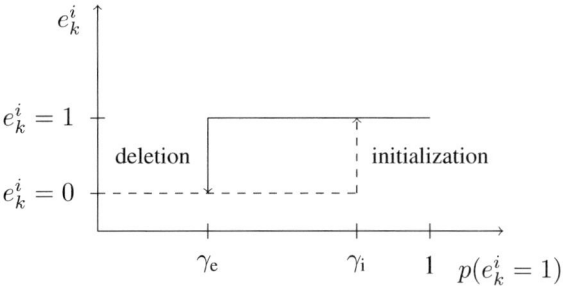

Figure 3.1: Hysteresis for the instantiation and deletion of objects.

3.2 Observation Model

A fusion of observations into the world model requires an observation model that relates the observation to an object. This observation model has to deal with the uncertainty of the object existence and the observation-to-object matching as in [VMB05, HM09]. The following fusion mechanism is presented as a special case of multiple tracks data association with the assumption that at each time step k, a single observation is received with regard to an arbitrary object.

The connection between the observation and the object is modeled with the association variable $d_k \in \{0, 1 \dots, N_k\}$. The probability that the observation at time step k regards the object d_k is $p(d_k|\underline{e}_k)$, with $\underline{e}_k := \left[e_k^1, \dots, e_k^{N_k}\right]^\mathrm{T}$ and N_k is the number of objects in the model. An observation that regards a new object, is represented with $d_k = 0$.

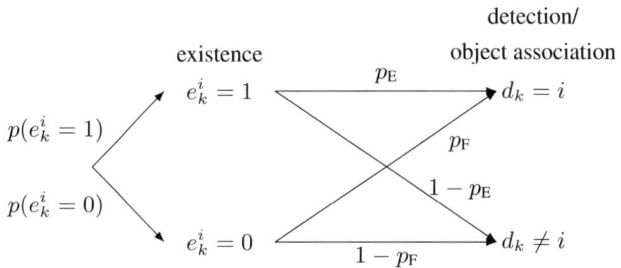

Figure 3.2: Schematic dependencies between the existence and observation of objects.

Fig. 3.2 shows four conditional DoBs regarding the observation and existence of a particular object i [DHS04]:

- $p(d_k = i | e_k^i = 1) = p_E$ describes the situation that the object i exists at the time step k and is observed;

- $p(d_k \neq i | e_k^i = 1) = 1 - p_E$ describes the situation that the object i exists at the time step k but it is not observed;

- $p(d_k = i | e_k^i = 0) = p_F$ describes the situation that an object i does not exist at the time step k but an observation is made;

- $p(d_k \neq i | e_k^i = 0) = 1 - p_F$ describes the situation that the object i does not exist at the time step k and it is not observed.

The observation probability which regards object i is

$$p(\underline{y}_k^i | \underline{a}_k^{i,1}, \ldots \underline{a}_k^{i,n_a}, t_k^i, e_k^i, d_k = i) := p(\underline{y}_k^{i,1} | \underline{a}_k^{i,m_1}) \cdot \ldots \cdot p(\underline{y}_k^{i,r} | \underline{a}_k^{i,m_r}) \cdot p(\mathcal{M}_k | t_k^i),$$

where $\underline{y}_k^i := \left[\underline{y}_k^{i,1}, \ldots, \underline{y}_k^{i,r}, \mathcal{M}_k \right]^{\mathrm{T}}$ is the observation vector, with $\underline{y}_k^{i,1}, \ldots, \underline{y}_k^{i,r}$ as observations of r given attributes and $\mathcal{M}_k = \bigcup_s m_s$ is the index set of observed attributes. The observation model for an attribute is given by $p(\underline{y}_k^{i,s} | \underline{a}_k^{i,m_s})$, where m_s marks the attribute observed by $\underline{y}_k^{i,s}$. The DoB $p(\mathcal{M}_k | t_k^i)$ models the DoB of observing the attributes $\mathcal{M}_k$, when the type of the instance is given.

The observation model for new objects is given by DoB

$$p(\underline{y}_k^i | \underline{a}_k^{i,1}, \ldots \underline{a}_k^{i,n_a}, t_k^i, e_k^i = 1, d_k = i).$$

3.3   Bayesian fusion

The observations to objects information fusion supposes calculation of the existence probabilities $p(e_k^i = 1 | \hat{\underline{y}}_{1:k})$ and the DoB distribution of descriptive attributes $p(\underline{a}_k^i | e_k^i = 1, \hat{\underline{y}}_{1:k})$ for all objects i. This is performed with prediction-correction scheme of Bayesian state estimation.

The Prediction Step   propagates the state of the environment model at time step $k - 1$ to the next time step k, which results in the predicted existence $p(e_k^i = 1 | \hat{\underline{y}}_{1:k-1})$ and the predicted attributes $p(\underline{a}_k^i | e_k^i = 1, \hat{\underline{y}}_{1:k-1})$ for all instances i.

The propagation is defined such that probabilities are altered according to some dynamic model, e.g. they decrease over the time. The predicted existence probability is calculated by using an exponential decreasing function, which results in the Markov model

$$p(e_k^i = 1|e_{k-1}^i = 1) = \beta^i,$$
$$p(e_k^i = 1|e_{k-1}^i = 0) = 0,$$

where $0 < \beta^i \leq 1$ is a constant. The predicted existence probabilities can be computed according to

$$p(e_k^i = 1|\underline{\hat{y}}_{1:k-1}) = \beta^i \cdot p(e_{k-1}^i = 1|\underline{\hat{y}}_{1:k-1}).$$

The predicted attribute probabilities result from the Chapman-Kolmogorov equation

$$p(\underline{a}_k^i|e_k^i = 1, \underline{\hat{y}}_{1:k-1}) = \int p(\underline{a}_k^i|\underline{a}_{k-1}^i) \cdot p(\underline{a}_{k-1}^i|e_k^i = 1, \underline{\hat{y}}_{1:k-1}) d\underline{a}_{k-1}^i$$

with the dynamic model $p(\underline{a}_{k+1}^i|\underline{a}_k^i)$ for descriptive attributes.

The Correction Step fuses the predicted state for time step k and the observation $\underline{\hat{y}}_k$. The updated probabilities for attributes can be written according to the Law Of Total Probability as a mixture

$$p(\underline{a}_k^i|e_k^i = 1, \underline{\hat{y}}_{1:k}) = \sum_{d_k} p(\underline{a}_k^i|e_k^i = 1, \underline{\hat{y}}_{1:k}, d_k) \cdot p(d_k|e_k^i = 1, \underline{\hat{y}}_{1:k}),$$

where the first term is the posterior distribution for a given association

$$p(\underline{a}_k^i|e_k^i = 1, \underline{\hat{y}}_{1:k}, d_k) \propto p(\underline{\hat{y}}_k^{d_k}|e_k^i = 1, \underline{a}_k^i) \cdot p(\underline{a}_k^i|e_k^i = 1, d_k, \underline{\hat{y}}_{1:k-1}).$$

The updated probability for the existence is

$$p(e_k^i = 1|\underline{\hat{y}}_{1:k}) = \sum_{d_k} p(e_k^i = 1, d_k|\underline{\hat{y}}_{1:k}).$$

In order to compute $p(e_k^i = 1, d_k|\underline{\hat{y}}_{1:k})$ and $p(d_k|e_k^i = 1, \underline{\hat{y}}_{1:k})$, we need the joint DoB of the updated existence and association variable

$$p(\underline{e}_k, d_k|\underline{\hat{y}}_{1:k}) \propto p(\underline{\hat{y}}_k|\underline{e}_k, d_k, \underline{\hat{y}}_{1:k-1}) \cdot p(\underline{e}_k, d_k|\underline{\hat{y}}_{1:k-1}),$$

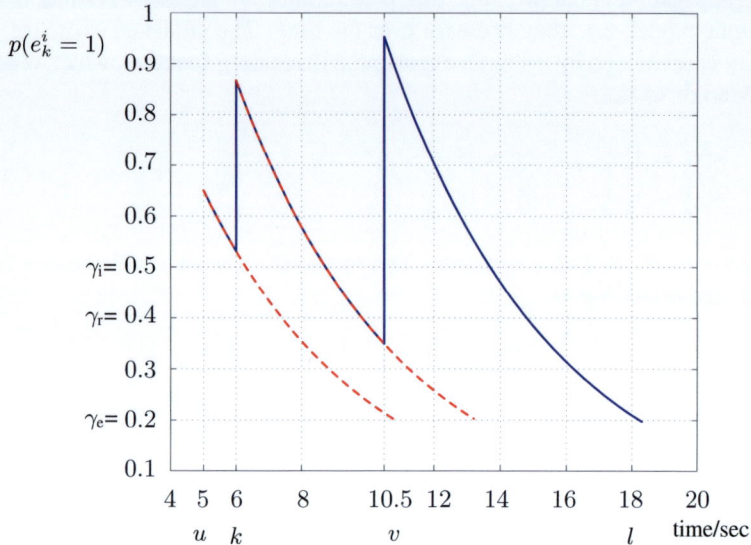

Figure 3.3: Example of the life-cycle of an instance. The red dashed line describes the propagation resulting from the aging mechanism, if no new observation is available. The continuous line describes the course of the DoBs when the existence of the entity is reconfirmed at the time steps $k = 6$ and $v = 10.5$.

where

$$p(\hat{\underline{y}}_k | e_k, d_k, \hat{\underline{y}}_{1:k-1}) = \int p(\hat{\underline{y}}_k^{d_k} | e_k^i, a_k^i, d_k, \hat{\underline{y}}_{1:k-1}) \cdot p(a_k^i | e_k^i, d_k, \hat{\underline{y}}_{1:k-1}) da_k^i$$

and

$$p(e_k, d_k | \hat{\underline{y}}_{1:k-1}) = p(d_k | e_k) \cdot p(e_k | \hat{\underline{y}}_{1:k-1}).$$

Creation of New Objects If the probability that the observation $\hat{\underline{y}}_k$ matches a new object exceeds the threshold γ_e: $p(d_k = 0 | e_k^0 = 1, \hat{\underline{y}}_{1:k}) > \gamma_e$, the observation cannot be assigned to one of the existing objects. Thus, a new object $\left[e_k^{N_k+1} \quad a_k^{N_k+1} \right]$ is created. If such instantiation was wrong (e.g. the object already exists), the deletion mechanism will remove this redundant "ghost" object after a while. Fig. 3.3 shows a typical example for the life-cycle of an instance according to the maximum of the DoB distribution for the attribute existence.

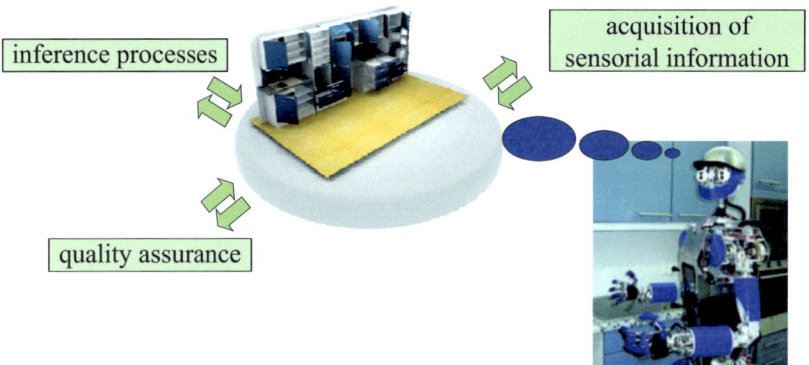

inference processes

acquisition of sensorial information

quality assurance

Figure 4.1: Humanoid robot in a test environment.

4 Realization

The three pillar information architecture was developed within the DFG project SFB 588 "Humanoid Robots – Learning and Cooperating Multimodal Robots" [SFB]. The project goal is to design humanoid robot assisting in household applications with learning and cooperating capabilities. Such complex systems require a comprehensive description of the environment. The described information management architecture has been developed and engaged. Fig. 4.1 shows the humanoid robot in a kitchen test area. Development and implementation details are given in [Bel10, KBS$^+$10].

5 Conclusion

The present contribution proposes an information management architecture for autonomous systems. The separation into three pillars (prior knowledge, world model, sensors) allows for an efficient information processing. The world model contains a comprehensive description of the surrounding environment. Other components provide sensor data and pre-defined prior knowledge. The world model acts as an information hub for all other modules of the autonomous system. The main advantage of the proposed architecture is the probabilistic approach based on the Bayesian framework. This includes mechanisms for instantiation, deletion, and update of objects as well as check mechanisms. Additionally, the notion of the abstraction pyramid enables retrieving information with different degrees of detail.

Bibliography

[Bau09]　　A. Bauer. Probabilistic reasoning on object occurrence in complex scenes. In *Image and Signal Processing for Remote Sensing XV, Proc. of SPIE*, volume 7477, 2009.

[Bel10]　　A. Belkin. Object-Oriented World Modelling for Autonomous Systems. Technical report, Karlsruhe Institute of Technology (KIT), 2010.

[Ber03]　　J. M. Bernardo. *Encyclopedia of Life Support Systems (EOLSS). Probability and Statistics*. UNESCO, 2003.

[Bey99]　　J. Beyerer. *Verfahren zur quantitativen statistischen Bewertung von Zusatzwissen in der Meßtechnik*. VDI Verlag, Düsseldorf, 1999.

[BGB⁺10a]　M. Baum, I. Gheta, A. Belkin, J. Beyerer, and U. D. Hanebeck. Data Association in a World Model for Autonomous Systems. In *Proceedings of IEEE International Conference on Multisensor Fusion and Integration for Intelligent Systems*, 2010.

[BGB⁺10b]　M. Baum, I. Gheta, A. Belkin, J. Beyerer, and U. D. Hanebeck. Three pillar information management system for modeling the environment of autonomous systems. In *Proceedings of IEEE Conference on Virtual Environments, Human-Computer Interfaces and Measurement Systems*, 2010.

[BHSG08]　J. Beyerer, M. Heizmann, J. Sander, and I. Gheţa. *Image Fusion – Algorithms and Applications*, chapter Bayesian Methods for Image Fusion, pages 157–192. Academic Press, 2008.

[BSDH09]　Y. Bar-Shalom, F. Daum, and J. Huang. The Probabilistic Data Association Filters. *Control Systems Magazine, IEEE*, 29(6):82 –100, Dec. 2009.

[DHS04]　Richard O. Duda, Peter E. Hart, and David G. Stork. *Pattern Classification*. John Wiley & Sons Inc, 2004.

[GHB08]　I. Gheţa, M. Heizmann, and J. Beyerer. Object oriented environment model for autonomous systems. In H. Boström, R. Johansson, and J. van Laere, editors, *Proceedings of the second Skövde Workshop on Information Fusion Topics*, pages 9–12. Skövde Studies in Informatics, November 2008.

[GHBB10]　I. Gheta, M. Heizmann, A. Belkin, and J. Beyerer. World Modeling for Autonomous Systems. In *KI 2010: Advances in Artificial Intelligence, Lecture Notes in Artificial Intelligence, Bd. 6359*, 2010.

[GRS03]　G. Görz, C.-R. Rollinger, and J. Schneeberger. *Handbuch der Künstlichen Intelligenz*. Oldenbourg, 2003.

[HGLB10]　M. Heizmann, I. Gheţa, P. F. León, and J. Beyerer. Informationsfusion zur Umgebungsexploration. In Fernando Puente León, Klaus-Dieter Sommer, and Michael Heizmann, editors, *Verteilte Messsysteme*, pages 133–152. KIT Scientific Publishing, March 2010.

[HL01]　　D.L. Hall and J. Linas. *Handbook of Multisensor Data Fusion*. CRC Press, May 2001.

[HM09]　　P. Horridge and S. Maskell. Searching for, Initiating and Tracking Multiple Targets using Existence Probabilities. In *12th International Conference on Information Fusion*, pages 611 –617, July 2009.

[KBS⁺10]　B. Kühn, A. Belkin, A. Swerdlow, T. Machmer, J. Beyerer, and K. Kroschel. Knowledge-Driven Opto-Acoustic Scene Analysis based on an Object-Oriented World Modelling Approach for Humanoid Robots. In *Proceedings of the 41st International Symposium on Robotics and the 6th German Conference on Robotics*. VDE-Verlag, 2010.

[MA02]   A. M. Meystel and J. S. Albus. *Intelligent systems: architecture, design, control. Wiley series on intelligent systems.* Wiley-Interscience Publication, 2002.

[ME02]   D. Musicki and R. Evans. Joint Integrated Probabilistic Data Association - JIPDA. In *Proceedings of the Fifth International Conference on Information Fusion*, volume 2, pages 1120 – 1125 vol.2, 2002.

[Nea93]   R. M. Neal. Probabilistic Inference Using Markov Chain Monte Carlo. Technical report, University of Toronto, 1993.

[PBB08]   Z. Papp, C. Brown, and C. Bartels. World Modeling for Cooperative Intelligent Vehicles. In *IEEE Intelligent Vehicles Symposium*, pages 1050–1055, 2008.

[RLBS96]   X. Rong Li and Y. Bar-Shalom. Tracking in clutter with nearest neighbor filters: analysis and performance. *Aerospace and Electronic Systems, IEEE Transactions on*, 32(3):995 –1010, july 1996.

[SFB]   SFB588. Humanoide Roboter.

[SM98]   S. Shlaer and S. J. Mellor. *Objekte und ihre Lebensläufe: Modellierung mit Zuständen.* Hanser, 1998.

[VMB05]   J. Vermaak, S. Maskell, and M. Briers. A Unifying Framework for Multi-Target Tracking and Existence. In *8th International Conference on Information Fusion*, 2005.

Developments in the Field of Deflectometry

Sebastian Höfer

Vision and Fusion Laboratory
Institute for Anthropomatics
Karlsruhe Institute of Technology (KIT), Germany
sebastian.hoefer@ies.uni-karlsruhe.de

Technical Report IES-2010-14

Abstract: Deflectometry has developed to the standard method for the inspection of specular surfaces, which usually defy inspection by optical metrology methods. Current research on deflectometry focuses on improving the technology for the challenges in industrial quality assurance. Additionally, deflectometric inspection will be made available to a broader range of materials. In this technical report, we will provide an overview of this research and give examples for future applications of deflectometry.

1 Introduction

Topological metrology plays an important role in industrial quality assurance. Especially methods based on optical sensors are used, because they allow for a fast and contactless inspection. By now there are optical sensors for nearly every visual inspection task, where the inspection of specular surfaces take up an special position. Considering the ubiquity of specular surfaces on objects in our environment, one might expect that there are established inspection methods. However, in practice the usual optical inspection methods are unsuitable for this task, due to the mirror-like reflecting properties of these surfaces. A perfect reflecting surface is virtually invisible and thus not directly observable.

This is where deflectometric methods excel. By including the surface to be examined within the imaging chain, deflectometric methods infer the geometry of a surface indirectly from the distortion it induces. Besides enabling the inspection of specular surfaces, the main difference to other methods is that they measure the slope of the surface instead of its height. Thereby deflectometric methods imitate the way a human observer examines a specular surface by looking at the reflection of a structured pattern on such a surface. This allows for an objective evaluation how possible surface defects would be perceived by a human, making it an appropriate tool for the quality assurance of consumer goods.

The first publication of the underlying function principle dates back to the work of Sanderson et al. [SWN88]. But only recently the first products became available, implementing deflectometric inspection for the application in industrial production lines. Nonetheless, these systems are still not using the full potential of deflectometry. Despite the easy function principle, is its practical application is still subject of ongoing research. In this technical report we are going to point out some of the work done at the *KIT Vision and Fusion Lab* to improve deflectometry for practical application.

The remaining part of the report is divided into four sections, each covering one research topic within the field of deflectometry. Section 2 introduces a novel approach for calibrating deflectometric sensors. Section 3 then briefly discusses the reconstruction of 3D data from multiple deflectometric measurements. Section 4 describes the possibility to extent deflectometric inspection into the infrared spectrum. Finally, we conclude the topic in Section 6.

2   Sensor Calibration

In order to take measurements with a camera system prior calibration is necessary. Only this makes the objective evaluation in terms of metric interpretation possible.

Although a typical deflectometric sensor consists of standard components for which there are already established calibration methods, their application in deflectometry has proven to be difficult. Figure 2.1 shows a setup in use at the *KIT Vision and Fusion Lab*. Main components are the monitor as pattern generator and a standard industrial camera for image acquisition. Even large scale specular surfaces can be examined, by mounting the sensor setup on an industrial robot. For the calibration of such a system at first the intrinsic parameters of the camera have to be determined, which is a trivial task using existing calibration techniques [Bou03, Zha99].

Knowing the cameras parameters, the challenging task is to determine the relative positions of each component. Figure 2.2 illustrates the geometry of a deflectometric sensor. Important for the interpretation of the measured data is the transformation H_{LCD} between monitor and camera.

The inspection of larger objects with multiple measurement positions requires knowledge of the relative movement between each position. Provided that the

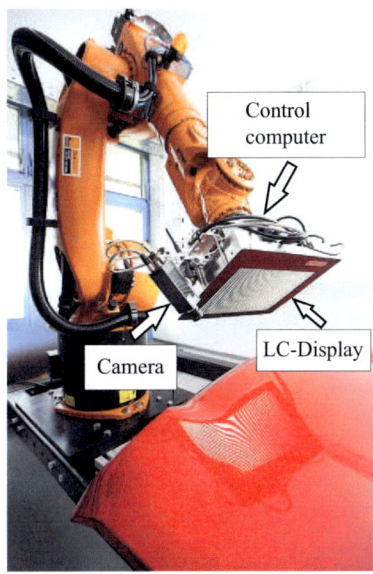

Figure 2.1: Measurement setup for deflectometric inspection of specular surfaces. Attaching the sensor to a robot arm enables flexible positioning in relation to the object under test.

object under test is steady relatively to a world coordinate system, this information can be derived from the respective camera position H_{world}. In case of the setup in Figure 2.1 this information is provided by the robot system. This requires additional so-called *hand-eye calibration* [TL89] between robot and camera.

A simple approach for a full system calibration would be the consecutive calibration of the single components and calculating the needed information from those, as previously done in [BWB07]. But this is a time consuming process which potentially needs assistance by an operator. In addition, special calibration patterns are required in each step. Considering the utilization in an industrial environment, where speed and autonomous operation are essential, this approach is not feasible. Therefore, we developed a new calibration procedure which integrates most of the necessary steps and handles them without special calibration patterns. The calibration procedure is presented in detail in [HWB10] and [Wer10].

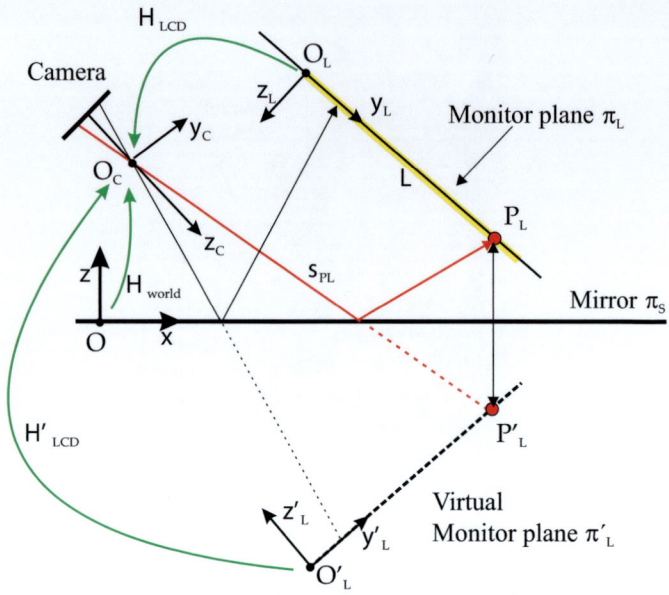

Figure 2.2: Geometry of the deflectometric sensor. The camera only sees a virtual image π'_L of the monitor. Its real image plane π_L and the mirror plane π_S are unknown beforehand.

2.1   Calibration Procedure

The functional principle of deflectometry requires an arrangement where the monitor is commonly outside the cameras field of view, since the camera looks at the reflection of the monitor on the surface to be examined. Thus, it is obvious to use a mirror to establish a line of sight between them for the calibration process. Apart from a plane mirror the aim for the new calibration technique is to forego additional auxiliaries. With this in mind, we introduce the concept of the *virtual monitor*, which refers to the reflected image π'_L of the real monitor (see Figure 2.2). Based on this concept we will deduce the mirror plane π_S and the monitor plane π_L from those virtual positions. Altogether the calibration of the sensor is subdivided into three tasks:

1. Calibration of the cameras intrinsics,

2. Calculating the Monitor/Camera-transformation,

3. Hand-Eye-calibration between robot and sensor.

Camera calibration Basis for our camera calibration is the work of Zhang [Zha99], which obtains the cameras intrinsic and extrinsic parameters from multiple views of a planar pattern. As replacement for the omitted calibration pattern we use the monitor plane of the deflectometric sensor. But instead of just displaying the calibration pattern, we employ the position-coding normally used for the deflectometric measurement. This allows us to determine the position P_L on the monitor plane π_L corresponding to every camera pixel, with sub-pixel accuracy. Compared with the usual checker-board pattern used for camera calibration, we obtain more reliable data this way. There is no need for an otherwise error-prone detection of the pattern.

For the calibration we take N_{Pos} deflectometric measurements of the planar mirror and apply the standard camera calibration algorithms on the obtained data. This provides us with the extrinsic position of the calibration pattern and the intrinsic parameters of the camera. In our case, those positions correspond to the positions of the virtual monitor plane π'_L, which gives us one plane $\pi'_{L,k}$ for each measurement position $k \in \{1, ..., N_{Pos}\}$.

Camera/Monitor-transformation Based on this positions, the next step is to derive the mirror positions $\pi'_{S,k}$ for each measurement and with that the real monitor plane π'_L which has a fixed position in relation to the camera. Each virtual monitor plane

$$\pi'_L : \langle \hat{\mathbf{n}}'_L | \mathbf{x_C} \rangle - d'_L = 0$$

provides us with four parameters: its normal vector $\hat{\mathbf{n}}'_L$ and distance d'_L to the camera's coordinate origin. We utilize the fact that the real monitor plane π_L is the reflection of each virtual monitor $\pi'_{L,k}$ plane about the corresponding mirror plane $\pi_{S,k}$:

$$\pi_{L,k} = \text{Refl}_{\pi_{S,k}}(\pi'_{L,k}), \tag{2.1}$$

where $\text{Refl}_{\pi_{S,k}}$ denotes the reflection about the plane $\pi_{S,k}$. These mirror planes are initially unknown. Using equation (2.1), we can now construct a system of linear equations:

$$\text{Refl}_{\pi_{S,j}}(\pi'_{L,j}) = \text{Refl}_{\pi_{S,k}}(\pi'_{L,k}), \tag{2.2}$$

with $(j, k) \in \{1, ..., N_{Pos}\} \times \{1, ..., N_{Pos}\}$ and $j \neq k$. From every equation (2.2) we obtain four constraints for the equation system. Given the data from at least three measurements, we can solve the equation system and get the mirror positions $\pi_{S,k}$. Any of those gives us the real monitor plane by inserting in equation (2.1) and therefore the wanted transformation $\mathbf{H}_{LCD}$.

Hand-eye calibration   The last step is the *hand-eye calibration* to obtain the transformation $\mathbf{H}_{world}$. This allows to combine the measurements in a world co-ordinate system. Tsai and Lenz described this calibration procedure in [TL89]. Hand-eye calibration requires knowledge of the robots position and the corre-sponding movement of the camera. While the robot's position is provided by its control system, the measurement of the camera's movement proves to be difficult in our calibration setup. The reflection in the mirror exhibits invariance towards translation and rotation in the mirror plane, i.e., movements of the camera parallel to the mirror plane result in the same reflection. Therefore, an additional marking or pattern on the mirror is necessary in order to obtain the camera's movement with all degrees of freedom. With this information we can now employ the algorithm from [TL89] which yields the transformation $\mathbf{H}_{world}$.

Although we can not sustain our self-imposed restriction to the solitary use of a mirror for calibration, our new technique reduces the calibration effort substan-tially. At the same time, we make optimal use of the deflectometric systems ca-pabilities. In the next section, we show a practical application which enables the combination of multiple measurements for the reconstruction of larger surfaces using a fully calibrated deflectometric sensor.

3   Reconstruction of Specular Surfaces

Once a deflectometric measurement of a surface is obtained one will desirably de-rive as much information as possible from this data. A common task in computer vision is the extraction of 3D shape from the acquired data. Due to the deflec-tometric principle, the raw data only contains the relation between the cameras rays-of-sight and the corresponding position on the sensor's monitor plane. Using the calibration from Section 2 and the law of reflection it is easy to extrapolate from this data to the surface normal for each rays-of-sight.

However, the normal field received is not a unique solution. Instead a whole set of possible surfaces is returned, each of which could have evoked the observed mea-surement. This ambiguity requires some kind of *regularization* to choose the real surface from the set of possible surfaces, by incorporating additional information. This additional information can arise from various sources: distance measurement through additional sensors, evaluation of surface properties like shading or polar-ization, fusion of the data from multiple measurements, to name but a few. A detailed survey can be found in [Wer10].

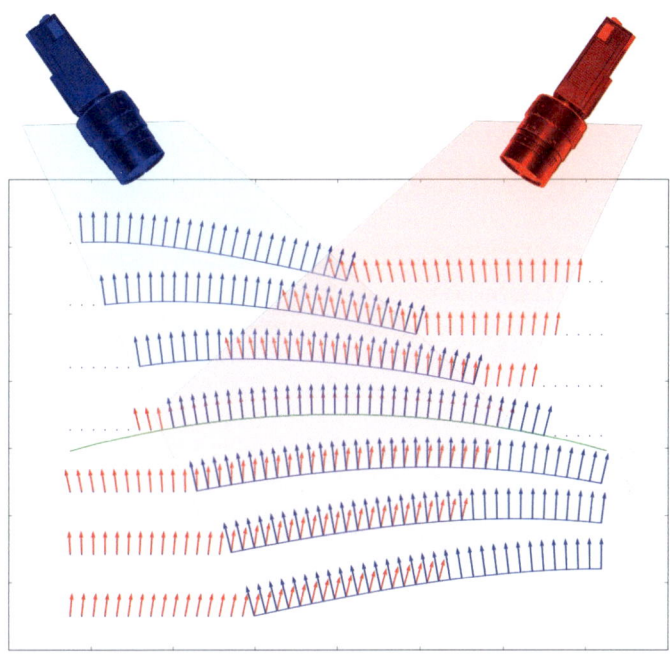

Figure 3.1: Principle of deflectometric stereo. Only at the position of the true surface the disparity between the normal fields attains a minimum.

As for the inspection of larger surfaces it seems natural to use the information from multiple measurements. Here, the redundant information in overlapping measurements is used for regularization while at the same time the measuring field is extended. Figure 3.1 illustrates the regularization for this case. Knowing the camera positions for both measurements, the proposed normal fields are superimposed. Only at the position of the true surface the disparity between the normal fields attains a minimum.

Following preparatory work in [Bal08] and [Wer10], we proposed in [BHWB10] a new approach for stereo reconstruction of specular surfaces. Therein we present a framework for reconstructing a surface under a strict data consistency constraint, while evaluating secondary information from multiple measurements. Our current research focuses on extending the reconstruction of large scale surfaces and will be subject of future publications.

By omitting additional sensors, the deflectometric setup is kept simple and lightweight. Thus enabling flexible construction and reconfiguration of the sensor, while providing the ability to inspect large surfaces.

4 Infrared-Deflectometry

The main advantage of deflectometry compared to other surface inspection methods is the ability to inspect specular surfaces. At the same time, this advantage is deflectometry's greatest disadvantage, because a specular reflection is indispensable for its function principle. Unfortunately, this limits the field of application for deflectometry to surfaces like polished metal, clear coating or glass, which all exhibit good reflective properties. This limitation arises only from the optical properties of the surface, more precisely, the reflectivity of the material and the roughness of the surface. Since the effect of these properties depends on the wavelength of the incident light it is obvious to adapt the deflectometric principle to operate in a more appropriate wavelength. This was first proposed by Horbach et al. in [HK05] and [Hor07], where they suggest the use of the far-infrared spectrum for deflectometric inspection.

In the following, we show how the deflectometric inspection benefits from this enhancement and what the problems in its practical implementation are.

4.1 Reflectivity of Rough Surfaces

Modeling the reflective properties of a surface can be a complex task. A common specification for these properties is the *bidirectional reflectance distribution function (BRDF)*. Here, for the sake of simplicity, we will concentrate on the two properties with the biggest impact for our case.

Material First there is the reflectivity of the material itself. Every material displays a different spectral response to incident light. Depending on the wavelength parts of the spectrum get reflected, absorbed or pass through the material, whereby no energy gets lost. In the visible light spectrum this wavelength-depended properties are perceived as color. Beyond the visible spectrum, especially metal surfaces reveal different reflective properties. While showing only moderate reflectivity in visible light, they become entirely specular with increasing wavelength. This effect is especially advantageous for the inspection of raw metal surfaces like, for example, car body parts before varnishing.

Roughness Besides the material itself the micro-structure of its surface also affects the reflective properties. It is impossible to find a descriptive model which fits all kind of surfaces. However, a good approximation of the reflective behavior is the *Rayleigh criterion*. Given a surfaces roughness, the Rayleigh criterion allows for an estimate of the minimal wavelength where the surface exhibits specular reflection. For that, the surface roughness is denoted by σ, its root mean square roughness. The angle of incidence is specified by θ. The Rayleigh criterion states that the wavelength λ of the incident light has to exceed the roughness σ by at least eight times to achieve a specular reflection:

$$\lambda > 8\sigma \cos(\theta).$$

The term $\cos(\theta)$ accounts for the fact that the reflectivity increases for shallow angles. Reflections with a wavelength below the limiting wavelength λ, are considered diffuse reflections, while they change to specular reflections above this limit. This effect is caused by interference when the light is reflected on different parts of the surface structure. Differing lengths between the light paths lead to constructive or destructive interference depending on the wavelength.

Both above-mentioned effects facilitate specular reflections with increasing wavelength. Compared to the visible light spectrum (400 - $700nm$) the long wavelength of the far-infrared spectrum in the range of 6 to $15\mu m$ allows inspection of surfaces with a surface roughness one magnitude higher.

4.2   Preliminary Material Tests

A set of preliminary tests were conducted to confirm the theoretical advantage of the infrared spectrum. Figure 4.1 shows some examples of the results. First, the reflection of an illuminated resolution test pattern is observed on different sample materials in the visible spectrum. The same experiment is repeated in the infrared spectrum with a thermal imaging camera and the resolution test pattern printed on a heated copper plate. Since the imprinted pattern exhibit a different thermal emission compared to the copperplate the pattern clearly stands out in the thermal image.

Particularly, test images with metal samples exhibit promising results. While the reflection in the visible spectrum displays a blurred image where the pattern is no longer recognizable, the infrared spectrum reveals a unblurred reflection of the thermal pattern. An untreated copper surface in Figure 4.1(a) looks like a perfect mirror and even milled aluminium with slight grooves on the surface (in Figure 4.1(b)) displays usable results.

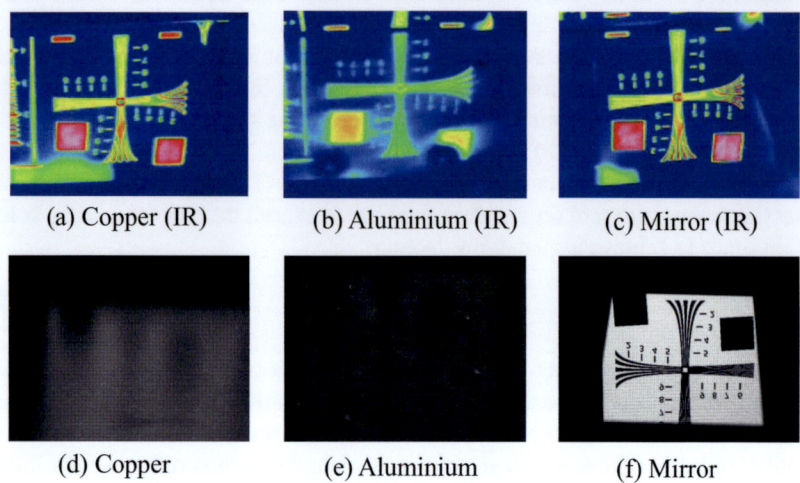

Figure 4.1: Comparison of reflectiveness of metals between the visible (d)-(f) and infrared (a)-(c) spectrum. The images show the reflection of a resolution test pattern with a comparable setup for both spectra.

Attention has to be be paid to materials that exhibit a high amount of absorption. Although most materials exhibit no perfect *black body* characteristics, they emit light in the far-infrared spectrum, depending on their temperature. Since the absorbed energy heats up the material, the emission of infrared radiation increases as well. This emission can possibly superimpose the reflection of the deflectometric measurement. If this effect can not be avoided, these disturbances have to be considered in the subsequent image processing.

4.3   Deflectometry in the Infrared-Spectrum

In theory, the deflectometric principle can be applied to the infrared spectrum in the same way as to the visible spectrum. Only the sensor composed of camera and monitor has to be adapted. While cameras for this spectrum are purchasable, there is practicably no replacement for the monitor in the infrared spectrum.

The camera can be replaced by an off-the-shelf thermal camera with a spectral sensitivity up to $14\mu m$. Although these cameras feature a comparatively low image resolution, they are still suitable for the application in deflectometry. However, the high prices of these devices increase the costs for the entire sensor.

The problem with transferring the deflectometric principle to the infrared spectrum is the lack of a monitor or other of dynamic pattern generators. Today, there is no purchasable technology for this function, apart from unavailable military developments. Future work in the field of infrared deflectometry will focus on the development of a suitable pattern generator. A simple approach would be the use of static patterns like we used for our tests in Section 4.2, as well as Horbach et al. for their measurements in [HK05]. However, a static pattern complicates the position coding which is necessary for the measurement. Dynamic pattern generators can base on different basic approaches:

1. An array of individually separated thermoelements, like resistors or peltier elements, which create the pattern pixel-wise,

2. Indirect pattern creation through optical absorption, e.g. writing the pattern with laser light onto a projection surface,

3. Switching a static pattern for every image of the code sequence,

to name but a few. It remains to be evaluated which approach is best suited for the application in infrared deflectometry.

5   Conclusion

We discussed three topics of current research in the field of deflectometry: A simplified calibration, which can be utilized for autonomous self calibration, new approaches which potentially enables deflectometry for large scale surface reconstruction and the extension of the deflectometric principle to the infrared spectrum, which enables the inspection of more surface materials.

All these developments aim towards an industrial application of deflectometric metrology. Further research will consolidate this preparatory work and extend deflectometry to a broad range of surface inspection tasks.

Bibliography

[Bal08]   Jonathan Balzer. *Regularisierung des Deflektometrieproblems – Grundlagen und Anwendung*. PhD thesis, Universität Karlsruhe (TH), Universitätsverlag Karlsruhe, 2008.

[BHWB10] Jonathan Balzer, Sebastian Höfer, Stefan Werling, and Jürgen Beyerer. Optimization on shape curves with application to specular stereo. *Lecture Notes in Computer Science*, 6376:41–50, 2010.

[Bou03]   J. Bouguet. Camera Calibration Toolbox for Matlab. Technical report, Microprocessor Research Labs and Intel Corp., 2003.

[BWB07]   Jonathan Balzer, Stefan Werling, and Jürgen Beyerer. Deflektometrische Rekonstruktion spiegelnder Freiformflächen. *tm - Technisches Messen*, 74(11):545–552, 2007.

[HK05]   Jan Horbach and Sören Kammel. Deflectometric inspection of diffuse surfaces in the far–infrared spectrum. In J. R. Price and F. Meriaudeau, editors, *Machine Vision Applications in Industrial Inspection XIII*, volume 5679 of *SPIE Conference Series*, pages 108–117, 2005.

[Hor07]   Jan Horbach. *Verfahren zur optischen 3D-Vermessung spiegelnder Oberflächen*. PhD thesis, Universität Karlsruhe(TH), 2007.

[HWB10]   Sebastian Höfer, Stefan Werling, and Jürgen Beyerer. Neuartige Strategie zur vollständigen Kalibrierung eines Sensorsystems zur automatischen Sichtprüfung spiegelnder Oberflächen. *Forum Bildverarbeitung*, 2010.

[SWN88]   Arthur C. Sanderson, Lee E. Weiss, and Shree K. Nayar. Structured Highlight Inspection of Specular Surfaces. *IEEE Transactions on Pattern Analysis and Machine Intelligence*, 10(1):44–55, 1988.

[TL89]   Roger Y. Tsai and Reimar K. Lenz. A New Technique for Fully Autonomous and Efficient 3D Robotics Hand/Eye Calibration. *IEEE Transactions on Robotics and Automation*, 5(3):345–358, 1989.

[Wer10]   Stefan Werling. *Deflektometrie zur automatischen Sichtprüfung und Rekonstruktion spiegelnder Oberflächen* . PhD thesis, Universität Karlsruhe (TH), Universitätsverlag Karlsruhe, 2010.

[Zha99]   Zhengyou Zhang. Flexible Camera Calibration By Viewing a Plane From Unknown Orientations. *Proceedings of the 7th International Conference on Computer Vision*, pages 666–673, 1999.

Feature Analysis for Maritime Object Classification in Single Images

Michael Teutsch

Vision and Fusion Laboratory
Institute for Anthropomatics
Karlsruhe Institute of Technology (KIT), Germany
teutsch@kit.edu

Technical Report IES-2010-15

Abstract: In order to implement a holistic image exploitation process for detecting, tracking and classifying maritime objects, it is necessary to understand the prospects and profits of the information coded directly in a single image. In this work, a big variety of features is extracted from given detection results. These features are analyzed automatically for their separability and benefit for classification tasks. This allows the innovation of a generic system, which is able to work independent of important properties such as perspective, object appearance, image quality and environmental condition. In two application examples, the scope and limits of this work are demonstrated and further ideas are outlined for improving the current results.

1 Introduction

Detection and classification of maritime objects with image exploitation algorithms especially in high distances can be very helpful for surveillance of fishery zones, ship monitoring, prevention of illegal immigration or piracy, and any similar request. Up to now, border protection agencies mostly use helicopters, airplanes or ships to observe wide maritime areas, but this process is very expensive and can hardly achieve satisfying spatial and temporal coverage. A useful support for human operators can be given by surveillance systems that use infrared or Synthetic Aperture Radar (SAR) image data of sensors located on unmanned buoys, unmanned aerial vehicles (UAVs) or satellites. They can take over the part for automatic detection and classification of suspicious objects around-the-clock.

This work considers the classification step of such systems. Preliminary obtained detection results are given for example as bounding boxes and features are extracted from them and analyzed for their capability to distinguish between desired object classes. There is no main focus on a specific feature or classifier type, but on the generality of the extracted features with respect to robustness, reliability, and to be independent of sensor perspective, object appearance, image quality and environmental condition. The temporal information available when considering image sequences is not utilized, yet. Just single images are used to extract the features.

1.1 Related work

The related work presented in this report centers on examples, where feature extraction is one of the main topics and is used to separate different object classes such as ship types (e.g., cargo ship, tanker, cruiser, carrier) or to identify suspicious objects (e.g., small boats). In most cases, the authors aim to determine ship types, but only few of them try to find suspicious objects [YA09], [LKF06]. Important criteria also are sensor type (visual-optical, infrared, SAR), perspective (buoy/ship/on-shore, airborne, spaceborne) and the extracted features themselves.

In images coming from a buoy, ship or on-shore camera, objects often have to be quite close to the sensor in order to analyze edges, shape or contour. In [AHR04], infrared images are processed by extracting edge-histograms and Hu moments. A neural network classifies different ship types. The authors in [LW08b] refer to the importance of a precise segmentation and use Hu moments and a Support Vector Machine (SVM) to gain better results than [AHR04]. The necessity of a good segmentation is one of the main topics in [YA09] and [LKF06], too. Both authors aim to identify suspicious – mainly small – boats either by using the Principal Component Analysis (PCA) [YA09] or by extracting region-based shape descriptors and using a k-Nearest-Neighbor (k-NN) classifier in visual-optical images [LKF06]. On similar data, in [FMS07] Scale-Invariant Feature Transform (SIFT) is used to extract class-specific object information.

Bird's eye view images generated by airborne or spaceborne sensors contain less information about object contours. However, the object distance is approximately known and, thus, mostly physical features like length, width, central axis can be extracted. This is the case in [SGHZ10] with an airborne visual-optical sensor, in [GK98] with an airborne SAR and finally in [ETP$^+$09] and [CHY$^+$06] with a spaceborne SAR sensor. Moreover, in [CHY$^+$06] also 3D scatter features are

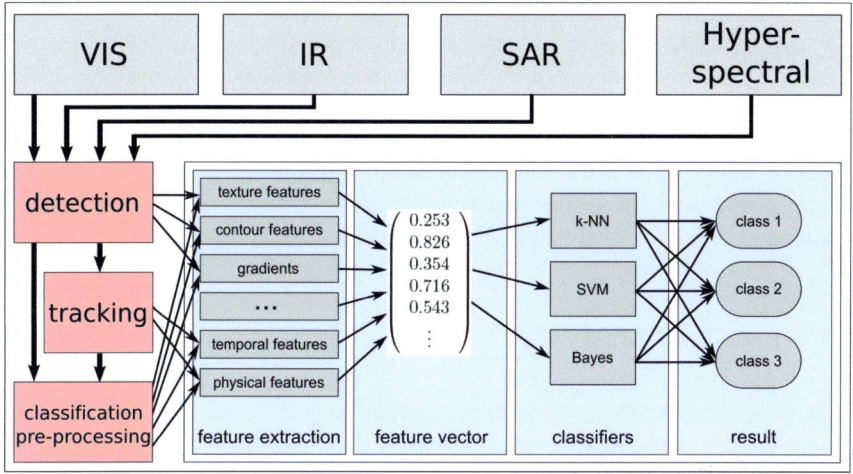

Figure 2.1: General processing overview.

used to specify a detected object. In [LW08a], precise segmentation, calculation of Zernike moments and classification with k-Nearest-Neighbor are applied to determine ship types in visual-optical images of an airborne camera.

1.2 Structure

The article provides the following organization: After a short general system overview in Section 2, the whole feature analysis process including feature extraction, normalization, evaluation and dimensionality reduction are presented in Section 3. Example applications for this method of feature extraction and the benefit for two different classification tasks are demonstrated in Section 4. Finally, a conclusion and an outlook to future work are given in Section 6.

2 General overview

The components for a classification process in the context of this work are shown in Fig. 2.1. As the focus lies on the generality of the extracted features, the input data should be as flexible as possible. Thus, different kinds of images such as visual-optical, infrared or even SAR can be processed. During the detection step, object hypotheses are generated using various approaches which will not be discussed in detail in this paper. Tracking can deliver temporal information and is used to verify object hypotheses, extract temporal features or reliable physical features. However, since only single images are considered here, tracking will not be specified in the follow-up. More attention will be paid to the pre-processing, where the segmentation plays a very important role as already mentioned in the related work. Main topic will be the classification module and particularly the feature analysis. The two examples in Section 4 will also provide the setup and comparison of classifiers as well as the choice of object classes.

3 Feature analysis

The classification process consists of an offline-stage for feature analysis and classifier training, and an online-stage for testing and processing. The feature analysis contains a *pre-processing module*, where precise segmentation of object pixels is performed, the *feature extraction*, where a high-dimensional feature vector with concatenated information of several feature classes is created, and finally the *feature evaluation*, where the features are normalized and tested for their separability of given classes in order to use only the best feature combination and reduce the feature vector's dimensionality for faster computation time. While pre-processing and feature extraction are also part of the online-stage – with an already reduced set of features and a feature vector of low dimensionality – the feature evaluation is a special sub-process of the feature analysis and conducted only in the offline-stage for initially setting up the feature vector.

3.1 Pre-processing

It is assumed, that the preceding detection or tracking module determines regions of interest (ROI) in the image, where objects are supposed to be, creates object hypotheses and passes them to the feature analysis for closer investigations. Each object hypothesis can be represented by a bounding box for example. As some of the features to be extracted need object segmentation first, background subtraction based on a single intensity-threshold is conducted:

The histograms of the ROI and the whole image are generated. By using an empirically determined scale-factor, the whole image histogram is downscaled bin-wise to adjust both histograms to each other. Now, the whole image histogram is subtracted bin-wise from the ROI one and the first bin of the difference histogram containing enough elements is taken as gray-value threshold. Some other histogram-based approaches have been analyzed, but this one proved to be most robust against unequal distributions of sea and sky as well as background irregularities like strong waves.

3.2   Feature extraction

With no specific expectation concerning the given data, the extraction of a big, but very generalized set of features has been implemented. Hence, no prior or background knowledge about the target class like characteristic contour, edge constellation, expected texture, scaling, distance, size, direction or any kind of model was considered. In this way, each kind of specialization shall be avoided to be as flexible as possible regarding heavy variations of perspective, image type, image quality, object appearance, and environmental condition. There are in total 342 features calculated and divided in several procedural related feature classes for better organization. The feature vector is created by concatenating all calculated features. An overview of the so far implemented feature classes is shown in Fig. 3.1. In the follow-up, these feature classes will be described more detailed:

- *Invariant moments*: Hu moments [Hu62], [Li92] are calculated for the ROI image.

- *Co-occurrence matrices*: Like in [HSD73], the co-occurrence matrices for the ROI image are calculated and features extracted like variance, contrast, entropy, sum variance, sum difference.

- *Texture analysis*: Mainly the same features like for the co-occurrence matrices are extracted, but directly on the ROI image.

- *Kernel analysis*: After segmentation, the object blob (*kernel*) is compared to its surrounding area (*frame*). Some clearspace next to the object blob is left unaffected to avoid merging effects. Feature extraction considers relations between the kernel and the frame like means difference, means ratio, variances difference, variances ratio.

- *Row analysis*: Values like mean, variance and standard deviation are calculated row-wise on the ROI in order to keep the object's vertical spatial information. Features are generated e.g. by comparing these values row-wise or by grouping them to compute ratios between upper and lower half of the ROI.

- *Blob analysis*: After object segmentation it is assumed that only the object blob is left. This object blob is analyzed by computing its mean, variance, centroid or central moments.

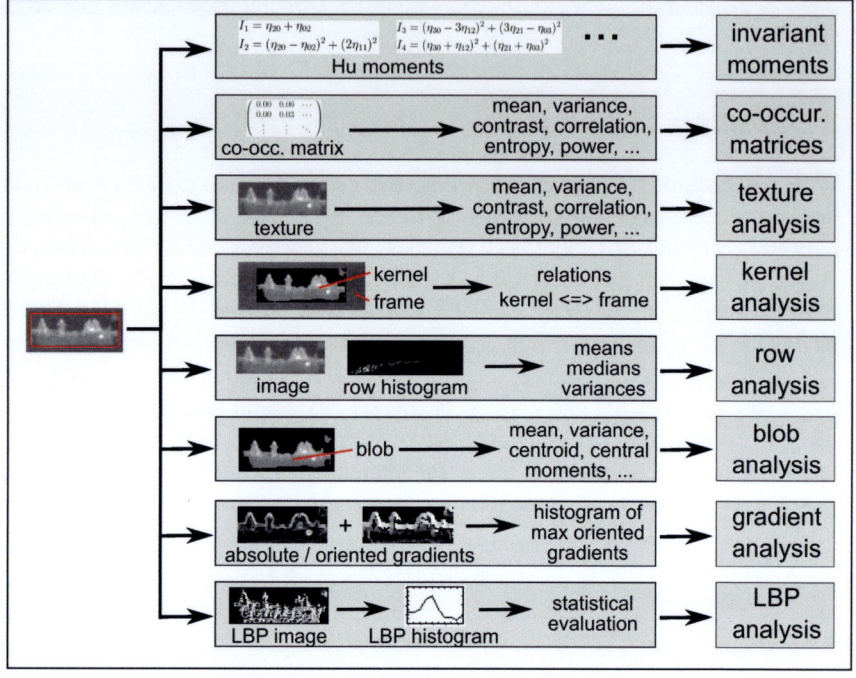

Figure 3.1: The extracted feature classes.

- *Gradient analysis*: Filters like Sobel or Normalized Gradients of Gaussians [Kor88] are applied to create absolute and oriented gradient images as well as Histograms of Oriented Gradients (HOGs). Texture analysis directly on the gradient image and miscellaneous statistical features of the HOGs specify the feature extraction process.

- *Local Binary Pattern analysis*: According to [OPM02], circular and "uniform" Local Binary Pattern (LBPs) are calculated. Favored benefit of LBPs is their invariance towards gray-values, rotation and scale. Texture analysis directly on the LBP-image and miscellaneous statistical features of LBP-histograms specify the feature extraction process.

Invariant moments, row analysis, gradient analysis and LBP analysis are performed with and without object pixel segmentation. The resulting feature vector containing 342 features can now be evaluated.

3.3   Feature evaluation

During the feature evaluation process, all features are tested towards their separability in a given classification task. Features with high separability are kept while features with poor separability are discarded. In this way, both the extraction and the classification become faster, as not all features have to be calculated and sent through the used classifier.

For equalization of the influence regarding the classification task, the features are normalized by downscaling the value range of each feature using its standard deviation. Thus, a bias towards a set of few features with high value range is avoided. As a Linear Discriminant Analysis (LDA) is applied for feature evaluation later, a set of labeled training samples has to be available. For normalization, only positive training samples are considered for autonomously learning a model for the target object's expected value range.

Now, in the evaluation process, features with highest variance for given labeled training data are identified by the LDA. Features with maximum variance between the two classes have best separability. A greedy algorithm chooses the best feature combination with respect to maximization of the overall separability and to guarantee good orthogonality and low covariance between the used features. This feature set is ready to be directly passed to the following classifier.

4   Applications

In this section, two example applications will be presented in order to demonstrate the generality of the just introduced approaches and methods. While the first one considers spaceborne SAR images, side view IR images coming from an unmanned buoy are processed in the second. Both sets of images contain maritime objects.

4.1   Ship classification in spaceborne SAR images

In [ST10], the authors aim to analyze SAR signatures in images coming from TerraSAR-X satellite for ship monitoring tasks such as surveillance of fishery zones or tracking of cargo ships and detection of offshore artificial objects such as small ships or lost containers.

Object hypotheses are produced by running pre-processing and detection steps. During these steps, the 16bit complex SAR data is downscaled to an 8bit gray-value image. An external land mask is applied to focus only on sea area and fast detection based on adaptive thresholding (CFAR) is performed. Finally, each object hypothesis is pre-processed for classification by cutting out its ROI, reducing speckle noise, and rotating the object to be paraxial to the horizontal image axis.

The classifier is trained to distinguish between ships and non-ships, which is a challenging task since objects and clutter often may appear very similar in the SAR data as shown in Fig. 4.1. The feature extraction is concentrated on these two classes, in which non-ships can be clutter, sidelobe effects, buoys, windmills or all kind of undefined reflections and unknown objects. After feature evaluation only the feature classes of kernel analysis and LBP analysis are taken for building up the feature vector as they are proven to offer highest separability. With 3-Nearest-Neighbor (3-NN) and SVM, two classifiers have been trained and tested on the available labeled data. The quantitative evaluation can be seen in Table 4.1, where the SVM outperforms the 3-NN and reaches 92 % of correct classifications on given data of 221 detection samples. False positives often occur when specific object classes are confused as ships often look like groins or windmills and vice-versa. Some examples for correct and incorrect classifications are displayed in Fig. 4.1.

Table 4.1: Ship classification in spaceborne SAR: Rate of correct classifications.

classifier	3-NN		SVM	
data set	test data	all data	test data	all data
overall rate	88.9 %	91.4 %	95.6 %	91.9 %
ship rate	96.7 %	98.9 %	96.7 %	95.8 %
non-ship rate	73.3 %	69.1 %	93.3 %	78.2 %

4.2 Small boat classification in side view IR images

In [TK10], an infrared camera on an unmanned buoy produces image sequences performing round-the-clock maritime surveillance to reveal criminal activities such as illegal immigration, drug trafficking or piracy. Often, small boats are used for such activities, because they are difficult to detect. Hence, they need to be identified and discriminated from irrelevant objects such as big boats, ships, buoys or clutter.

Three different approaches for object detection are applied and fused to guarantee high robustness which is important due to the strongly varying object appearance, image quality and weather condition. After a spatio-temporal check for stability

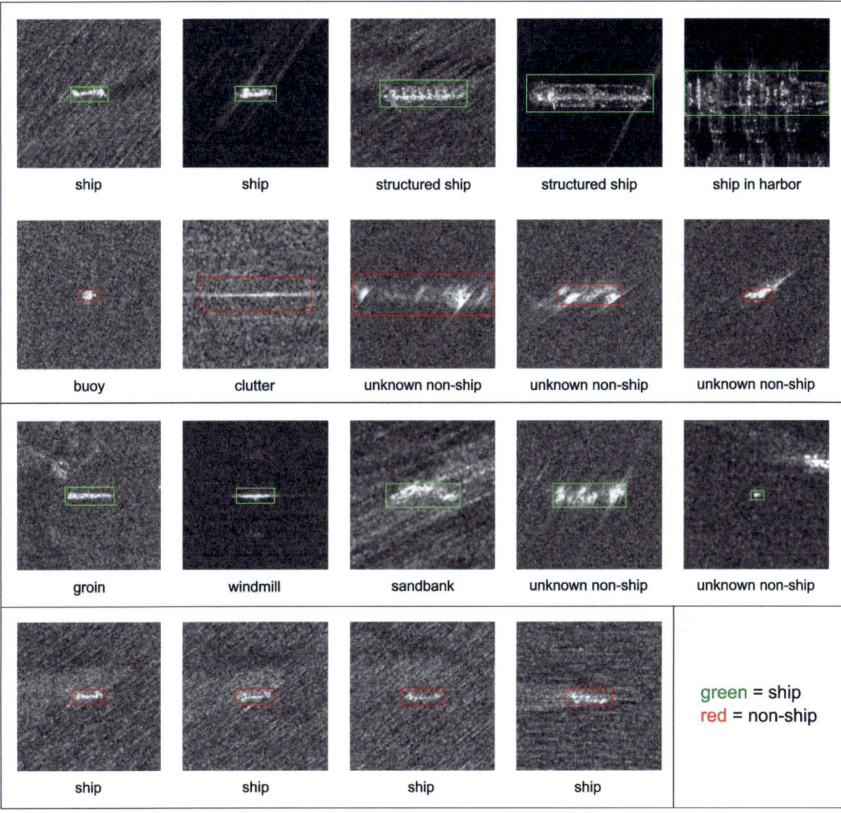

Figure 4.1: Ship classification in spaceborne SAR: Correct classifications in row 1 and 2, false positives in row 3 and false negatives in row 4. Different SAR-data-types can be seen in the different scalings e.g. in row 1 [ST10].

of the detection result, an alarm hypothesis is generated and passed to the feature extraction and classification module.

The classification is subdivided into two stages: Separating objects from clutter in the first stage and suspicious boats from irrelevant objects in the second stage. A SVM is trained with a customized feature set for each stage. The first stage is mainly a cross-check of the given alarm hypothesis as it is assumed that clutter is filtered by the alarm generation process. Feature evaluation determined a combination of eleven features composed from co-occurrence matrices, texture analysis, kernel analysis, row analysis and gradient analysis to reach best separability of clutter and objects in first stage. As many different features classes are involved, low covariance beneath the used features is achieved. Same situation with the second stage: With a set of seven features coming from co-occurrence matrices, texture analysis and gradient analysis, high orthogonality of the feature vector dimensions is guaranteed.

The SVMs were trained on a training data set of 1877 samples in total with 1256 clutter objects, 386 irrelevant objects and 235 suspicious boats. Afterwards, the evaluation was performed with the test data set of 200 clutter objects, 74 irrelevant objects and 54 suspicious boats. As presented in Table 4.2, the two-stage-classification achieved a correct classification rate of 96.78 %, while the SVM separating clutter and objects reached 99.10 % and the SVM distinguishing between irrelevant objects and suspicious boats 97.66 %. Some classification examples are shown in Fig. 4.2.

Table 4.2: Small boat classification in side view IR: Rate of correct classifications.

classifier	SVM 1 (clutter)	SVM 2 (objects)	2-stage-SVM
correct rate	99.10 %	97.66 %	96.78 %
false positives	0.90 %	0.00 %	0.54 %
false negatives	0.00 %	2.34 %	2.68 %

5   Conclusion and future work

In this report, the extraction and analysis of a big variety of feature classes in different image types for classification tasks has been presented. Main focus was laid on the generality of the used features and approaches in order to be as flexible as possible regarding image type, sensor perspective, object appearance, image quality and environmental condition. 342 features of eight different feature

Figure 4.2: Small boat classification in side view IR: Suspicious boats in red, irrelevant objects in yellow and clutter in green [TK10].

classes were extracted including invariant moments, co-occurrence matrices, texture analysis, kernel analysis, row analysis, blob analysis, gradient analysis and LBP analysis. By applying normalization and LDA, the features were evaluated and analyzed with respect to their separability and covariance towards given classification tasks keeping only the strongest feature combination. Outcome is a low-dimensional feature vector, which is assumed to be good input for classification and is subsequently passed to a classifier like SVM.

Two very different applications with spaceborne ship classification in SAR images and side view classification of small boats in IR images were presented, where the proposed feature extraction method reaches good results of more than 90 % correct classifications for given image data in each application. But experiments also uncovered the fact that the main advantage of this approach simultaneously is the main limit: The generality. Often, special or background knowledge is necessary especially for difficult classification tasks as mainly seen in the false positives for ship classification in spaceborne SAR. Groins or windmills often appear very similar to ships, so it is not possible to reliably distinguish between them automatically. Hence, in most applications a specialized object description e.g., using expert knowledge will improve the classification process. Nevertheless, the general point of view towards feature extraction and evaluation seems to be a good fundament for gaining first good results and for further specializations.

Future work will basically aim to expanding the existing approach by temporal and physical features. In the side view IR data, the analysis of image sequences can deliver temporal information, which can massively support the classification process. After the introduction of tracking to receive temporal object attributes, these attributes can be used for calculating temporal features. Furthermore, with tracking reasonably reliable physical information such as approximate object size, distance or velocity is accessible, which can be compared to known values from a prior knowledge database for example.

Bibliography

[AHR04]   Jorge Alves, Jessica Herman, and Neil C. Rowe. Robust Recognition of Ship Types from an Infrared Silhouette. In *Command and Control Research and Technology Symposium*, San Diego, CA, USA, 2004.

[CHY+06] Peng Chen, Weigen Huang, Jingsong Yang, Bin Fu, XiuLin Lou, and Huagon Zhang. Characters of merchant vessels in spaceborne SAR imagery. In *Proceedings of SPIE Vol. 6406, Remote Sensing of the Marine Environment*, November 2006.

[ETP+09] Stéphane Estable, Frank Teufel, Lars Petersen, Stefan Knabe, Günter Saur, and Tobias Ullmann. Detection and Classification of Offshore Artificial Objects in TerraSAR-X Images:

First Outcomes of the DeMarine-DEKO project. In *Proceedings of the IEEE OCEANS Conference*, Bremen, Germany, May 11–14 2009.

[FMS07]   Patricia A. Feineigle, Daniel D. Morris, and Franklin D. Snyder. Ship Recognition using Optical Imagery for Harbor Surveillance. In *Proceedings of Association for Unmanned Vehicle Systems International (AUVSI)*, Washington, D.C., USA, June 2007.

[GK98]   Langis Gagnon and R. Klepko. Hierarchical Classifier Design for Airborne SAR Images of Ships. In *Proceedings of SPIE Vol. 3371, Automatic Target Recognition VIII*, Orlando, FL, USA, April 1998.

[HSD73]   Robert M. Haralick, K. Shanmugam, and Its'hak Dinstein. Textural Features for Image Classification. *IEEE Transactions on Systems, Man and Cybernetics*, 3(6):610–621, November 1973.

[Hu62]   Ming-Kuei Hu. Visual pattern recognition by moment invariants. *IRE Transactions on Information Theory*, 8(2):179–187, February 1962.

[Kor88]   Axel Korn. Toward a Symbolic Representation of Intensity Changes in Images. *IEEE Transactions on Pattern Analysis and Machine Intelligence*, 10(5):610–625, September 1988.

[Li92]   Yajun Li. Reforming the theory of invariant moments for pattern recognition. *Pattern Recognition*, 25(7):723–730, July 1992.

[LKF06]   Qiming Luo, Taghi M. Khoshgoftaar, and Andres Folleco. Classification of Ships in Surveillance Video. In *Proceedings of the 2006 IEEE International Conference on Information Reuse and Integration*, pages 432–437, Waikoloa Village, HI, USA, September 16–18 2006.

[LW08a]   Jinhui Lan and Lili Wan. Automatic ship target classification based on aerial images. In *Proceedings of SPIE Vol. 7156, 2008 International Conference on Optical Instruments and Technology: Optical Systems and Optoelectronic Instruments*, Beijing, China, 2008.

[LW08b]   Heng Li and Xinyu Wang. Automatic Recognition of Ship Types from Infrared Images Using Support Vector Machines. In *Proceedings of the 2008 International Conference on Computer Science and Software Engineering*, pages 483–486, Wuhan, China, December 12–14 2008.

[OPM02]   Timo Ojala, Matti Pietikäinen, and Topi Mäenpää. Multiresolution Gray-Scale and Rotation Invariant Texture Classification with Local Binary Patterns. *IEEE Transactions on Pattern Analysis and Machine Intelligence*, 24(7):971–987, July 2002.

[SGHZ10]   Bo Sun, Wei Guo, Jun He, and Xiaoming Zhu. A special algorithm based on structure for ship classification. In *Proceedings of SPIE Vol. 7701, Visual Information Processing XIX*, Orlando, FL, USA, April 2010.

[ST10]   Günter Saur and Michael Teutsch. SAR signature analysis for TerraSAR-X-based ship monitoring. In *Proceedings of SPIE Vol. 7830, Image and Signal Processing for Remote Sensing*, Toulouse, France, September 20–22 2010.

[TK10]   Michael Teutsch and Wolfgang Krüger. Classification of small Boats in Infrared Images for maritime Surveillance. In *Proceedings of the 2nd WaterSide Security Conference (WSS)*, Carrara, Italy, November 3–5 2010.

[YA09]   Cenk Yaman and Vijayan Asari. Long-Range Target Classification in a cluttered Environment using Multi-Sensor Image Sequences. In *3rd International Conference on Recent Advances in Space Technologies (RAST)*, Istanbul, Turkey, June 14–16 2009.

On Adaptive Open-World Modeling Based on Information Fusion and Inductive Inference

Achim Kuwertz

Vision and Fusion Laboratory
Institute for Anthropomatics
Karlsruhe Institute of Technology (KIT), Germany
achim.kuwertz@kit.edu

Technical Report IES-2010-16

Abstract: In this technical report, a conception for adaptive open-world modeling for cognitive information systems is presented. In cognitive systems, a world model serves as information storage for sensor data and thus represents an abstract, simplified copy of the observed environment. In order to allow for a high-level information processing on a semantic layer, the represented objects are backed by a semantically enriched domain model containing a priori knowledge. Such prior knowledge generally contains only a fixed number of object concepts, thus constituting a closed-world model. However, in many real-life applications, the considered environment is not closed. For coping with changing environments, a cognitive system must be equipped with an adaptive world model able to adjust to an observed open environment. For designing such an open-world model, this report evaluates and summarizes information fusion and concept learning techniques.

1 Introduction

In modern society, information is prevalent. The developments in sensor technologies over the last decades allow for an almost universal information acquisition. The amount of processable data and information is constantly rising. In order to make beneficial use of all this information, a structured and managed approach is necessary. On the one hand, data must be gathered, assessed for relevance and, in a timely manner, disseminated to the requiring authorities, departments and decision makers. Furthermore, acquired information often has to be persistently stored. On the other hand, the sheer amount of data can not efficiently be processed by a human being without appropriate technological support. Here, modern technologies like data mining, (semi-)automated image exploitation and video analysis, information fusion frameworks, distributed data sharing architectures, or knowledge management systems can help to efficiently determine and subsequently process relevant data. The use of such technology allows to provide a more understandable situational overview based on a vast amount of initially unstructured data.

Information management is thus an important process for providing situation-related solutions and satisfying specific information requests. It is applicable to many domains of modern life, ranging from economy and business management over disaster management, civil security and military operations to areas like environmental monitoring or health administration. Concrete tasks like security and safety in public places, maritime and land border surveillance, strategic and tactical reconnaissance, or atmospheric monitoring can all be characterized by producing large amounts of data, acquired by multiple sensors which possibly support heterogeneous sensing modalities.

In information processing, this raw data is transformed into data products by manual or automated exploitation, enriching the data by value in the form of contextual information and semantics. In order to obtain meaningful information, this single enriched data element has to be related to other relevant observations by employing techniques for data or information fusion. As a result of this processing, an integrated overall picture of the situation at hand is then to be established.

For enhancing the performance of information integration, the processed sensor data can be combined with *a priori knowledge* existent for the specific domain of interest. Such knowledge, established by domain experts, provides a semantic grounding to evaluate, efficiently classify and consistently integrate sensor observations into a knowledge base in order to represent the current state of the observed real-world domain. Managing the acquired sensory information with the objective of providing a sophisticated real world representation is then the task performed by a *world model*. A world model thereby serves as a central information hub, connecting information acquisition processes to exploitation, integration and representation systems, as well as providing a persistent information storage for static and dynamic information elements. The tasks to be performed within world modeling therefore comprise:

- acquiring and providing access to a priori domain knowledge in an operational form of representation,

- integrating sensor data and enriched information into the representation of the current domain state,

- processing information elements and inferring new information,

- representing the stored information on different abstraction levels.

The ability to represent the current state of a given domain in a world model strongly depends on the domain model contained in a priori knowledge. This model generally embodies knowledge acquired from domain experts in combination with general knowledge and facts from previous experience. It describes all entities that are likely to be observed and processed in the given domain of interest. Therefore, the overall expressiveness of a world model is limited by its ability to internally represent observed real-world objects as a priori modeled concepts. As a consequence, only a closed and a priori considered world segment can be represented. To allow for an integration of unforeseen events and entities, the world model has to be able to dynamically adjust its prior knowledge. This adjustment then should be based on the current state of the observed domain. An adaptive world model consequently must be capable of learning yet unrepresented concepts from real world observations.

The task of *concept learning* in information management and cognitive system goes hand in hand with the fusion and abstraction capabilities of a world model. In an adaptive system, the relevance of newly learned concepts has to be evaluated in terms of their usefulness for information integration and state representation tasks in the system. Successfully managing this requirement, an adaptive open-world model is than able to support human operators in tasks like situation assessment and decision making. By focusing on task-relevant data and presenting a role-adapted abstraction level of information, this can be done even in light of large amounts of sensor data. By integrating new aspects into its knowledge base, the system can further evolve with and to both its user and the current situation at hand.

This technical report gives an overview on topics revolving around adaptive open-world modeling. In Section 2, the concepts and notions of world modeling and knowledge representation in general are presented. Section 3 then gives a short introduction to information fusion. Section 4 is concerned with inductive inference and presents an outline on concept learning. In Section 5 then a conception for adaptive open-world modeling is introduced.

2   World Modeling

By modeling, one generates an abstract representation of a considered real-world scenario. A generated model contains abstract, possibly simplified concepts of real-world objects and represents these concepts in a structured way, e.g., as mathematical or graphical formalization. In this report, the term *world model* is used to describe the process of conceptually representing a considered segment of the real world. The abstractions applied in modeling can for instance be given as constrains on the spatial extension of the real-world segment, as limitations to the considered time frame as well as a domain-specific level-of-detail view to the segment.

An important feature of world modeling for cognitive information systems is the ability to capture *semantic relations* between real-world objects. These relations can for instance represent a spatial connection, e.g., a cup standing on a table, or a functional dependency, e.g., a driver steering a car. Often, the semantics of a world model are established when a model is build, derived from a priori knowledge about the considered real-world domain. These semantics then serve as a basis for information processing, e.g., semantically relating current sensor observations to each other. A world model as described above thereby consists of several parts.

2.1   Conceptions of World Modeling

The conceptions and notions of world modeling as used in this report are illustrated in Figure 2.1. As can be seen, a world model is employed to represent the considered *real world*, which here means a spatio-temporal segment of the physical world, possibly regarded from a domain-specific perspective. The background knowledge about this real-world segment and the considered domain is formalized in *prior knowledge*, depicted on the left-hand side. This prior knowledge initially contains all information that is known a priori, i.e., prior to any sensor observations, and can therefore be considered as a static model of the real world.

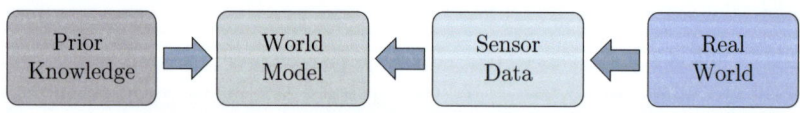

Figure 2.1: World modeling conception and notions.

In prior knowledge both the features and semantic relationships of relevant real-world entities are formalized. A real-world *entity*, denoting anything existent in the real world (like tangible objects, abstract concepts, etc.), is thereby mapped to an entity concept in prior knowledge. A feature of a real world object (e.g., its height) is for example mapped to an attribute concept (e.g., height being a non-negative real-valued variable). A relationship between entities is mapped to a relation concept (e.g., describing the kind of relationship and the number of entities involved). A real-world object with its defining features and relationships is then represented in prior knowledge as an object concept, i.e., a named set of attributes and relation concepts.

Observations of the real world are depicted in Figure 2.1 as *sensor data*. Sensor data represents a view or projection of the real world according to the sensing modalities, e.g., the visible electro-magnetic spectrum for imagery data. In world modeling, sensor data constitutes the input to the dynamic *world model*. A dynamic world model represents the current state (as known from observations) of the real world, possibly in combination with a history of recent state information. This world model is time-dependent and therefore is denoted as dynamic. The state represented in the world model for a given time step is a result of integrating current sensor data with information drawn from prior knowledge (e.g., semantic relations) and previously acquired already processed observations.

2.2   Knowledge Representation

In world modeling, acquired information has to be represented, processed and stored. The subject of information processing is covered in Section 3 by an introduction to information fusion methods. The next two sections deal with the problem of how to formally represent knowledge and information. First, the notions of data, information and knowledge should be formalized following [Das08, Ack89]. In Figure 2.3, an information hierarchy is illustrated. At the bottom of the hierarchy, data is situated. *Data* represents the most basic unit in information management, having by itself only little purpose and meaning. Data is just symbols, for example, the measured values of a physical signal. On the middle level of the pyramid, *information* is located. Information constitutes semantically enriched or processed data, e.g., annotated data. Information is also given by meaningful relationships between data, e.g., the results of data fusion. On the top level of the hierarchy, knowledge is placed. *Knowledge* is the possession and application of data and information, sometimes regarded as a process. Knowledge is thereby in general subjective and in a certain way connected to consciousness. Furthermore, data, information and knowledge are especially relevant in the context of communication (between humans and/or systems) or decision making (and consecutive actions).

Another set of notions that has to be clarified is given by the terms entity, concept and symbol. As noted previously, an *entity* shall represent everything existing (physically or conceptually) in the real world. In order to exchange information about entities, these entities have to be uniquely identified, by assigning *symbols* to them, e.g., names. Now, derived from previous experience with real-world entities,

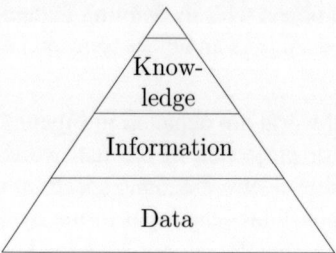

Figure 2.2: Data, information and knowledge pyramid.

human communication in everyday life works more or less effectively just on the basis of symbolic names. This means that humans are mostly able to understand to meaning behind a communicated symbol, due to the fact that the human mind is able to generalize common entity features and internally has built an abstract entity model based on its experience. However, in machine communication (either system-to-system or human-to-system), communication based just on symbols is not sufficient. Here, a formal definition of the features of a real world entity is necessary for successfully interchanging information. This definition, constituting a formal equivalent to the internal human model, is now named a *concept*.

Concept thus are the formal description of named real world entities. In defining concepts, two different approaches are possible [Stu09]. The generalization approach is to find and point out all the common features of a considered set of entities. This results in an intensional, feature-based concept description. Another approach is to regard the domain of interest and to build concepts by separating or partitioning this domain into different classes. This approach foregrounds not the similarities but the differences of the various concepts. Furthermore, an alternative way of describing concepts should be noted: rather than describing their features, a concept can be given by explicitly enumerating all its contained entities. For information management, the use of concepts is beneficial as they formalize the meaning of a notion, i.e., a symbol, and in doing so capture its semantics.

Adequately capturing the semantics of a notion generally is an important aspect of knowledge representation. The problem can be made clear by considering the so-called semiotic triangle [Stu09], depicted in Figure 2.3(a). As can be seen here, a symbol (e.g., a notion or entity name, respectively) is standing for a real-world entity, here called the referent. By being mentioned to a human being, the symbol induces a certain thought or mental image, linked to human expectations about the referent. Now, the entity being actually represented by the symbol and the entity being expected by the human being do not necessarily have to match, as is

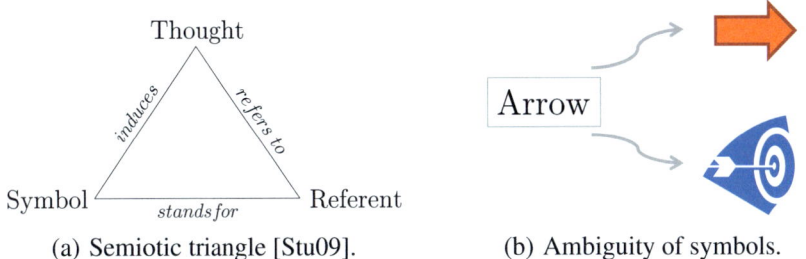

(a) Semiotic triangle [Stu09].　　　　(b) Ambiguity of symbols.

Figure 2.3: Semantic knowledge representation.

illustrated in Figure 2.3(b). Thus, only if the meaning of a symbol has been clearly captured, the symbol is useful for information processing in cognitive systems.

2.3　Ontologies

One way of representing knowledge in a structured manner, with semantics attached to it, is the use of ontologies. The notion of an ontology, being a part of philosophy for a long time, has become more and more popular recently. Ontologies, defined as "an explicit specification of a conceptualization" [Gru93], thereby serve in the process of acquiring and formalizing human knowledge [Stu09]. Ontologies allow for semantics in information management by formalizing the link between symbols and expectations. They enable systems and their users to function in an interoperable way by acting as interfaces between different kinds of representation [Sch06].

An ontology thus can be considered as a formally ordered representation of a set of conceptualities (i.e., entities) along with existing relations, for a given domain of interest. There exist several definitions for ontologies (e.g. [Sch06]). An ontology can thereby be defined as a tuple

$$\mathcal{O} \;=\; (\,\mathcal{C},\mathcal{R},\mathcal{H},\mathcal{A},\mathcal{D},\mathcal{I}\,)\;,$$

where $\mathcal{C}$ denotes the set of concepts represented in the ontology, $\mathcal{R}$ the set of relations in between these concepts or their current instances, $\mathcal{H}$ a set of hierarchies or taxonomies on the concepts, and $\mathcal{A}$ the set of axiomatic rules used for reasoning. Furthermore, $\mathcal{D}$ represents the domain of interest, and $\mathcal{I}$ the current set of actual instances, i.e., the knowledge base.

Ontologies themselves can be represented in different ways. In this report, two possibilities will be presented following [Stu09]. As a graphical representation, a *semantic network* can be considered. Based on a graph $G = (\mathcal{G}, \mathcal{E})$ with the set of nodes $\mathcal{G}$ and the set of edges $\mathcal{E}$, the set of concepts $\mathcal{C}$ is mapped to the set of nodes $\mathcal{N}$, and the set of relations $\mathcal{R}$ is mapped to the set of edges $\mathcal{E}$. Thereby, different types of edges are allowed in order to represent different kinds of relations. An advantage of this graph-based representation is that it can be easily used in computer systems, with many processing algorithms available.

Another way of representing an ontology is given by formal logic. Ontologies inherently contain logical axioms in their set of rules $\mathcal{A}$. These axioms e.g. allow for the integration of universal facts into an ontology and constitute an efficient way to build complex concepts, as well as enabling deductive inference within the knowledge base $\mathcal{I}$. Ontologies therefore can be represented by first order predicate logic. Concepts and relations can e.g. be mapped to unary and binary predicates, concept instances and attribute values to term variables and constants. Furthermore, a transformation from a semantic network representation to a logic-based description is possible, for more details see e.g. [Stu09].

3 Information Fusion

In a world model, various kinds of observations, differing for example in employed sensor modalities, covered area, creation time, abstraction level or content, have to be combined consistently. In order to enable a consistent handling of acquired data and information, fusion methods can be employed.

Fusion can be defined as the process of combining potentially heterogeneous data and information from different sources in order to obtain improved information of higher value [PLR08]. The actual improvement thereby can consist of more reliable information with reduced uncertainty or higher precision (e.g., in the case of combining homogeneous measurements), of a higher area of sensor coverage, or of an increased number of known object attributes (e.g., in case of heterogeneous information fusion).

In world modeling, sensor data and derived exploitation information is fused with facts from prior knowledge and previous observations. The fused information then gets stored into the dynamic world model, where further fusion processes (e.g., for abstraction, generalization, or inference) can be applied.

3.1 Fusion Models

Fusion can take place at different levels of information management. For example, different methodologies for data and information fusion do exist. In order to define the different levels of fusion processes, several fusion models have been developed.

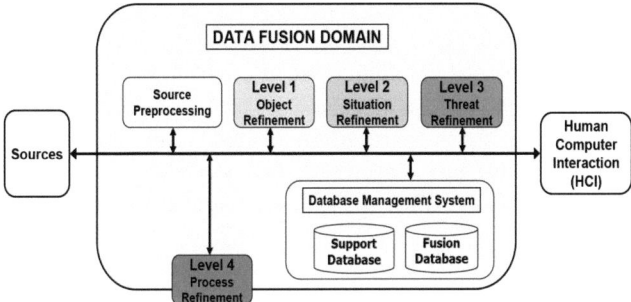

Figure 3.1: The JDL data fusion model, from [Whi88].

A prominent one is given by *the JDL data fusion model*, illustrated in Figure 3.1 [Das08, LBR+04]. In this model, several fusion levels are defined, distinguished by the kind of information they produce. Data and information from heterogeneous sources is preprocessed on a signal level, e.g., for noise reduction, alignment, signal estimation, or feature extraction. On Level 1, sensor data is combined to obtain an accurate state estimate of a (physical) object, e.g., by estimating its attribute values. On Level 2, relationships among the determined entities are inferred based on the previous results, i.e., the entity estimates. Finally, on Level 3, inference on the current situation is performed in order to predict its possible impacts.

Following [Das08], the notions of data fusion versus information fusion can now be mapped to the fusion levels of the JDL model. Data fusion thereby denotes all information processing situated at Level 1 and below, whereas information fusion takes place on the levels equal to Level 2 or higher. Furthermore, knowledge gets involved on Level 3.

3.2   Fusion methods

Related to the fusion levels, different fusion methodologies do exists. For data fusion, probabilistic methods and Bayesian inference can for example be applied. The well-known Kalman filter belongs to this class of fusion methods. For high-level information fusion on the other hand, a logic-based approach can be taken.

In world modeling, generally Bayesian as well as logic-based fusion methods are applied. For estimating attribute values of modeled entities based on observations, Bayesian inference can be employed, as e.g. in [GHB08]. Here, the attributes are described by Gaussian densities in a degree-of-belief interpretation, represented by their mean values (denoting the assumed attribute values) and variances (expressing the uncertainty or belief in the denoted attribute values). Furthermore, several modeled entities can be combined to higher-level concepts by logic-based fusion (e.g., by abstracting several vehicles to a convoy). A connection between Bayesian and logic-based inference is established by methods like Markov-Logic-Networks [RD06]. Connecting the fusion levels one and two, Markov-Logic-Networks thus constitute another fusion method applicable to world modeling.

4 Concept Learning

In this report, an approach to modeling an open world is considered. In order to allow for open-world modeling, the employed model has to be capable of actively adapting to the environment it perceives. The model thereby has to be able to learn relevant facts about its environment based on observations. Such a task of trying to gain abstract information from a limited number of exemplary observations is known as a learning problem and constitutes a typical example of inductive inference [BBL04]. Automatically solving learning problems belongs into the realms of machine learning and computational learning theory. In the following, a brief overview of inductive inference and concept learning is given.

4.1 Inductive Inference

The term *inference* generally denotes the process of gaining information either by concluding from known facts, denoted as deductive inference, or by generalizing from observed data samples. The latter process is known as inductive inference or statistical inference. The goal of *inductive inference* is to find laws and regularities underlying a given set of observation [Grü07]. These laws can then be used to gain information about the process generating the data, predict future observations, make decisions or construct models of relevant features [BBL04].

Inductive inference is a general principle. It is the process successfully employed by human beings in their everyday life in tasks concerning learning and generalization [Mic83]. The ability to learn from only a few examples thereby is regarded as a core capability of human cognition [Ten99]. On the other hand, seen from a philosophical perspective, induction does not even constitute a valid method for logical conclusion since it cannot be properly justified by deductive means [Hum93]. This problem can be made clear by the fact that inductive inference extends the knowledge of a system with a non-zero probability of error. This means that an inductive inference always allows for the possibility of a wrong conclusion. For example, having seen only apples of green color, one could draw the conclusion that all apples are green. Nevertheless, induction is one of the most basic principles for knowledge acquisition as well as learning, and is prominent in various disciplines, specifically in machine learning.

For the general task of learning from examples, a set of samples or training data $\{(x_1, y_1), (x_2, y_2), \ldots, (x_n, y_n)\}$ is given, where the x_i represent the observable part of the data and the y_i represent a valuation of this data. If a functional relationship between the x- and y-values is to be discovered, this task is called regression in the statistics domain or supervised learning in the machine learning domain [Grü07]. The more special case where the y-values are restricted to some finite set is called classification, or, in computational learning theory, concept learning.

Automatically learning from a small number of examples is a difficult task, especially when the resulting functional relationship or classifier should also be able to perform well on previously unseen data, e.g., future observation. For successful learning in addition to given training samples, further assumptions on the problem at hand are necessary. These assumption can have a strong influence on the inferred generalization, and are therefore known as *inductive bias* [Mit80]. A prominent example of inductive bias for concept learning is given by the structure of the space of possible hypotheses. Since inference procedures can only choose from this hypotheses space when learning, non-representable concepts therefore are excluded a priori from being learned.

4.2   Principles of Inductive Learning

As a consequence of inductive bias, one has to carefully choose the assumptions made during the design process of a learning algorithm. Another problem which automated learning has to deal with, also being connected to prior assumptions, is the level of complexity that a learning algorithm can represent. In the case of regression, a given set of training data might for example have been generated by a process governed by some cubic law. However, if a learning algorithm can only represent second degree polynomials, it might never be able to infer an appropriate model for the given process. On the other hand, considering for example linearly distributed but noisy data samples, a high-order polynomial learning algorithm might admittedly be able to accurately reproduce the training data. But it could possibly fail to perform well on the prediction of future data, since it could have learned not only the data, but also the inherent noisy. In machine learning, this phenomenon is known as *overfitting*.

Since the success of learning depends on wisely choosing the inductive bias as well as the complexity of a learning algorithm, several general *principles for inductive inference* have been proposed. In statistical learning theory, for example, the structural risk minimization principle has been established [Vap99]. This principle tries to simultaneously optimize both the complexity class of functions that possibly can be learned and the deviation of an actually learned regression to training data. It thus defines a trade-off between approximation quality for training data and complexity of the set of possible functions.

A similar approach is taken by the *minimum description length* (MDL) principle, as described in [Grü07]. In MDL, learning is understood as finding regularities in data and using them to compress the data. The more a data set can be compressed by a given algorithm, the more we have learned about the data. To illustrate this following [Grü07], one can for example consider two lengthy binary strings, one consisting of randomly drawn "0s" and "1s", and the other given as 0100101001010010100101001010100101001.... Now, the second string can be compressed by describing it as the number 01001 repeated for a certain number of times, as soon as one has identified that kind of regularity in the string. For the first string, this is not possible, due to its random nature. So, by learning the law underlying for the second string, it is possible to describe it in a compressed way.

In consequence, MDL regards functions that are to be learned as methods of describing a given set of data. In this approach, the *MDL principle* then prefers hypothesis, i.e., description methods, which achieve a shorter overall description length [Grü07]. To fairly measure description length, MDL employs a so-called universal coding, which maps functions to descriptions in a pre-defined way and, for example, measures the number of bits needed to encode the resulting description. Similarly to structural risk minimization, MDL chooses the hypothesis that best fits the training data by actually considering both the description length of the particular hypothesis and the description length of the data when encoded with the help of that hypothesis [Grü07]. Due to its two parts structure, this approach inherently protects MDL against overfitting.

The MDL principle further can be seen as an implementation of Occam's razor, in which one is generally advised to prefer the most simple explanation for a considered problem amongst other suitable explanations.

4.3   Classical Concept Learning

For adaptive open-world modeling, prior knowledge must be extensible to incorporate new concepts. Furthermore, the modeling system must be equipped with a method for learning new concepts based on acquired observations. The classical approach to concept learning is concerned with learning boolean functions from examples [Mit97]. A concept is regarded as a boolean function mapping instances, represented by their attribute values, to a value of 1 (denoting concept membership) or 0 (denoting extraneousness). The set of possible instances is thus defined by the outer product of the considered attribute domains, which often are comprised of discrete values. Each instance in the set of training data is thereby marked as a positive or negative example of the concept.

In order to learn a target concept, concepts are represented as hypotheses, i.e., conjunctions of restrictions on allowed attribute values. Thereby, for a given attribute e.g. any value could be allowed, or just one specific value. The inductive bias of classical concept learning thus is partially determined by the chosen structure of hypotheses representation (e.g., if the given target concept is not representable, it hence cannot be learned).

The task of concept learning then consists of finding a hypothesis that matches the training data. This task then can be performed as a directed search in hypotheses space by exploiting a preexisting ordering relation, the so-called general-to-specific ordering of hypotheses. A hypothesis thereby is more general than another if its set of allowed instances is a superset to the set of instances belonging to the other hypothesis. Based on this ordering, several concept learning algorithms have been developed, including the well-known version space algorithm [Mit79].

5   Adaptive Open-World Modeling

In world modeling, combining sensor data to a situation-specific operational picture is achieved by information fusion based on the concepts stated in prior knowledge. These concepts are originally obtained by a priori modeling the considered domain, i.e., the process of acquiring and formally representing the knowledge of domain experts. Prior knowledge, represented for example in an ontology, usually constitutes a fixed and static set of information. As a consequence, only a fixed segment of the real world can be modeled a priori, and thus only a closed world can be (semantically) represented in the dynamic world model.

In order to allow for *open-world modeling*, i.e., a semantic representation of real-world entities which originally were not considered during a priori modeling, an information management system must support adaption of its prior knowledge. An adaptive open-world modeling thereby automatically should detect the need for or the usefulness of extensions to its prior knowledge during operation. Furthermore, additions to prior knowledge in form of newly built concepts should be

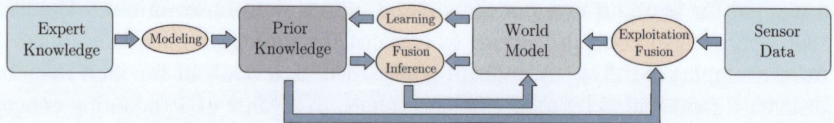

Figure 5.1: An adaptive open-world modeling conception.

automatically inferred from the information currently contained in the dynamic world model as well as from current sensor data. This task of concept learning shall be performed by an inductive inference technique, applying for example the MDL principle for deciding on useful concepts.

An overview of adaptive world-modeling is depicted in Figure 5.1. As can be seen, domain knowledge is employed to initially set up prior knowledge. This modeled knowledge then serves as a basis for exploiting and fusing newly acquired sensor data as well as inferring on already stored information. The fusion results as usual get stored in the dynamic world model, where the modeled entities (as instances of prior knowledge concepts) semantically represent real-world entities.

The adaptiveness of world-modeling now is given by the learning process connecting the dynamic world model and prior knowledge. The idea behind the adaptive system is a follows: in usual operational mode, modeled entities in the dynamic world model are induced from sensor data and mapped to entity concepts. If a situation occurs in which modeled entities are created that cannot be mapped to existing prior knowledge concepts, a learning process is started. This process then extends prior knowledge by inductive inference based on the information from the dynamic world model, learning necessary new entity concepts.

In order to perform this step, the information stored in prior knowledge can be operationalized in some way, e.g., it could be transformed into a form of representation well-suited for logic-based, Bayesian or graphical inference.

For designing an adaptive world model, several questions have to be considered:

- How to recognize to necessity of adaption by creating or reorganizing the concepts contained in prior knowledge?

- If adaption is necessary, what kind of adaption should be done (reorganization versus new concepts)?

- How should the usefulness of different adaption approaches (e.g., different concept hypothesis) be rated?

- Should adaption be made persistent in prior knowledge?

- Is there a need for adapting prior knowledge by removing ("forgetting") entity concepts?

6 Conclusion

In this technical report, a conception for an adaptive open-world model in cognitive information systems has been proposed. For this purpose, an overview over several aspects of knowledge management, information fusion, machine learning and inductive inference has been presented. All these areas thereby play an important role in designing an adaptive system for world modeling.

Future work will be considered with research on suitable methods for adaptive concept learning, including logic-based information fusion, and implementing an example application for proof of concept.

Bibliography

[Ack89]   Russell L. Ackoff. From Data to Wisdom. *Journal of Applied System Analysis*, 16:3–9, 1989.

[BBL04]   Olivier Bousquet, Stéphane Boucheron, and Gábor Lugosi. Introduction to Statistical Learning Theory. In *Advanced Lectures on Machine Learning*, pages 169–207. Springer, 2004.

[Das08]   Subrata Das. *High-Level Data Fusion*. Artech House, Boston, 2008.

[GHB08]   Ioana Gheta, Michael Heizmann, and Jürgen Beyerer. Object Oriented Environment Model for Autonomous Systems. In Henrik Boström, Ronnie Johansson, and Joeri van Laere, editors, *Proceedings of the second Skövde Workshop on Information Fusion Topics*, pages 9–12. Skövde Studies in Informatics, November 2008.

[Grü07]   Peter D. Grünwald. *The Minimum Description Length Principle*. The MIT Press, June 2007.

[Gru93]   Thomas R. Gruber. A Translation Approach to Portable Ontology Specifications. *Knowl. Acquis.*, 5(2):199–220, 1993.

[Hum93]   David Hume. *An Enquiry Concerning Human Understanding*. Hackett Pub Co Inc, December 1993.

[LBR+04]   James Llinas, Christopher Bowman, Galina Rogova, Alan Steinberg, and Frank White. Revisiting the JDL Data Fusion Model II. In *In P. Svensson and J. Schubert (Eds.), Proceedings of the Seventh International Conference on Information Fusion (FUSION 2004*, pages 1218–1230, 2004.

[Mic83]   Ryszard S. Michalski. A Theory and Methodology of Inductive Learning. *Artificial Intelligence*, 20(2):111 – 161, 1983.

[Mit79]   Tom M. Mitchell. *Version Spaces: An Approach to Concept Learning.* PhD thesis, Stanford, CA, USA, 1979.

[Mit80]   Tom M. Mitchell. The Need for Biases in Learning Generalizations. Technical report, 1980.

[Mit97]   Tom M. Mitchell. *Machine Learning.* McGraw-Hill Education (ISE Editions), 1st edition, October 1997.

[PLR08]   Fernando Puente León and Heinrich Ruser. Information fusion - Overview and taxonomy. In Fernando Puente, editor, *Reports on Distributed Measurement Systems*, pages 1–18. Shaker Verlag, 2008.

[RD06]   Matthew Richardson and Pedro Domingos. Markov Logic Networks. *Machine Learning*, 62:107–136, 2006. 10.1007/s10994-006-5833-1.

[Sch06]   Rainer Schönbein. *Agenten- und ontologiebasierte Software-Architektur zur interaktiven Bildauswertung.* Universitätsverl. Karlsruhe, Karlsruhe, 2006.

[Stu09]   Heiner Stuckenschmidt. *Ontologien: Konzepte, Technologien und Anwendungen (Informatik Im Fokus).* Springer, Berlin, 1 edition, 2009.

[Ten99]   Joshua B. Tenenbaum. Bayesian modeling of human concept learning. In *Advances in neural information processing systems 11*, pages 59–65. MIT Press, 1999.

[Vap99]   Vladimir Vapnik. *The Nature of Statistical Learning Theory (Information Science and Statistics).* Springer, 2nd edition, November 1999.

[Whi88]   Franklin E. White. A Model for Data Fusion. In *Proceedings of the 1st National Symposium on Sensor Fusion*, volume 2, 1988.

Karlsruher Schriftenreihe zur Anthropomatik
(ISSN 1863-6489)

Herausgeber: Prof. Dr.-Ing. Jürgen Beyerer

Die Bände sind unter www.ksp.kit.edu als PDF frei verfügbar oder
als Druckausgabe bestellbar.

Band 1   Jürgen Geisler
Leistung des Menschen am Bildschirmarbeitsplatz. 2006
ISBN 3-86644-070-7

Band 2   Elisabeth Peinsipp-Byma
**Leistungserhöhung durch Assistenz in interaktiven Systemen zur
Szenenanalyse.** 2007
ISBN 978-3-86644-149-1

Band 3   Jürgen Geisler, Jürgen Beyerer (Hrsg.)
Mensch-Maschine-Systeme. 2010
ISBN 978-3-86644-457-7

Band 4   Jürgen Beyerer, Marco Huber (Hrsg.)
**Proceedings of the 2009 Joint Workshop of Fraunhofer IOSB and
Institute for Anthropomatics, Vision and Fusion Laboratory.** 2010
ISBN 978-3-86644-469-0

Band 5   Thomas Usländer
Service-oriented design of environmental information systems. 2010
ISBN 978-3-86644-499-7

Band 6   Giulio Milighetti
**Multisensorielle diskret-kontinuierliche Überwachung und Regelung
humanoider Roboter.** 2010
ISBN 978-3-86644-568-0

Band 7   Jürgen Beyerer, Marco Huber (Hrsg.)
**Proceedings of the 2010 Joint Workshop of Fraunhofer IOSB
and Institute for Anthropomatics, Vision and Fusion Laboratory**
ISBN 978-3-86644-609-0